AND BEYOND

Complete English as a Second Language for Cambridge Secondary 1

Chris Akhurst, Lucy Bowley, Lynette Simonis

Series editor: Rachel Beveridge

ASPIRE SUCCEED PROGRESS

7

TEACHER PACK

Oxford excellence for Cambridge Secondary 1

OXFORD

OXFORD
UNIVERSITY PRESS

Great Clarendon Street, Oxford, OX2 6DP, United Kingdom

Oxford University Press is a department of the University of Oxford. It furthers the University's objective of excellence in research, scholarship, and education by publishing worldwide. Oxford is a registered trade mark of Oxford University Press in the UK and in certain other countries

© Oxford University Press 2016

The moral rights of the authors have been asserted

First published in 2016

All rights reserved. No part of this publication may be reproduced, stored in a retrieval system, or transmitted, in any form or by any means, without the prior permission in writing of Oxford University Press, or as expressly permitted by law, by licence or under terms agreed with the appropriate reprographics rights organization. Enquiries concerning reproduction outside the scope of the above should be sent to the Rights Department, Oxford University Press, at the address above.

You must not circulate this work in any other form and you must impose this same condition on any acquirer

British Library Cataloguing in Publication Data
Data available

978-0-19-837818-1

9 10

Paper used in the production of this book is a natural, recyclable product made from wood grown in sustainable forests.
The manufacturing process conforms to the environmental regulations of the country of origin.

Printed and bound by CPI Group (UK) Ltd, Croydon, CR0 4YY

Acknowledgements
The publishers would like to thank the following for permissions to use their photographs:

Cover image: Jenny Wheatley/Bridgeman Images.

Artwork by Aptara Inc. and Erwin Haya.

We are grateful to the authors and publishers for use of extracts from their titles and in particular for the following:

Jacqueline Wilson: Interview from https://clubs-kids.scholastic.co.uk/clubs. Reprinted by permission of David Higham Associates.

Any third party use of this material, outside of this publication, is prohibited. Interested parties should apply to the copyright holders indicated in each case.

Although we have made every effort to trace and contact all copyright holders before publication this has not been possible in all cases. If notified, the publisher will rectify any errors or omissions at the earliest opportunity.

Links to third party websites are provided by Oxford in good faith and for information only. Oxford disclaims any responsibility for the materials contained in any third party website referenced in this work.

®IGCSE is the registered trademark of Cambridge International Examinations.

All sample questions and answers within this publication have been written by the authors. In examination, the way marks are awarded may be different.

Contents

Introduction iv

Scope and sequence vi

1 Our natural world 2

2 Fit for life 18

3 Work around the world 34

4 Leisure 50

5 Friends 66

6 Where we learn 82

7 Culture and customs 98

8 Cookbook 114

9 Communication 130

Grammar reference 146

Use of English glossary 150

Introduction

Welcome to *Complete English as a Second Language for Cambridge Secondary 1*.

Each Student Book 7, 8 and 9 introduces students to nine engaging themes designed to help them to develop the vocabulary needed in a range of different contexts. Each level is carefully aligned to the latest Cambridge Secondary 1 English as a Second Language curriculum, providing strong coverage of five key skills: reading, listening, speaking, writing, and use of English. The Teacher Packs will help you to lay a firm foundation for students preparing for the Checkpoint test and further study of English as a Second Language at IGCSE®.

This Teacher Pack 7 is designed to help you guide your students through the *Complete English as a Second Language for Cambridge Secondary 1 Student Book 7*, and provides resources to develop students' skills in class, as well as to set homework and prepare them for assessment. Each unit comprises of seven spreads, which are mapped closely to the Student Book 7 content. Some of the features in the book are explained below.

1. Unit scope and sequence chart

A scope and sequence chart can be found on pages 2–3 of the Teacher Book and is designed to help you easily navigate the book. This provides a full overview of the Student Book and the themes, learning objectives and writing genres covered in each unit.

2. Learning objectives

Each unit opens with a list of all of the learning objectives covered in that unit, with a reference to the page in the Teacher Book where these are covered. You will also find a syllabus matching grid on the CD which lists all of the learning objectives from the Cambridge curriculum framework and where they are covered in both the Teacher Book and the Student Book.

3. Student Book activities

Student Book activities are divided by key skills: reading, listening, speaking, writing and use of English. Each activity in the Student Book has a corresponding box in the Teacher Book, with guidelines for you to get the most out of the activities. These include ways in which you can prepare students, help them to understand any difficult vocabulary and extend the activities in order to stretch them and better ensure learning. Here, you will also find the answers to all Student Book activities to check students' understanding.

4. Workbook activities

The Workbook provides supplementary work for students to complete independently, at home or in class. The Workbook 7 unit themes match those in Student Book 7, and extra practice is provided for the key skills covered in the Student Book. Answers for the Workbook activities are provided in the Teacher Book to enable you to go through these with your students in class, as a class or individually, to check students' understanding.

5. Extension activities

If you have time to fill, we have provided additional activities not in the Student Book for students to complete in-class. These comprise of more research-based, creative or collaborative tasks for students to complete individually, in pairs or in groups. They provide an opportunity for students to put into practice and consolidate the vocabulary and skills they have learned.

6. Challenge activities

We recognise that your students will learn at different paces, so all of the activities in the Student Book are differentiated from A to C. Each unit also includes at least one more stretching Challenge activity, which you can set more able students to complete on their own in class or at home.

7. Reading corner

The Reading corner in each unit is a longer and more engaging extract designed to expose students to a range of different writing genres. These include non-fiction, fiction and poetry, and we hope these will encourage your students to find pleasure in reading in English, while also improving their reading and writing skills.

8. Writing workshop

In addition to smaller writing tasks throughout the unit, the Writing workshop gives students the opportunity to practise writing an extended piece (to help prepare students for the writing part of the Checkpoint test). Each Writing workshop will mirror the writing genre in the corresponding Reading corner, thereby covering a wide range of writing genres, and will be supported with careful scaffolding.

9. End-of-unit activity

These short activities focus on one of the skills learned in that unit, to summarise and consolidate learning. Worksheets and audio recordings needed for these activities can be found on the CD.

10. Reflection on learning

Each Student Book unit ends with an opportunity for students to check their progress by completing a short Progress check quiz on what they have learned, with answers in the Teacher Book. Students also complete a Progress assessment chart which helps them to think about how well they have understood each of the skills covered in the unit, and where they need help. Both of these help you to ascertain each student's understanding and any areas for development.

11. Teacher reflection

You are also encouraged to reflect on what students enjoyed, what they learned, what they found difficult, how you performed as a teacher, what you have learned from teaching the unit, and where you might improve next time. This is part of an ongoing commitment to excellence to raise lifelong learners of English who are confident, responsible, reflective, innovative and engaged.

CD content

You will find some additional material on the CD, including:

- audio recordings to accompany activities in the Student Book, Teacher Book and Workbook
- transcripts of audio recordings
- printable classroom resources
- curriculum matching grid.

Unit contents

Unit	Theme	Reading and comprehension	Listening and comprehension
1	Our natural world	Non-fiction: Ten facts about space! Fiction: adventure/description: *Sky Hawk*	Zoo keeper talks about her work at Singapore Zoo
2	Fit for life	Non-fiction: Report about The Youth Olympic Games Blog: Bear Grylls	Interview with a footballer
3	Work around the world	Informal letter: Letter to a friend about transport in Hong Kong Newspaper job advertisements	VSO volunteer describes his work in Nepal
4	Leisure	Interview: interview with a film actor (Star Chat: *Into the Woods*) Fiction: *The Lion, the Witch and the Wardrobe*	Interview with an author (Jacqueline Wilson)
5	Friends	Emails: emails between friends	Conversation between old friends
6	Where we learn	Non-fiction: The School of the Air Non-fiction: Online newspaper article	Radio broadcast: Learning new things every day
7	Culture and customs	Non-fiction: Birthday celebrations around the world Poetry: The Boab Festival	Mu Lan describes the preparations for Chinese New Year Interview: New Year celebrations
8	Cookbook	Recipe Review of a cookbook	Friends talk about different recipes
9	Communication	Non-fiction: The first telephone call	Four different kinds of signalling systems
Unit	Theme	Reading and comprehension	Listening and comprehension

Language, grammar, spelling, vocabulary	Writing	Speaking
Countable and uncountable nouns Determiners Quantifiers Compound adjectives Participle adjectives Comparative adjectives and comparative structures	Non-fiction: writing facts about space Non-fiction: writing an advertisement (persuasive language) Fiction: Descriptive writing	Expressing opinions Spoken presentation Speaking to persuade Expression of ideas Negotiating classroom tasks Using subject-specific vocabulary
Indefinite pronouns Quantitative pronouns Present perfect tense Proofreading and editing Language for discussions: asking and giving reasons and opinions	Non-fiction: writing a paragraph about sporting role model Writing a blog	Asking questions Expressing opinions Giving reasons for opinions Taking part in a role-play interview Class presentation
Active and passive present simple Causative forms (*have, get done*) Present continuous Past continuous	Letter: writing a formal letter Writing a persuasive paragraph Writing a letter to a friend Writing an advertisement for a school council position	Expressing opinions Organisation of ideas Role-playing a job interview Devising a spoken advertisement Class presentation
Comparative adverb structures Sentence adverbs (*too, either, also*) Pre-verbal, post-verbal and end position adverbs	Non-fiction: Writing a text message Non-fiction: Writing interview questions Playscript: writing a playscript	Expressing opinions Organisation of ideas Asking questions Using subject-specific vocabulary
Compound nouns Abstract nouns Gerunds as subjects and objects Noun phrases Determiners Proofreading and editing	Non-fiction: short paragraph about what makes a good friend Informal letter: writing an informal letter to a penfriend	Expressing opinions Using subject-specific vocabulary Negotiating classroom tasks Role-play an interview between old friends
Language for asking closed, open and rhetorical questions Modal verbs Conjunctions Informal and informal language	Non-fiction: Writing an online newspaper article	Expressing opinions Asking questions Using subject-specific vocabulary
Prepositions and prepositional phrases Conditional sentences, using 'If only' and 'wish'	Writing an invitation Writing an informal email Writing a description of a festival Writing a poem	Asking questions Role-play an interview Expressing opinions Using subject-specific vocabulary
Reported speech Determiners Present continuous Active and passive verbs	Writing a book review	Expressing opinions Asking questions Using subject-specific vocabulary
Verbs and adjectives, followed by infinitives *-ing* forms after verbs and prepositions Phrasal verbs Prepositional verbs	Writing a formal email (responding to an advertisement) Planning, writing, editing and proofreading	Class presentation Negotiating classroom tasks Expressing opinions Asking questions Using subject-specific vocabulary

Our natural world

Learning objectives

In this unit, students will:

- Understand the main points in texts. **pages 4, 14** *7Re1*
- Read a limited range of extended fiction and non-fiction texts on familiar and some unfamiliar general and curricular topics with confidence and enjoyment. **pages 4, 14** *7Re8*
- Understand specific information in texts. **pages 4, 14** *7Re2*
- Brainstorm, plan and draft written work at text level, with some support. **pages 5, 8, 15** *7W1*
- Compose, edit and proofread written work at text level, with some support. **pages 5, 8, 15** *7W2*
- Use a range of quantifiers for countable and uncountable nouns including *several, plenty, a large/small number/amount*. **pages 6–7** *7Uw2*
- Use a growing range of compound adjectives and adjectives as participles and a limited range of comparative structures to indicate degree including *not as … as, much … than*. **pages 10–11** *7Uw3*
- Understand, with little or no support, the main points in extended talk. **page 8** *7L1*
- Understand, with little or no support, most specific information in extended talk. **page 8** *7L2*
- Give an opinion, at discourse level. **pages 3, 13** *7S3*
- Interact with peers to negotiate classroom tasks. **page 9** *7S6*

Setting the scene

Our natural world

Write the unit title on the board. Explain to the students that the theme of this unit is the natural world and it will focus on space, animals and the environment. Look at the photographs on page 8 of the Student Book together. Read the quotations and discuss the meaning of 'astronaut' (a person who travels in space) and 'natural history' (the study of animals and plants). Ask the students whether they have heard of Tim Peake, Stephen Hawking or David Attenborough. If possible, show pictures of each and tell the students a little about them. Tim Peake is a British astronaut who flew into space to join the International Space Station in December 2015. Stephen Hawking is a physicist at Cambridge University who talks about space and time. He has motor neurone disease and the film *The Theory of Everything* was made about him in 2014. David Attenborough is a naturalist and broadcaster who has been making television programmes about the natural world for over 60 years.

Thinking ahead

The purpose of the Thinking ahead activity on page 9 of the Student Book is to introduce students to the different topics that they will focus on in this unit. Start by asking students what they know about Earth and the solar system. Then ask students the meaning of the term 'wild animal'. Explain that most wild animals live freely in their natural environment but some live in zoos. Discuss the meaning of the verb 'recycle' and elicit what students know about recycling. Now ask the students to think about the questions in small groups.

Suggested responses:

1. Stars, the moon, planets, comets, shooting stars.
2. Students' own answers. Encourage students to give reasons for their choice.
3. Recycling preserves the world's resources for future generations and reduces the amount of waste that is buried in landfill sites.
4. Students' own answers. Encourage responses that mention taking an interest in the world we live in.

Our natural world

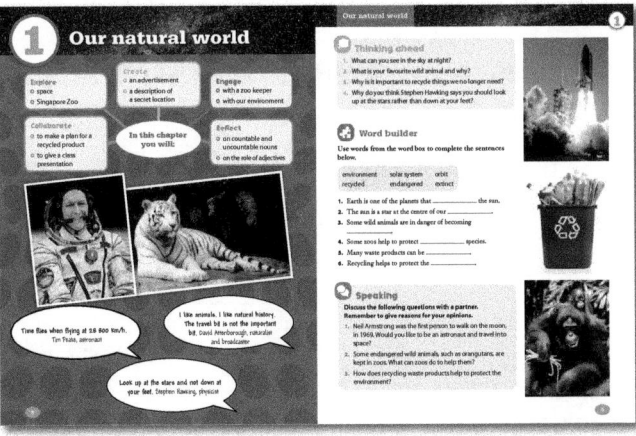

Theme opener

Workbook page 2: Our natural world

Page 2 of the Workbook gives students practice in answering questions relating to the theme of the unit.

Example responses:

1. This free choice of ideas might include: family, a teacher, the school library, television.
2. The thing I like most about the natural world is the sea.
3. I would like to learn more about animals that live in the sea.
4. The change I would like to make would be to have less rubbish on the beach.
5. I will put up posters asking people to take rubbish away from the beach. (Make sure students complete this answer as a sentence.)
6. Dear Ronnie

   I want to tell you about how people should be encouraged not to leave their rubbish on the beach because it can hurt the birds and animals that live in the sea. I am planning to put up posters to tell people about this. Can you help me draw the posters? It will be great for the animals if you can.

   Thanks and see you soon

   Charlie

Vocabulary

Word builder

The questions in this section introduce students to some of the new vocabulary that they will find in the unit. Ask students to fill the gaps in the sentences, working on their own. When they have finished, ask them to check their answers with a partner. Then ask them to read the sentences out loud and check their pronunciation is correct.

Answers:

1. Earth is one of the planets that <u>orbit</u> the sun.
2. The sun is a star at the centre of our <u>solar system</u>.
3. Some wild animals are in danger of becoming <u>extinct</u>.
4. Some zoos help to protect <u>endangered</u> species.
5. Many waste products can be <u>recycled</u>.
6. Recycling helps to protect the <u>environment</u>.

Speaking

Speaking

Students can start by thinking about the questions independently before discussing their opinions with a partner. Before they start, remind them to use the words from the Word builder activity in their discussion. You could also put other vocabulary on the board to help the students in this task. (Examples: space, rocket, float, gravity, breed, conserve, resources, etc.) Write on the board some other words and phrases that will help them to express their opinions. (Examples: In my opinion …, I think that …, I believe that …, What I mean is …, I am not sure …, I agree that … .) Encourage the students to listen to each other's opinions and ask questions to ensure they understand.

Extension

Animal names

Explain to the students that when an animal or plant is discovered for the first time it is given a name and sometimes it is named after a person. The attenborosaurus, for example, is an extinct sea creature that was named after the naturalist David Attenborough. Ask the students to use the Internet to find out about the attenborosaurus.

When they have done their research, ask the students to imagine that they have just found the bones of a dinosaur that has never been discovered before. Tell them that the dinosaur will be named after them. They can add 'saurus' to their own name to make the name of the dinosaur. Then, ask them to work in small groups and describe their dinosaur to each other.

Reading

Ten facts about space!

Prior knowledge

Students read an informative text with factual information about the solar system and then answer some questions before writing some facts about one of the planets. Elicit from students what they have learned about the solar system in other lessons in school, or from their own reading or other sources. Ask them to think of as many words as they can that relate to space and the solar system.

Students may be familiar with the terms 'non-fiction', 'fiction', 'fact' and 'opinion' from primary level. Write the terms on the board. Then focus the students' attention on the title of the text 'Ten facts about space!' Ask them what kind of text they think this will be (non-fiction). Give some other examples of non-fiction text (newspapers, biographies, reference books, etc.). Discuss the meaning of the word 'fact' (something that is true or certain) and how a fact differs from an opinion (an opinion is someone's view or belief about something and may not be based on fact or knowledge). Ask students for examples of non-fiction text they have read and ask whether it included facts or opinions, or both. Ask what kind of information they think the 'Ten facts about space!' will contain (facts, not opinions).

Reading

 Ten facts about space!

Read the text with the class before they start on the Understanding section. Ask the students what tense the text is written in (present tense). Look together at the words and definitions in the Glossary box. Stop at any other unfamiliar words (for example, considered, leftovers, construction). Tell the students that with the English they already know, they can work out what a word means. For example, they know that a bicycle has two wheels and they know that a triangle has three sides, so they could work out a tricycle has three wheels. They can apply this to any new word, especially where there are prefixes (for example, bi–, tri–) which they're already familiar with. Now ask them to look at 'leftovers' – they should be able to say that it combines something

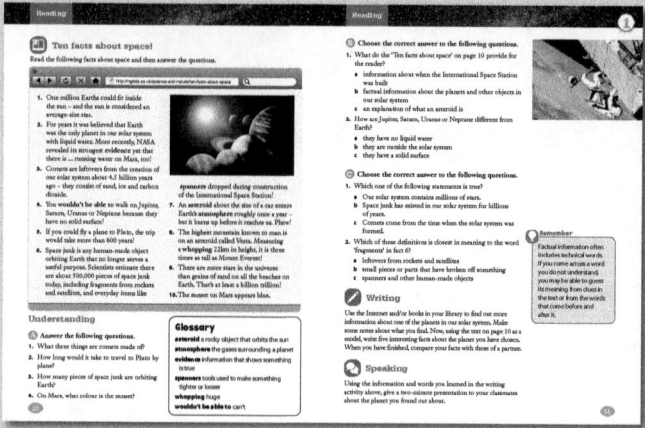

which has been left with something which is more (over) than what is needed, to find the meaning of the word. Can the students guess the meanings of other words from the context? Explain that factual information often includes technical words.

Student Book answers

Understanding

Ask the students to read the text again and then answer the questions on their own.

Answers:

A 1. sand, ice and carbon dioxide
   2. more than 800 years
   3. about 500,000
   4. blue

B 1. b factual information about the planets and other objects in our solar system
   2. a they have no liquid water

C 1. c Comets come from the time when the solar system was formed.
   2. b small pieces or parts that have broken off something

Reading

Writing

 Writing

In this activity students will use the Internet or books in the library to research information about one of the planets in the solar system. They will then write five interesting facts about their chosen planet. Before the students begin their research, explain that in a library they might choose to look in the reference book section, which will include encyclopedias and other reference books. If they use the Internet for their research, you could suggest that they find information on the NASA website (www.nasa.gov). Remind the students to check in a dictionary (online or printed) to find out the meaning of any words they come across during their research that they do not understand. Before they start writing, remind students about the features of the 'Ten facts about space!' text that they have read: technical words, present tense, information that is true. Explain that they should use these features when they write their own five facts. When the students have written their facts, ask them to compare them with those of a partner.

Speaking

 Speaking

Students will present their five facts about their chosen planet to the class. Let them have up to two minutes for their presentations. Encourage them to use some of the vocabulary from the Word builder exercise on page 9 of the Student Book and check that they are speaking fluently. If they are having difficulty, encourage them to speak in shorter sentences (they can lengthen these when they are more confident). At the end, ask them which fact they liked the most about their planet.

Reading

Workbook page 3: Koalas

Page 3 of the Workbook gives students practice in reading a non-fiction text and answering questions on the text.

Answers:

1. **B** marsupials
2. **A** Koalas can sleep for as many as 20 hours a day.
3. A koala needs a good sense of smell to select the best leaves to eat/for the selection of the best leaves. (either of these)
4. A koala needs a good sense of hearing to detect predators./A koala needs a good sense of hearing for the detection of predators. (either of these)
5. If the eucalyptus trees are cut down, there will be less food for koalas to eat./If the eucalyptus trees are cut down, koalas might become endangered. (either of these)

Extension

Researching the International Space Station

Ask the students to use the Internet or school library to find out more information about the International Space Station. Ask them to write three interesting facts they find out. Then ask them to write three sentences explaining how daily life on the International Space Station is different from how it is on Earth. (Check students understand there is lower gravity at the International Space Station and that means astronauts and all other objects there will be floating and they can think about what problems that will cause.) This will enable students to practise giving reasons and explanations for ideas. Explain to the students that there are no right or wrong answers, but when they have finished they should check their sentences and the reasons they give with a partner.

Use of English

Countable and uncountable nouns

Grammar

Countable and uncountable nouns

In this section students develop their knowledge of countable and uncountable nouns. Most students will be familiar with the term 'noun' from primary level. Remind them that a noun is a word that names a person, place or thing. Work through the explanation and examples of countable nouns on page 12 of the Student Book. Give some more examples of nouns they can see in the classroom (examples: 'chair', 'table', 'pen', 'book'). Ask them to think of other countable nouns and use numbers to say exactly how many there are.

Now read through the explanation of uncountable nouns and the examples. Explain that uncountable nouns often name things such as ideas or concepts. Give some more examples, such as 'happiness', 'love', 'knowledge' and 'advice'. Explain that uncountable nouns also name substances that we cannot count, such as 'rice' and 'sugar' and things such as 'travel' and 'money'.

Read the explanation about using 'a' or 'an' or 'some' with countable and uncountable nouns and give some more examples to ensure understanding before students answer the questions.

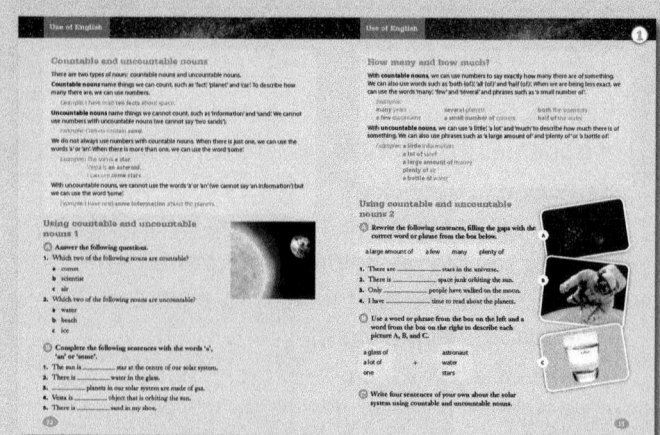

Grammar

How many and how much?

In this section students develop their knowledge of quantifiers that can be used with countable and uncountable nouns. Read through the examples of words and phrases (quantifiers) that can be used with countable nouns, such as 'many', 'a few', 'several' and 'a small number of'. Give the students other examples of quantifiers we use with countable nouns (examples: 'lots of', 'a number of', 'not many', 'most of', 'enough'). Now read the examples of the quantifiers we can use to describe how much there is of an uncountable noun and give some more examples (examples: 'much', 'not much', 'any', 'a bag of', 'a box of'). Ask the students to give some examples of nouns that could be used with these quantifiers before they start the exercises.

Student Book answers

Using countable and uncountable nouns 1

Ask the students to complete the answers in pairs and then check their answers with another pair.

Answers:

A 1. a comet   and   b scientist
   2. a water   and   c ice

B 1. The sun is <u>a</u> star at the centre of our solar system.
   2. There is <u>some</u> water in the glass.
   3. <u>Some</u> planets in our solar system are made of gas.
   4. Vesta is <u>an</u> object that is orbiting the sun.
   5. There is <u>some</u> sand in my shoe.

6

Use of English

Student Book answers

Using countable and uncountable nouns 2

Ask the students to complete the answers in pairs and then check their answers with another pair.

Answers:

A   1. There are <u>many</u> stars in the universe.
    2. There is <u>a large amount of</u> space junk orbiting the sun.
    3. Only <u>a few</u> people have walked on the moon.
    4. I have <u>plenty of</u> time to read about the planets.

B   a lot of stars (picture A)
    one astronaut (picture B)
    a glass of water (picture C)

C   Students' own answers. Accept any sentences that use countable and uncountable nouns correctly.

I also saw a <u>rocket</u> – I wonder where it landed? I can't wait to camp again – it was so much <u>fun</u>!

4. Suggested responses:

    Eva: I love being able to see <u>plenty of stars</u> in the sky.

    Lucia: Sometimes it is cloudy, but there are only <u>a few clouds</u> tonight.

    Eva: It's very dark, but there is <u>a bit of light</u> from the moon.

    Lucia: If I were an astronaut, I would want to take <u>lots of photos</u> of the Earth from space.

    Eva: I'm cold and thirsty now. Shall we go inside and have <u>a cup of hot chocolate</u>?

    Lucia: Yes. Are you hungry, too? I brought <u>a bunch of bananas</u> with me.

Use of English

Workbook page 4: Countable and uncountable nouns

Page 4 of the Workbook gives students more practice in countable and uncountable nouns.

Answers:

1. Countable nouns: planet; rocket; helmet; spacesuit; star

    Uncountable nouns: water; weather; dust; ice; mud

2. The two questions are free response, but here are some suggestions:

    How many rockets have been into space?/ How many spacesuits does an astronaut have?

    How much water is there in the solar system?/ How much ice would you like in your drink?

3. For the completed diary entry, make sure students have used countable or uncountable nouns correctly, and a singular or plural where necessary.

    Tonight I camped in the garden and looked at the night <u>sky</u>. I saw the bright round <u>moon</u>, surrounded by many <u>stars</u>, all twinkling clearly.

Extension

Practising quantifiers with nouns

This task gives students more practice using quantifiers with countable and uncountable nouns. Either write the questions on the board or use the photocopiable sheets available on the CD.

Choose the correct word or phrase from the box below to complete the following sentences.

| enough | much | a lot of |
| some | a few | |

1. I have _____ homework to do.
2. We haven't got _____ time to finish our game.
3. There isn't _____ rice left.
4. There are only _____ people coming, so I think we have enough chairs.
5. I need _____ advice as I don't know what to do!

Answers:

1. I have <u>a lot of</u> homework to do.
2. We haven't got <u>enough</u> time to finish our game.
3. There isn't <u>much</u> rice left.
4. There are only <u>a few</u> people coming, so I think we have enough chairs.
5. I need <u>some</u> advice as I don't know what to do!

Listening

Singapore Zoo

Prior knowledge

Explain to the students that they are going to listen to a recording of a zoo keeper who works at Singapore Zoo and then answer questions about what she says. As a pre-listening activity, ask the students whether they have ever visited a zoo and, if so, where it was. Ask them what animals they saw and which they found most interesting. Discuss why we keep animals in zoos (for example: to conserve endangered animals; to see animals we might not otherwise see; to learn more about how the animals behave; to breed the animals).

Show the students where Singapore is on a world map or globe. Then ask them to work in small groups to find out about the zoo on the Internet. When they have done their research, discuss with the whole class what they have found out (for example: the zoo attracts over 1.5 million visitors a year; the zoo has over 300 species of animal; some of the animals there are endangered in the wild, including orangutans and white tigers; the animals are kept in spacious enclosures rather than cages with bars).

Listening

 Track 1.1: Singapore Zoo

Play Track 1.1 once and ask the students whether they think the zoo keeper enjoys her work at the zoo. Which animals does the zoo keeper mention? Discuss the meaning of difficult words such as 'sections' and 'stimulating'. Write the phrase 'protected for the future' on the board. Ask the students what they think this means. Can they work out the meaning from the context? Play the recording a second time before the students answer the questions. The full transcript for Track 1.1 can be found on the CD.

Student Book answers

Understanding

Answers:

A 1. 16
   2. happy
   3. orangutans
   4. breakfast

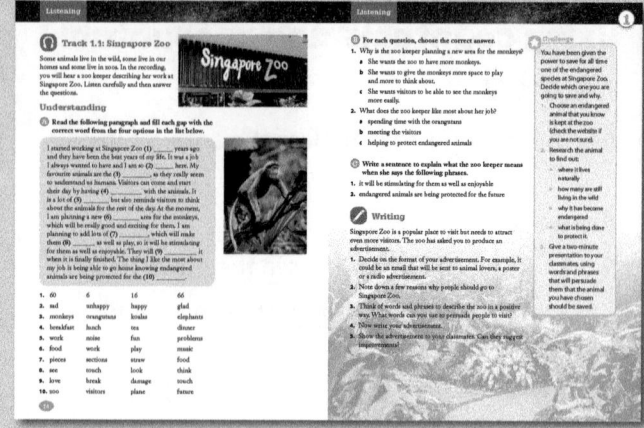

   5. work
   6. play
   7. sections
   8. think
   9. love
   10. future

B 1. b She wants to give the monkeys more space to play and more to think about.
   2. c helping to protect endangered animals

C Example answers:
   1. The new area will give the monkeys interesting things to do and think about as well as somewhere fun to play.
   2. The zoo is helping to protect endangered animals so they will not become extinct in the future.

Writing

 Writing an advertisement

Explain to the students that they are going to produce an advertisement for Singapore Zoo. First, ask the students what an advertisement is (something that tries to persuade someone to do something, such as buy something or visit somewhere). Give some examples of different kinds of advertisements (leaflets, magazine advertisements, radio advertisements, posters, etc.). Find some examples of persuasive language in the advertisements you have shown. (Examples: short sentences, persuasive adjectives such as 'best', 'fantastic', 'brilliant', rhetorical questions such as 'Do you want a great day out?') Explain to the students that they should use features such as these to make their advertisements as persuasive as possible.

8

Listening

⭐ Challenge

In this task students will research an endangered animal before giving a presentation to the class about why it should be saved. Tell the students that they should first find out more about the endangered animals at Singapore Zoo. You may wish to give some students some support by giving them some examples: panda, white tiger, orangutan, king cobra, Malayan tapir, golden lion tamarind, white rhino, douc langur, white rhinoceros, etc. They can research in school or at home, using school computers, library books or any other resources that are available. Tell them to make some notes, including words and phrases they can use in their presentation that will convince or persuade the class that their animal should be saved. Give them up to two minutes to give their oral presentations. Ask the groups to ask one question to each presenter at the end of their presentation.

Extension

💬 Planning a new animal enclosure

Ask the students to imagine they are zoo keepers. Which zoo animal would they like to be a keeper for and why? Ask the students to plan how they would design their enclosure. Tell them to think about the size and shape of the enclosure, as well as the features they might include to keep the animals entertained.

When they have decided on their plans, ask the students to present them to each other, working in small groups. Who has come up with the most innovative plan for their animal? Ask the students to vote for their favourite plan (but they can't vote for their own plan).

Listening

Workbook page 5: Recycling

Page 5 of the Workbook gives students more practice in listening and answering questions on what they have listened to.

Answers:

1. There is a huge <u>crane</u> on the building site.
2. The finished products travel on a <u>conveyor belt</u> to be packed into boxes.
3. Rubbish is sorted at the local <u>recycling plant</u>.
4. The man who works in our local museum is an <u>expert</u> on paintings.
5. My mother has a beautiful <u>jade</u> necklace.
6. Athens, in Greece, was built in <u>ancient</u> times.
7. B smaller
8. A sewing machine
9. B glass
10. A history expert.
11. This is a free response. Suggested response:

No, I don't think Katya is upset that she could not keep the object. I think she is pleased it is in the national museum and pleased she has a free ticket to visit the museum.

Use of English

Adjectives

Grammar

Adjectives

In this section students will develop their knowledge of adjectives, including compound adjectives and participle adjectives. Start by reminding students that an adjective is a word that we use to describe a noun and write some simple examples on the board. The students may be familiar with the word 'compound' from primary level. Read through the explanation of compound adjectives on page 16 of the Student Book. Write some more examples on the board (examples: 'well-known', 'part-time').

Remind students of the meaning of the word 'participle' (a word formed from a verb, often ending in '–ing' or '–ed'). Explain that participle forms of verbs are often used as adjectives. Adjectives that end in '–ed' describe emotions or how people feel about something (examples: surprised, bored). Adjectives that end in '–ing' describe the thing that causes the emotion (examples: boring, surprising). Read the examples on page 16 of the Student Book and write some other examples on the board (examples: 'Monkeys are interesting', 'I am interested in monkeys'; 'He thinks tigers are frightening', 'He is frightened of tigers').

Student Book answers

Using adjectives

Answers:

A multi-coloured

    snow-covered

    sweet-smelling

    high-speed

B 1. The zoo keeper has an <u>interesting</u> job.

    2. I was <u>surprised</u> to see so many giraffes.

    3. I saw some <u>endangered</u> white tigers.

    4. The monkeys had an <u>amazing</u> area to play in.

C Accept any sentences that make sense using the compound adjectives and nouns correctly. Suggested responses:

    There is a multi-coloured parrot in the trees. (picture A)

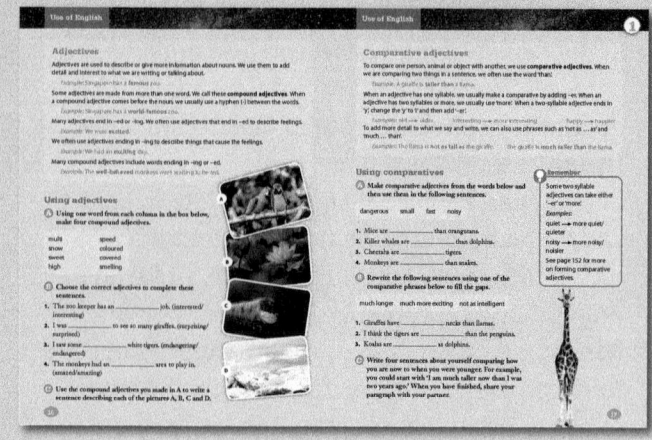

That is a sweet-smelling flower. (picture B)

I like the new high-speed train. (picture C)

In the distance, they could see the snow-covered mountains. (picture D)

Grammar

Comparative adjectives

In this section students will develop their knowledge of comparative adjectives. Start by explaining that comparative adjectives are used to compare two things. Draw the outline of two trees on the board – one much bigger than the other. Explain that if we want to compare the two trees, we can use comparative adjectives (examples: 'The tree on the left is bigger than the tree on the right'; 'The tree on the right is smaller than the tree on the left'). Ask students to pick out the comparative adjectives (bigger, smaller).

Work through the explanation and examples in the box on page 17 of the Student Book. Give the students some more examples of words and phrases we can use when comparing two things (examples: 'much … than' or 'not … as'). Tell them how these can be used in sentences (examples: 'The tree on the left is much taller than the tree on the right'; 'The tree on the right is not as tall as the tree on the left'). Ask students to think of other examples.

Explain that when an adjective has one syllable, we usually add '–er' to make a comparative adjective (fast, faster). When an adjective has two syllables we sometimes add '–er' (narrow, narrower) and sometimes we use the word 'more' (famous, more famous). When an adjective has three or more syllables, we use the word 'more' (powerful, more powerful).

Use of English

Remind the students of the spelling rules when adding '–er'. When an adjective ends in 'e', we drop the 'e' before adding '–er': late, later. When an adjective ends in 'y' we change the 'y' to 'i' before adding '–er': early, earlier. When an adjective ends in a consonant, vowel and consonant, we double the consonant before adding '–er': big, bigger. Draw students' attention to the 'Remember' feature on page 17 of the Student Book and give the students some more examples of two-syllable adjectives that can take either '–er' or 'more'.

Student Book answers

Using comparatives

Students can work in pairs for these exercises.

Answers:

A 1. Mice are <u>smaller</u> than orangutans.
   2. Killer whales are <u>more dangerous</u> than dolphins.
   3. Cheetahs are <u>faster</u> than tigers.
   4. Monkeys are <u>noisier</u> than snakes.

B Students continue to work in pairs and you can check their answers. Here are some possible responses:
   1. Giraffes have <u>much longer</u> necks than llamas.
   2. I think the tigers are <u>much more exciting</u> than the penguins.
   3. Koalas are <u>not as intelligent</u> as dolphins.

C Students might need some support with this exercise. You could give them some examples of nouns they could use in their sentences (for example: hair, legs, arms, feet, shoes, clothes).

   Example sentences:

   I wear bigger shoes than I did when I was younger.

   My hair is not as long as it was last year.

   I am not as shy as I used to be.

   My bedroom is much more untidy than it used to be.

Use of English

Workbook page 6: Adjectives

Page 6 of the Workbook gives students more practice in the use of compound adjectives, participle adjectives and comparative adjectives.

Answers:

1. sharp-toothed, well-known, snow-topped, bad-tempered, icy-cold
2. It sounded like a <u>mouth-watering</u> menu.
3. The children were <u>excited</u> about the nature trip.
4. My grandpa is so <u>kind-hearted</u>.
5. Suki has a lot of energy. She is much <u>more high-spirited</u> than her brother.
6. Luke said, "That spelling test was far <u>trickier</u> than the one we had last week."
7. The traffic is far <u>more slow-moving</u> today than yesterday.
8. "I have so much work to do," said Rosa. "I'm <u>busier</u> than ever!"

Extension

Practising comparisons

This task will give students some extra practice in using comparative adjectives. Write the following pairs of nouns on the board. Then ask the students to work in pairs and write a sentence that compares each of the two nouns.

1. Earth/Neptune
2. sun/Pluto
3. Mount Everest/Vesta
4. pandas/lions
5. elephants/mice

Example sentences:

1. Earth is closer to the sun than Neptune.
2. The sun is much bigger than Pluto.
3. Mount Everest is not as high as Vesta.
4. Pandas are more endangered than lions.
5. Elephants are much heavier than mice.

Speaking

Recycle, recycle, recycle

Prior knowledge

In this section students will discuss the subject of recycling before working with their peers to plan a new product from something that has been previously used. To introduce them to the subject, elicit from students what they know about recycling. They may be familiar with recycling certain items at home, in their school or in their community. Explain that many communities are becoming more concerned about what happens to the rubbish we throw away and try to reduce the volume of waste that is produced. Ask what items they think can be recycled and whether they have recycled any waste this week. Ask the students to look at the photographs on page 18 of the Student Book and then answer the questions.

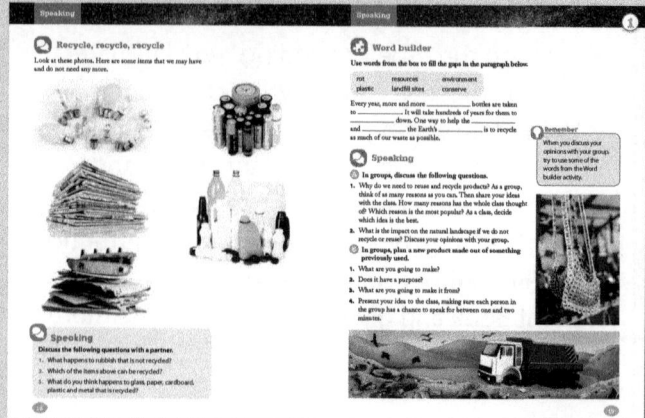

Speaking

 Speaking

Organise the students into pairs for this activity. Before they start, ask the students what products they can see in the photographs on page 18 of the Student Book. Write these on the board with some other vocabulary that will help them when discussing the questions (for example: plastic, glass, battery, cardboard, metal, light bulb, rubbish dump, waste, reuse, etc.). Elicit responses in a short class discussion afterwards.

Possible responses:

1. Rubbish that is not recycled is usually taken to large rubbish dumps to be buried.
2. They can all be recycled in part.
3. They can be broken down and reused to make more of the same product or other products.

Vocabulary

 Word builder

This activity will help students to learn some new vocabulary that they can use in their discussions about recycling. Ask students to use the words in the word box to fill the gaps in the sentences, working on their own. When they have finished, ask them to check their answers with a partner.

Answers:

Every year, more and more <u>plastic</u> bottles are taken to <u>landfill sites</u>. It will take hundreds of years for them to <u>rot</u> down. One way to help the <u>environment</u> and <u>conserve</u> the Earth's <u>resources</u> is to recycle as much of our waste as possible.

Speaking

💬 Speaking

Organise the students into small groups for this activity. In the first part of the activity, the students discuss with their group the importance of recycling and the impact on the environment if we do not recycle our waste. Remind the students of the vocabulary they can use for giving their opinions (see page 3). Ask the students to share their ideas with the class, giving as many reasons for recycling as they can.

In the second part of the activity, students work in their group to plan to make a new product from something that has previously been used. Encourage them to brainstorm ideas as a group. What waste product are they going to use? Will their new product be useful or will it be ornamental, like a work of art? When they have decided on their plan, ask them to present their ideas to the whole class. Encourage them to decide what each person will talk about, with each student speaking for between one and two minutes. They should cover the following points:

- what waste product will be used
- where the waste product will obtained
- what they plan to make
- what the new product will look like
- whether the new product has a purpose
- what other materials will be needed to make it.

Listening

Workbook page 7: Living in space

Page 7 of the Workbook gives students practice in answering questions relating to a recording and in acting out a conversation with a partner.

Answers:

1. **C** 12
2. **B** a soapy cloth
3. **B** they are thrown away
4. scientists on the ground
5. For this activity, ask the students to work in a pair at home if they can. If no one can, then you could do the speaking part as a class activity in the following lesson.

Speaking

Suggested response:

Controller: Hello, is that Astronaut <u>Ahmed</u> on the International Space Station?
Astronaut: Yes, it is, hello Mission Control.
Controller: So, what can you see?
Astronaut: <u>I can see Earth from space. It looks so beautiful.</u>
Controller: Wow, that sounds amazing. What is the first thing you did today?
Astronaut: <u>Well, I had a wake-up call. Then I washed with a soapy cloth before breakfast.</u>
Controller: And what else have you done today?
Astronaut: <u>I've carried out some scientific experiments. I've also done my daily exercises to keep fit.</u>
Controller: That is great to hear. See you back on Earth in 18 days.
Astronaut: <u>Yes, see you then.</u>

Extension

✏️ Writing a formal letter

This task will give students practice in writing a formal letter as well as an opportunity to use some of the vocabulary they have learned in this section. Ask them to write a letter to their local community leader asking them to recycle more waste products in their area. Before they start, remind them how a formal letter should be laid out with the address of the sender in the top right corner, the date below, and the name and address of the person the letter is being sent to on the left. Remind them of the kind of language that should be used in a formal letter and how the letter should be signed off (Yours sincerely or Yours faithfully). They should explain what kind of waste or which products they think should be recycled and why. Ask them to write about 100 words. When they have finished, ask them to exchange their letter with a partner and check they have given reasons for their points and that they have followed the correct format for a formal letter.

Reading corner

Reading corner

Prior knowledge

Students read an extract from *Sky Hawk*, a wildlife adventure story by Gill Lewis. They answer some questions about the text before writing their own description of a setting for a story. Before they read the text, elicit examples of other adventure stories the students have read. The students may be familiar with the word 'setting' from primary level. Remind them that a setting is the place where the events in a story happen. Explain that in adventure stories, writers use powerful adjectives to describe the setting of their story. They include words and phrases that help the reader imagine what they can see, hear, smell and touch there.

Before they read the text, explain to the students that the two main characters in the story are Iona and Callum. Iona has found a hawk (a type of bird) in a forest that she wants to keep safe, so she is keeping it secret. Callum follows Iona to the forest and she shares her secret with him.

Reading

 Sky Hawk

Read the extract with the class as well as the Glossary words and their definitions. Students may need support with other difficult vocabulary, so discuss the meaning of any other unfamiliar words (for example, moss, lightning, cracks, grip, wedge, ridges, disappeared, hauled, platform, spreading, crates, balanced, driftwood, high tide, random). Can the students guess the meaning of the words from the context?

Ask the students where the text is set (a forest). Ask them to find some powerful adjectives that the writer uses to describe the setting (sunlit, damp, pale, tiny, etc.). Can they find examples of words and phrases that appeal to the readers' senses ('sunlit space', 'pulled some damp moss with my fingers', 'slid her fingers and toes into the tiny cracks in the bark', 'tried to grip the tree trunk', 'small ridges of bark', 'my feet and hands slid', 'I whispered', 'Open your eyes Callum', etc.).

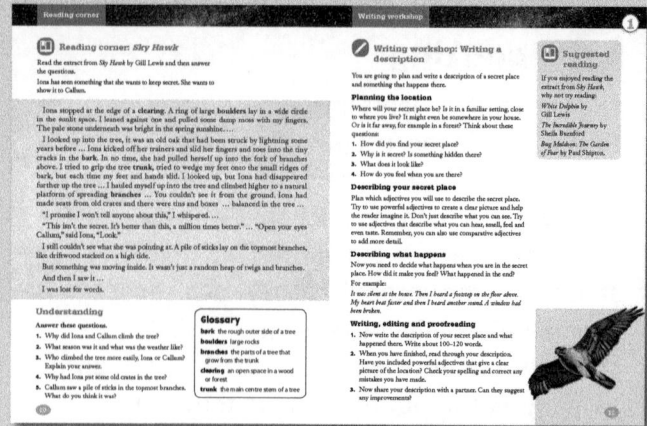

Student Book answers

Understanding

Ask students to answer the questions on their own.

Answers:

1. So that Iona could show Callum her secret (the hawk at the top of the tree).
2. It was spring and it was sunny.
3. Iona climbed it more easily. She had climbed it before. The writer uses phrases such as 'In no time' and 'pulled herself up' to describe how Iona climbed the tree. To describe how Callum climbed the tree, the writer uses phrases such as 'each time my feet and hands slid' and 'hauled myself up' to describe how Callum climbed the tree.
4. To make seats, so she could sit in the tree.
5. A nest.

Writing workshop

Writing

Writing a description

Tell the students that they are going to plan and write a description of a secret place and describe something that happens there. Remind them of the forest setting in the *Sky Hawk* extract they have read. Remind them also about the powerful adjectives used to describe the setting, as well as the words and phrases that appealed to the senses, helping us imagine the setting. Ask students as a class to suggest settings where a secret place might be. Before they plan their setting, explain to the students that they can use one of the places they discussed as a class or use another idea of their own.

Now encourage them to think of powerful adjectives to describe their setting, including words and phrases that appeal to the senses as well as some comparative adjectives. Now they need to think of something that happens in the secret place.

When they have finished planning, ask the students to write their description of the setting and what happened. When they have finished, ask them to check their spelling and punctuation and correct any mistakes. Then they can proofread their partner's work.

Reading

Suggested reading

If the students liked reading the text from *Sky Hawk*, ask them to pick one book in the list – they can either read it alone, or you could choose it as your next class reading book.

Writing

Workbook page 8: Describing an animal

Ask the students to choose an animal they would like to write about and make some notes about it.

Suggested responses:

My wild animal is a <u>Bengal tiger</u>.

It lives in <u>India</u>.

It eats <u>meat</u>.

It looks like <u>a big cat with orange and black stripes</u>.

I am interested in it because <u>I wonder how such a large animal can move so quietly</u>.

The students then use the Internet to find out more about their animal before writing a paragraph about it. If students do not have Internet access, ask if they would be able to ask a relative or a friend to help them complete the information.

Suggested responses:

- The tiger lives in a warm place.
- It usually lives alone.
- It hunts and kills its food.
- It is endangered.
- It has been affected by humans because not only have the forests where it lives been chopped down, it has also been hunted.

Students now write their paragraph.

Suggested response:

I have chosen to write about the Bengal tiger because I have always been interested in it and wanted to find out more about this dangerous but beautiful animal. It lives in a warm place and usually lives alone. It is very powerful and hunts and kills its food. However, it is endangered because the forests where it lives have been chopped down and the tiger has also been hunted.

Extension

Continuing the story

Ask the students to continue the story about Iona and Callum in the same style as the section they have read and use their imagination to write about what could happen next in the story. Tell them to write the next paragraph of the story, saying what happens to Iona and Callum.

15

Progress assessment

Progress check

Student Book answers

Progress check

1. One mark. a the sun is a star at the centre of the solar system. [1]
2. One mark. Accept either spanner or space junk. [1]
3. One mark for each item (examples: newspaper, paper cup, plastic bottle). [3]
4. One mark for each noun – one countable and one uncountable. [2]
5. One mark for each countable noun used to fill the gaps (examples: When I go to my <u>nature reserve</u>, I like to take a <u>notebook</u> and a <u>pair of binoculars</u>). [3]
6. One mark each.
   a Singapore Zoo has <u>a large number of</u> monkeys.
   b I would like <u>some</u> information about recycling.
   c We have <u>plenty of</u> time, so we will not be late. [3]
7. Two marks. Award-winning is an example of a compound adjective. Example sentence: He created an award-winning zoo. [2]
8. One mark each: smaller, more entertaining, colder, slower [4]
9. One mark for each sentence that uses the comparative adjectives correctly.
   Example responses:
   • Cheetahs are smaller than tigers.
   • Monkeys are more entertaining than snakes.
   • Penguins live in colder parts of the world than lions.
   • A bus is slower than a train. [4]
10. Example responses:
    • Where the setting is.
    • Which adjectives to use. [2]

Total marks: 25

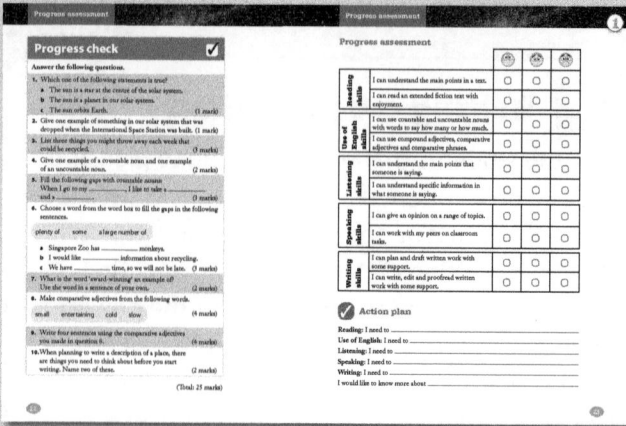

Answers:
1. B types
2. countable noun: telescope; uncountable noun: space
3. a large amount of
4. C The jade frog was worth a lot of money.
5. Example responses: man-eating, sharp-toothed, short-haired, big-eyed
6. Example responses: A lion is faster than a tortoise. A tortoise is quieter than a lion.
7. C going to sleep
8. Example answer: There is a high mountain near my home and the views all around are beautiful. On a clear day, you can see three different countries from the top!

Reflection

Reflecting on your learning

Have a discussion with the class about how they will continue to use the different skills they have covered in this unit. Students should then work independently on the progress assessment task. For each of the skills, ask them to tick the box that they think most fits how well they are doing. Now move on to the action plan questions. The aim is to encourage students to identify which skills they think they need more practice in, while reinforcing the skills they can do well. Give students the opportunity to practise the skills they have identified and revisit the action plan after a few weeks, encouraging students to compare later attempts with the first.

End-of-unit quiz

Workbook page 9: Our natural world quiz

Students can do this quiz in the class under timed conditions or on their own at home.

Progress assessment

Listening

End-of-unit activity

This activity will allow students to evaluate the unit and identify what they have found easy and interesting in the unit. Explain to the students that they will hear a conversation between Mohammad and Abdul about the topics in this unit. Listen to Track TB1.1 together and then ask them to answer the questions below. A transcript of Track TB1.1 can be found on the CD.

1. What fact does Mohammad say he has learned about the solar system?
2. What does Mohammad say he is using more of in his writing?
3. Where is the zoo that Mohammad has heard about?
4. What are Abdul and Mohammad going to do next?

Let the students answer the questions while they are listening. Give them the answers when they have listened to the recording twice (see the photocopiable sheet on the CD).

Answers:
1. That it takes more than 800 years to fly from the Earth to Pluto.
2. adjectives
3. Singapore
4. Plan a trip to visit a zoo.

When they have answered the questions, ask them to think of a fact that they have learned about the solar system and something they have learned about Singapore Zoo. Ask them to share their responses with the class.

Reflection

Teacher reflection

1. Which parts of the unit did the students enjoy most? Why was this?
2. Was there anything that the students found difficult in this unit? How can I make sure this is easier next time?
3. Considering the learning objectives and content, what did the students successfully learn while studying this unit?
4. Considering the learning objectives and content, what did the students struggle with while studying this unit? Why was this? What could I do to help them more?
5. Which parts of the unit did I teach well? How did I achieve this?
6. Which parts of the unit did I struggle to teach well? What can I do to improve this?
7. Next time I teach this unit, is there anything I can do to improve the learning experience for my students?

2 Fit for life

Learning objectives

In this unit, students will:

- Understand specific information in texts. **pages 20, 30** *7Re2*
- Recognise the attitude or opinion of the writer. **page 30** *7Re5*
- Deduce meaning from context. **page 20** *7Re6*
- Use familiar and some unfamiliar paper and digital resources to check meaning and extend understanding. **pages 25, 29** *7Re9*
- Brainstorm, plan and draft written work. **pages 24, 31** *7W1*
- Compose, edit and proofread written work at text level, with some support. **pages 24, 31** *7W2*
- Write, with some support, with moderate grammatical accuracy. **pages 24, 31** *7W3*
- Use, with some support, style and register appropriate to a limited range of written genres. **page 31** *7W5*
- Punctuate, with accuracy, a growing range of written work. **page 25** *7W8*
- Use a range of pronouns including indefinite pronouns *anybody, anyone, anything* and quantitative pronouns *everyone, everything, none, more, less, a few*. **pages 22–23** *7Ug3*
- Use a range of simple perfect forms to express [recent, indefinite and unfinished] past. **pages 26–27** *7Ug4*
- Understand, with little or no support, the main points in extended talk. **page 24** *7L1*
- Understand, with little or no support, most specific information in extended talk. **page 24** *7L2*
- Recognise, with little or no support, the opinion of the speaker(s) in extended talk. **page 24** *7L5*
- Ask questions to clarify meaning. **pages 19, 28–29** *7S2*
- Give an opinion, at discourse level. **pages 28–29** *7S3*
- Use appropriate subject-specific vocabulary and syntax. **pages 19, 29** *7S7*

Setting the scene

Fit for life

Write the unit title on the board and explain to the students that in this unit they will be focusing on fitness and health. Discuss the meaning of the word 'fit' (healthy and strong from plenty of exercise). Ask the students why it is important to stay physically fit and active (because it helps with overall health). Ask the students to look at the photos on page 24 of the Student Book and discuss what each photo shows. Then ask them to read the three quotations. Explain to the students that Jim Rohn was an American author, who was born into a poor farming family and went on to become extremely wealthy. He used his own story to inspire others. Explain that Change 4 Life encourages people to make a small change in their lives that will benefit their health. The students may be familiar with the American tennis player, Serena Williams. Tell them that she is one of the most successful female tennis players of all time.

Thinking ahead

In this activity, students will think about some questions relating to how they stay fit and healthy. You could start by asking them how they get to school in the morning. Do they walk or cycle or travel by bus or car? Ask which of these is likely to keep them more fit. Now ask the students to think about the questions in the Thinking ahead activity. Students may keep fit and healthy by doing sports in school, by doing physical exercise outside school and by eating healthy food. The sport they like watching most could be one they watch at school or on television. They might have a favourite sporting personality who plays their favourite sport or they might like a sports personality and not be very interested in the sport they play. When discussing the final question, ask the students whether they do most or all of their exercise in school or whether they do a lot outside school. What are the reasons for this?

Fit for life

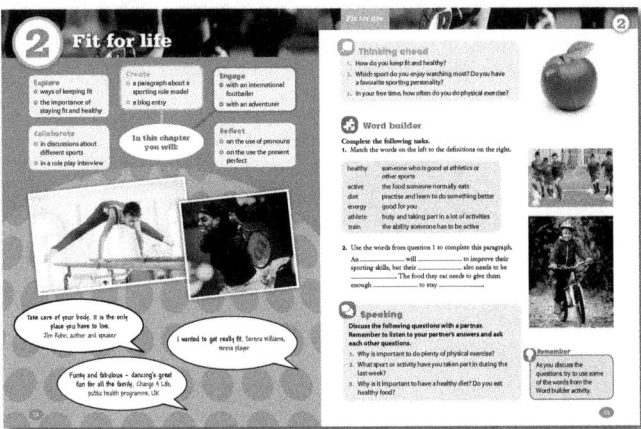

before they begin to discuss the questions in the activity. Now direct the students' attention to the questions. Ask them to discuss their answers in pairs. Encourage them to use words from the Word builder activity as well as some of the words you have written on the board.

Theme opener

Workbook page 10: Fit for life

Page 10 of the Workbook gives students practice in answering questions relating to the theme of the unit. Students will listen to two friends talk about how they keep healthy. They will show their understanding by answering some multiple-choice questions, and then practise their writing skills by writing a letter to a friend.

Answers:

1. Example: This week, I am keeping healthy by going swimming. Next week, I will eat more fruit and vegetables to be healthier.
2. **C** he plays football   3. **B** a banana
4. **C** Novak Djokovic   5. at the weekend
6. Check that the students have started (for example, 'Dear David') and ended (for example, 'Write back soon, Roman') as is appropriate for an informal letter. Check that they have given some factual information in the letter and that they have asked their friend a question.

Vocabulary

Word builder

This section introduces students to some of the vocabulary that they will find in the unit. Ask them to match the words in the left-hand column with their definitions on the right and then use the words to fill the gaps in the paragraph.

Answers:

1. healthy: good for you

   active: busy and taking part in a lot of activities

   diet: the food someone normally eats

   energy: the ability someone has to be active

   athlete: someone who is good at athletics or other sports

   train: practise and learn to do something better

2. An <u>athlete</u> will <u>train</u> to improve their sporting skills, but their <u>diet</u> also needs to be <u>healthy</u>. The food they eat needs to give them enough <u>energy</u> to stay <u>active</u>.

Extension

Class fitness

Explain to the students that they are going to decide on one thing they could do as a class to become more fit and healthy. For example, they could do more exercise together or eat less sugar. Ask the students to get into groups to plan what they want the class to do to be healthier. Encourage them to think of at least two reasons why this will make the class healthier. Ask one member of each group to speak for about a minute on their chosen method and reasons why they think it is a good idea. When someone from each group has spoken, everyone can vote on the best method. You will have the casting vote if there is a draw. Why not actually do it next week and see if everyone in the class feels healthier as a result?

Speaking

Speaking

Students may like to have some vocabulary on the board to help them with this speaking activity. Here are some examples you could write on the board for each question:

1. health, fitness, heart, body, circulation
2. lesson, club, after-school club, gymnasium, competition
3. vitamins, minerals, calcium, carbohydrate, protein

Ensure the students understand the meaning of the words you have written on the board

19

Reading

The Youth Olympic Games

Prior knowledge

Students will read some information about the Youth Olympic Games. Students will probably have heard of the Olympic Games but may be less familiar with the more recent Youth Olympic Games. Ask the students how often the Olympic Games are held (every four years) and which season they are held in (one summer, one winter). Ask them to give some example sports from each (summer – athletics, javelin, long jump, high jump, swimming, diving, equestrian; winter – skiing, ice-skating, bobsleigh, ice hockey, curling).

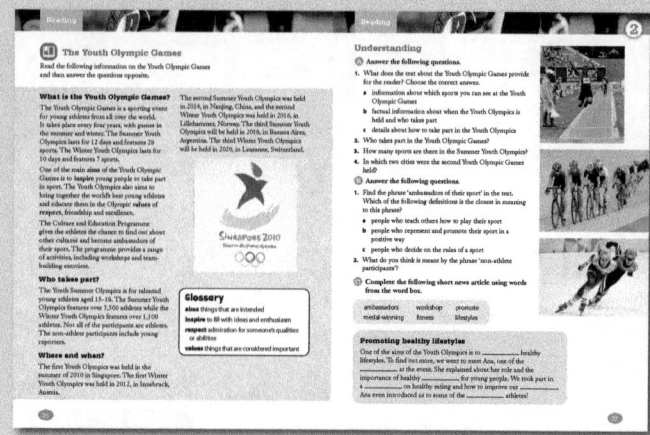

Reading

 The Youth Olympic Games

Before the students read the text, explain that it is a piece of non-fiction that gives the reader factual information. Remind them of the factual information about the solar system that they read in Unit 1 and of the features of factual text, such as present tense and the use of facts rather than opinions. Elicit other examples of non-fiction writing (examples: information leaflets, articles in magazines and newspapers, diary entries, letters, reports).

Read the text together and discuss the meaning of the words in the Glossary. Stop at any other unfamiliar words and discuss their meaning (examples: features, ambassadors, talented, workshops, participants). Can the students guess the meaning of the words from the context, using clues in the text and words on either side?

Ask the students to find the main heading (The Youth Olympic Games) and the subheadings (What is the Youth Olympic Games? Who takes part? Where and when?). Discuss how these subheadings help the reader know what information will be included in each paragraph.

Student Book answers

Understanding

Give the students time to read the text again on their own and then answer the questions.

Answers:

A 1. b factual information about when the Youth Olympics is held and who takes part
 2. Talented young athletes from all over the world.
 3. 28
 4. Nanjing and Lillehammer

B 1. b people who represent and promote their sport in a positive way
 2. People such as reporters who are taking part in the games but are not athletes.

C Ask the students to complete this exercise on their own. When they have completed it, they may check their answers with their partner.

One of the aims of the Youth Olympics is to <u>promote</u> healthy lifestyles. To find out more, we went to meet Ana, one of the <u>ambassadors</u> at the event. She explained about her role and the importance of healthy <u>lifestyles</u> for young people. We took part in a <u>workshop</u> on healthy eating and how to improve our <u>fitness</u>. Ana even introduced us to some of the <u>medal-winning</u> athletes!

20

Reading

Reading

Workbook page 11: Youth Olympic Games

Page 11 of the Workbook revisits the theme of the Youth Olympic Games. Students read an interview with Burzo Ciprian, from Romania, who designed the medals given out at Lillehammer in 2016. Then they answer questions about the reading to test their understanding.

Answers:

1. Either of: the Youth Olympic Games spirit or the look of the Winter Games
2. the outline of the mountains in Norway
3. glass
4. B   symbol
5. Example: Burzo chose two lines to represent skis, sledges and skates because these come in pairs, and leave a trail of two lines behind them.

Extension

Writing a report

Ask the students to imagine they have seen an event at the Youth Olympic Games and they are going to write a report about the event. Explain that reports or accounts of events are usually written in the past tense and they often use the first person. They usually include facts and may include some of the writer's opinions.

When the students have decided on the event they will write about, ask them to plan their report. Explain that they should try to make their report as interesting as possible, using a lively style to catch the reader's attention. You may wish to provide a writing frame. For example:

- Opening paragraph: Introduce the event – was it an important event? Who was taking part? Include any relevant facts and the most important details about the event.

- Main body of text: Describe what happened during the event in the order it happened. Give an opinion about the event.

- Closing paragraph: Sum up the event and your opinions about it.

Now ask the students to write the report. When they have finished, ask them to check their reports and correct any mistakes in punctuation, spelling or grammar before reading them to a partner.

Use of English

Pronouns

Grammar

Pronouns

In this section students build on their knowledge of pronouns. Students may be familiar with personal pronouns from primary level. Remind them that pronouns are words we use instead of nouns in a sentence. Read the examples of personal pronouns in the language focus box and in the Remember feature on page 28 of the Student Book. Then explain that we use indefinite pronouns to refer to people or things without saying exactly who the people are or what the thing is. Go through the examples of indefinite pronouns in the language focus box and write some others on the board. (Examples: another, either, neither, any, others.) Explain that these words can sometimes function as other parts of speech as well. For example, when they are used before nouns (examples: another person; neither book), they are not used as indefinite pronouns (they are not replacing nouns). When they are used before nouns they are known as 'determiners'. Give some examples of how the indefinite pronouns in the language focus box and on the board can be used in sentences. (Examples: Everyone was ready for the match. I saw somebody score a goal. No one knew what was happening. He gave me an apple and then he gave me another.)

Student Book answers

Using pronouns

Ask the students to complete the exercises on their own and then check their answers with a partner.

Answers:

A 1. Jamal picked up the ball and threw <u>it</u> to me.
   2. Nara phoned her friend Kiko and invited <u>her</u> to lunch.
   3. Please can you give <u>me</u> that book?

B 1. Does <u>anyone/anybody</u> have a football I could borrow?
   2. I hope you have <u>everything</u> you need.
   3. I like watching gymnastics but I don't know <u>anything</u> about it.

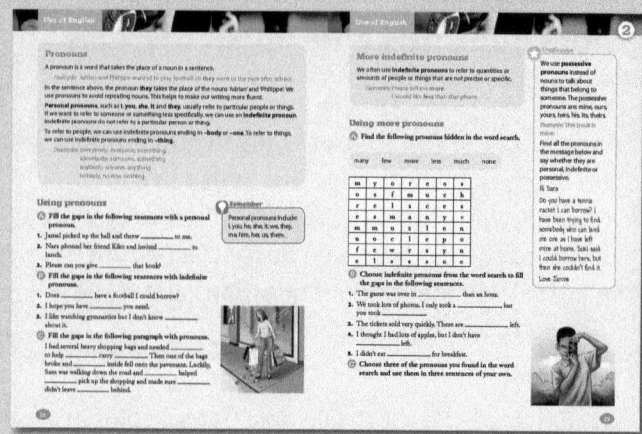

C   I had several heavy shopping bags and needed <u>someone</u> to help <u>me</u> carry <u>them</u>. Then one of the bags broke and <u>everything</u> inside fell onto the pavement. Luckily, Sam was walking down the road and <u>he</u> helped <u>me</u> pick up the shopping and made sure <u>I</u> didn't leave <u>anything</u> behind.

Grammar

More indefinite pronouns

This section builds on students' understanding of indefinite pronouns, focusing on the quantitative pronouns, such as more, less and a few. Read through the language focus box together and provide some more examples of pronouns we use to refer to quantities or amounts (examples: many, little, much, none, several, enough, most, plenty). Remind students that the words can also function as determiners when they are used before a noun. Read the examples in the language focus box. Give some further examples of how indefinite pronouns can be used in sentences. (Examples: I had eaten enough. He didn't know much about history. I wanted some information and you have given me plenty.)

⭐ Challenge

This activity gives students practice in distinguishing different types of pronouns, including possessive pronouns. Students may be familiar with possessive pronouns from primary level, but remind them that these are used to express ownership and ask them to read the list of possessive pronouns in the Challenge feature.

Answers:

you (personal), I (personal), somebody (indefinite), me (personal), mine (possessive), hers (possessive), she (personal), it (personal)

22

Use of English

Student Book answers

Using more pronouns

A Ask the students to find the pronouns in the word search on their own and then check with a partner that they have found them all.

m	y	o	r	e	o	s
o	s	f	m	u	c	h
r	e	l	s	c	e	s
e	s	m	a	n	y	v
m	m	u	z	i	e	n
u	o	c	l	e	p	o
f	e	w	r	s	y	n
e	l	s	s	s	o	e

B Ask the students to complete the sentences using the pronouns they have found in the word search.

Answers:

1. The game was over in <u>less</u> than an hour.
2. We took lots of photos. I only took a <u>few</u>, but you took <u>more</u>.
3. The tickets sold very quickly. There are <u>none</u> left.
4. I thought I had lots of apples, but I don't have <u>many</u> left.
5. I didn't eat <u>much</u> for breakfast.

C Students write three sentences of their own. This is a free response so check that students have written three sentences and that each contains an indefinite pronoun that has been used correctly.

Use of English

Workbook page 12: Indefinite pronouns

Page 12 gives students practice in using indefinite pronouns. Set as homework or as an in-class exercise and go through the answers together, making sure to stop at any difficulties.

Answers:

1. She won prizes for <u>everything</u> she did.
2. We waited for a long time, but <u>no one</u> came.
3. I looked in the box, but there was <u>nothing</u> in it.
4. <u>Everyone</u> knows they should be healthy.
5. They all waited quietly until <u>somebody</u> got up and left the room.
6. <u>Many</u> agree that we need to look after the natural world. ✓
7. I was so thirsty I finished all the water in my glass, but I still wanted <u>more</u>.
8. Aleeza hoped to buy some mangoes, but there were <u>none</u> left. ✓
9. How <u>much</u> does that sports bag cost?
10. The bus is due in <u>less</u> than an hour. ✓
11. Example response:

    Although I have done some practice for Sports Day, I think I need to do <u>more</u>. Tomorrow, I'll ask if <u>anyone</u> wants to join me in running round the field. If I practise enough, then on Sports Day, <u>nobody</u> will beat me!

Extension

Practising pronouns

This activity will give students more practice with using pronouns, including personal, indefinite and possessive pronouns. Students who completed the Challenge activity on page 29 of the Student Book will have some knowledge of possessive pronouns, but those who have not may need some guidance. Write the possessive pronouns on the board and explain that these are used when we are talking about ownership. Write some examples of how they can be used in sentences and explain that possessive pronouns should not be confused with possessive adjectives/determiners, which are used before nouns.

Now give the students a copy of the incomplete commentary (see the photocopiable sheet on the CD) and ask them to fill the gaps with pronouns.

Answers:

So now it is the Indonesian athlete who is coming to collect a gold medal and <u>she</u> looks very happy. "This gold medal is <u>yours</u>," says the person giving the medals. <u>Everyone</u> in the crowd is cheering. <u>Someone</u> has thrown flowers for the gold medallist and <u>she</u> bends down to pick <u>them</u> up. "These are <u>mine</u> too," she laughs. Now the gold medal winner is giving a brief speech. "Thank you. This medal is not just <u>mine</u> but it is <u>yours</u> as well because I only achieved it with your support." <u>Everyone</u> in the crowd starts to clap.

Listening

Sporting role models

Prior knowledge

Explain to the students that they are going to listen to an interview with a professional footballer. As a pre-listening activity, ask students if they can name any professional footballers or sportsmen or sportswomen from other sports that they like and admire. Ask them why they like the people they have named. Ideas might include: being a talented player, winning a lot of matches, scoring a lot of goals, being a good team player, being a good team captain. Discuss the meaning of the phrase 'sporting role model' and ask the students whether they think people who play sport professionally can have an influence on young people. They can then tell you how sports people influence young people – ask them for examples of famous sports people who have had an influence on others, either good or bad. Ask them whether they think sports people should set an example to young people in the way they behave. You may wish to put some names on the board of some possible sporting role models: David Beckham, Sergei Bubka, Usain Bolt, Michael Phelps, Serena Williams, Jessica Ennis, Roger Federer.

Listening

 Track 2.1: Sporting role models

Listen to Track 2.1 together. Then discuss the meaning of the words in the Glossary. Give examples of how each word can be used in a sentence to ensure the students understand their meanings before they answer the questions. A full transcript of Track 2.1 is available on the CD.

Student Book answers

Understanding

Ask the students to listen to the recording again and answer the questions individually.

Answers:

A 1. Two of Adam's biggest influences are his <u>parents</u> and his club.

2. Adam has enjoyed the <u>friendship</u> and support he has received at the club.

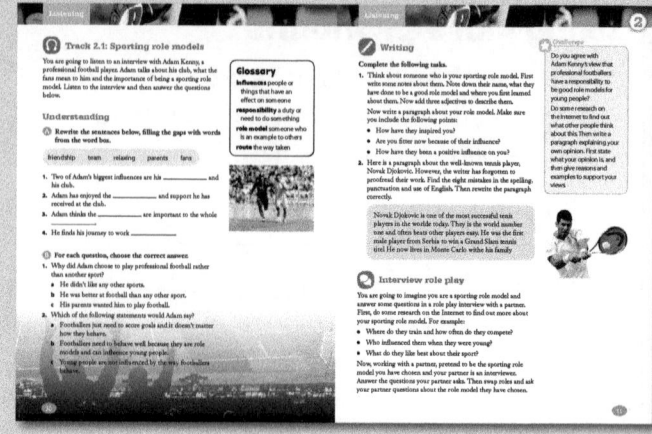

3. Adam thinks the <u>fans</u> are important to the whole <u>team</u>.

4. He finds his journey to work <u>relaxing</u>.

B 1. b He was better at football than any other sport.

2. b Footballers need to behave well because they are role models and can influence young people.

Writing

 Writing

1. Explain to the students that they are going to write a paragraph about a sporting role model. Ask them to include the three bullet points mentioned on page 31 of the Student Book.

2. Ask students to proofread and correct the paragraph about Novak Djokovic. Explain that when they are proofreading, they need to look for several types of error. These could include: spelling mistakes; subject-verb agreement; subject-pronoun agreement; and punctuation.

Answer:

Novak Djokovic is one of the most successful <u>tennis</u> players in the <u>world</u> today. <u>He</u> is the world number one and often beats other players <u>easily</u>. He was the first male player from Serbia to win a Grand Slam tennis <u>title.</u> He now lives in Monte Carlo <u>with</u> his family.

24

Listening

Speaking

Interview role play

Ask the students to research some more about a sporting role model – they could use the Internet, school library, local public library, or ask friends or family for information. While they are doing their research, they will find some words that are specific to the particular sport. Ask them to make sure they have written this vocabulary down so they can use it later.

When they have completed their research, ask them to imagine they are the sporting role model being interviewed by a partner. They should listen to their partner's questions and give accurate answers. Then the partner should ask one question about what they have heard that they wish to clarify (either a fact or an opinion).

Extension

You, the sporting role model

Tell the students to imagine they have won a gold medal at the Olympic Games. They now have to make sure they become a sporting role model. What are they going to do to help others? They need to plan what they are going to do. Write some ideas on the board for them to read and be inspired by:

- set up a sports school (the same sport they did in the Olympics)
- take a class once a week after school
- take some students running before school
- give students a talk on how to stay fit
- set up a website where students can find a daily challenge.

Ask the students to write a few sentences to describe their plans.

Challenge

In this activity, students write a paragraph giving their opinion about whether professional footballers have a responsibility to be good role models for young people. Ask the students to do some research to find examples of footballers who are good role models and have had positive effects on young people. Can they also find examples of professional footballers who are not good role models? If a footballer breaks the rules or behaves badly off the pitch, could this have an effect on young people? Does it matter how footballers behave off the pitch if they are playing well and scoring goals? Students then write their paragraph giving their own opinion, with reasons and examples to support their views.

Listening

Workbook page 13: Sporting role models

Page 13 of the Workbook is a listening exercise, for students to complete on their own as homework or in class. When students have completed the exercise, you may want to listen to Track WB2.2 together, stopping at any unfamiliar words. Check students' answers and play again if necessary to make sure students have understood.

Answers:

1. role model: someone who sets a good example to others

   wheelchair: a chair fitted with wheels

   champion: someone who has won a contest or competition

   Paralympic Games: a major sporting event for athletes with disabilities

2. A good athlete might compete at the Olympics or the Paralympic Games. However, a good sporting role model will use their fame for good causes, for example, to help children do better in schools.

3. **B** Wales
4. **A** wheelchair racing
5. **B** 11
6. London
7. Example response:

   Tanni is a good sporting role model because she is committed to her sport but also helps all disabled people.

25

Use of English

The present perfect

The present perfect

In this section students will build on their knowledge of tenses, focusing on the present perfect. Read through the first part of the language focus box on page 32 of the Student Book, which explains how the present perfect is formed. Remind students that in regular verbs the past participle is made by adding '–ed' to the verb stem (or just '–d' if the verb ends with the letter 'e'). In irregular verbs it is formed in different ways. Give some examples (taken, spoken, bought, got, lost, put, done, seen, found, etc.). Read through the rest of the language focus box describing the different uses of the present perfect. Give some more examples of each case. (Examples: 'I have been on holiday to Italy', 'I have lost my keys', 'They have been married for five years.')

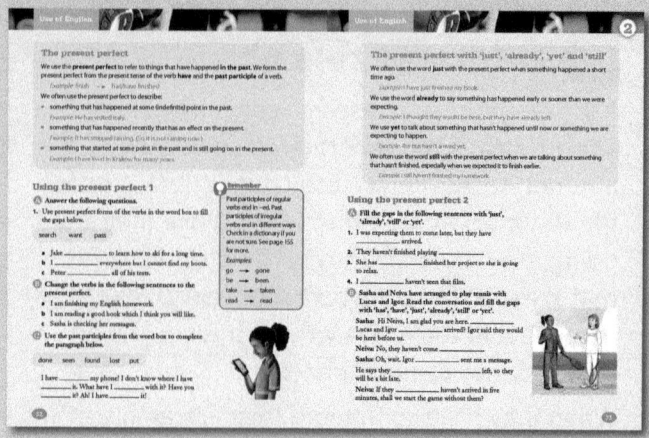

Student Book answers

Using the present perfect 1

Ask the students to answer the questions on their own.

Answers:

A   1. Jake <u>has wanted</u> to learn how to ski for a long time.
   2. I <u>have searched</u> everywhere but I cannot find my boots.
   3. Peter <u>has passed</u> all of his tests.

B   a   I <u>have finished</u> my English homework.
   b   I <u>have read</u> a good book which I think you will like.
   c   Sasha <u>has checked</u> her messages.

C   I have <u>lost</u> my phone! I don't know where I have <u>put</u> it. What have I <u>done</u> with it? Have you <u>seen</u> it? Ah! I have <u>found</u> it!

Grammar

The present perfect with 'just', 'already', 'yet' and 'still'

In this section students focus on the use of the words 'just', 'already', 'yet' and 'still' with the present perfect to add further information about when something has happened. Read through the information in the language focus box on page 33 of the Student Book. Give some more examples, focusing on the meanings of the words in each case. (Examples: The game has just started. The plane has just landed. The game has already started. The plane has already landed. The game hasn't started yet. The plane hasn't landed yet. The game still hasn't started. The plane still hasn't landed. The game hasn't started yet. The plane hasn't landed yet.) Focus students' attention on the position of the words 'just', 'already', 'still' or 'yet' in the examples. Explain that when we use these words with the present perfect 'already' and 'just' usually come between the two parts of the verb, 'still' usually comes between the subject and the first part of the verb and 'yet' usually comes at the end of the sentence.

Use of English

Student Book answers

Using the present perfect 2

Answers:

A 1. I was expecting them to come later, but they have <u>already</u> arrived.
   2. They haven't finished playing <u>yet</u>.
   3. She has <u>just</u> finished her project so she is going to relax.
   4. I <u>still</u> haven't seen that film.

B **Sasha:** Hi Neiva. I am glad you are here. <u>Have</u> Lucas and Igor <u>already</u> arrived? Igor said they would be here before us.

   Neiva: No, they haven't come <u>yet</u>.

   Sasha: Oh, wait. Igor <u>has</u> sent me a message. He says they <u>have just</u> left, so they will be a bit late.

   Neiva: If they <u>still</u> haven't arrived in five minutes, shall we start the game without them?

Use of English

Workbook page 14: The present perfect

On page 14 of the Workbook, students can practise using the present perfect. Set as homework or as an in-class exercise, and go through the answers together. Make sure students have correctly used irregular past participles.

Answers:

1. I <u>have stayed</u> in the same caravan near the sea for many of my holidays. (R)
2. He <u>has travelled</u> to Paris frequently for business. (R)
3. They <u>have watched</u> a tennis match at Wimbledon every year for the last ten years. (R)
4. Meera <u>has seen</u> a really good film at the cinema. (I)
5. Today, I <u>have eaten</u> some fruit and some cereal. (I)
6. Did you see the model boat that Sam and Jack <u>have made</u>? (I)
7. Since Elena was young, she <u>has been</u> very active. She <u>has jogged</u> twice a week since she was 14. Recently, she <u>has attended</u> a yoga class on Saturdays too. Through the class, she <u>has met</u> some people who also like running. So she <u>has started</u> a running group with her friends and they <u>have run</u> every week for the last year. As a group, they <u>have trained</u> to run a marathon.
8. Students' own answers. Make sure that they have correctly used the present perfect in their sentence.

Extension

Message to a friend

Ask the students to write a message to a friend about something that has just happened, something they have just done, or somewhere they have just been. Tell them to give as much detail as they can about what has happened and use at least three verbs in the present perfect. When they have finished, tell them to show their message to a partner. The partner should check how many times they have used the present perfect.

Speaking

Keeping fit

Prior knowledge

The photographs on page 34 of the Student Book will serve as stimuli for students to discuss different kinds of physical activity, from indoor sports to outdoor adventure sports. Before the students begin the speaking activities, discuss what they know about adventure sports and ask them for some examples. (Examples: trekking/kayaking/rock climbing/canoeing.) Ask the students if they have ever taken part in any adventurous activities and whether they enjoyed them. Explain that safety is important when doing all kinds of activities and these activities should only be done with the help of an adult. You may wish to provide some vocabulary on the board to help the students in their discussions. (Examples: indoors, outdoors, mountain climbing, rafting, extreme sport, exciting, risky, frightening, dangerous, safe, life jacket, helmet, ropes.)

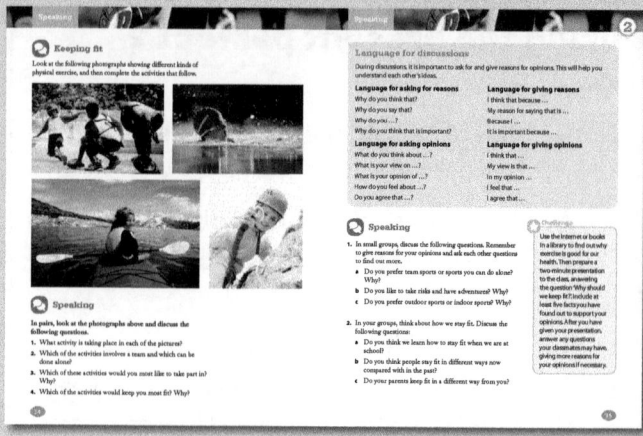

Speaking

 Speaking

In this activity students discuss the pictures on page 34 of the Student Book in pairs. The questions relate closely to the photographs and will encourage students to start thinking about whether they would like to take part in adventurous activities. For the first question, encourage students to describe the sport or activity shown in each picture. Can it be done outdoors or indoors? Is it an adventurous sport? Are there any risks involved? The students then discuss which of the activities can be done alone and which involves a team, before giving their opinion about which of the activities they would most like to take part in, and which would keep you most fit. Encourage the students to give at least two reasons for their choice.

Language for discussions

Explain to the students that certain words and phrases help the participants in a discussion follow and respond to the discussion. Direct the students' attention to the language focus box on page 35 of the Student Book. Elicit from the students the meaning of 'opinion' (what you think about something or a belief) and 'reason' (why something happens or why you think something). Read through the examples of language that can be used to give opinions and reasons with the students. Give some further examples.

Now ask the students a question about which they will have an opinion. (Examples: Should children do more sport at school? Should children have to wear a uniform at school? Should the school holidays be longer?) Ask them first to think what their opinion is and use one or more of the phrases from the language focus box to give their opinion to a partner. Then, ask them why they have that opinion. They should then use one or more of the phrases to give their reasons.

Speaking

 Speaking

In this section students will give their opinions on different kinds of sports and how we stay fit. First, remind them of the words and phrases they have discussed for giving opinions and write some other examples on the board. (Examples: My thoughts on this are …; What I think is …; From my point of view …; What I feel about this is … .)

Before the students discuss question 1, elicit some more examples of team sports not shown in the pictures (hockey, cricket, rugby, basketball, netball) and sports they can do alone (diving, running, archery, long jump, javelin). Give reasons why taking risks and having adventures might be good (sense of achievement, excitement, fun) and why there might be problems (dangerous, could get injured, might get lost).

Speaking

For question 2, give some examples of places where we can do activities that help us stay fit (school, gym club, sports centre, outdoors, park, etc.). Discuss whether their parents and other adults take part in sports or other activities that help to keep them fit. Now ask students to get into small groups to discuss the questions in the Student Book.

⭐ Challenge

In this activity students find out reasons why exercise is good for our health. Then they give a class presentation answering the question 'Why should we keep fit?' When they are doing their research, encourage them to find out facts about the health benefits of exercise. Are people who do lots of exercise healthier than people who do not? Can exercise help to prevent some illnesses? Is there evidence to show that if we do not keep fit, we will be less healthy? When they have finished their research, ask them to plan their presentation, with at least five facts to support their opinion. When they have given their presentation, they answer any questions their classmates have, including unexpected questions that may require them to give further examples and reasons.

Speaking

Workbook page 15: Language of discussion

Page 15 of the Workbook gives students extra practice in using language of discussion. First, they will hear a recording of teenagers planning a holiday and will answer questions to test their comprehension. Then, they will write answers to questions to help them prepare for the spoken element.

Answers:
1. **B** a boat
2. **C** an owl
3. **B** gymnastics
4. They can write their history project about it.

5. Examples: I love being by the sea/I don't agree with you/I also want to be relaxed on holiday/I wouldn't feel relaxed on a boat/that does not sound relaxing at all!/I think that sounds a bit scary/I don't want to be surrounded by wild animals/I think we should go on a fitness holiday/that sounds interesting

6. Students should back up their suggestions with reasons for their answer. Example: I would like a sports holiday where we play team games and try some new sports, so I can have fun and get fitter.

7. Students will have completed this exercise at home, but may not have had the opportunity to speak aloud to a partner. Remind them that when they are working on a speaking exercise, it is helpful if they speak aloud, even if they are alone. You could ask students to work in pairs to practise their short speeches in class. While they are doing this, circulate to check their pronunciation and that they are giving reasons for their responses.

Extension

A new gymnasium

This activity gives students more practice in giving opinions and reasons. Tell the students that their school is going to build a new gymnasium. Ask them to give you three reasons why this is a good thing. Write on the board some language for giving reasons to remind them: because, therefore, as a result.

Now, tell the students that the school is going to charge the students to use the gym. Ask them to work in small groups and discuss their opinons about this. Write on the board some language for giving opinions to remind them: I think this because …, My view is that …, I believe that …, In my opinion … .

Reading corner

Reading corner

Prior knowledge

Explain to the students that they are going to read a blog about the adventurer and explorer Bear Grylls. They will then answer some questions before writing a blog entry of their own. Start by telling the students a bit about Bear Grylls' life – for example, he was born in 1974 and from an early age enjoyed climbing and sailing. As a teenager, he learned to skydive. Discuss the meaning of 'skydiving' (jumping from a plane and falling freely before opening a parachute). As a child, he had always wanted to climb Mount Everest, the highest mountain in the world. He achieved his ambition when he was just 23 years old, becoming one of the youngest people ever to reach the top of the mountain. Since then he has continued to explore different parts of the world and now presents television programmes about his adventures.

Reading

Bear Grylls' blog

Before the students read the blog entry, remind them that a blog is a piece of writing that is uploaded onto the Internet. The person who writes a blog is called a blogger. Explain that a blogger often writes about particular things or events in their life, or they may use their blog as an online diary for others to read. Draw students' attention to the title of the blog 'Taste for adventure'. What do they think this means? (If someone has a taste for something it means they like or enjoy it.) Now read the blog with the class. Students may need support with some of the vocabulary, so read the Glossary words and their definitions and discuss the meaning of any other difficult words or phrases (examples: 'without a doubt', 'Isle of Wight', 'cliffs', 'get in trouble'). When you have finished reading, discuss what the blog tells us about Bear Grylls (something about his childhood and where his love of adventure came from; his personal opinions and feelings about adventures and being outdoors). Explain that blogs often contain facts and other information about things that have happened, but they often also contain opinions and the blogger's personal

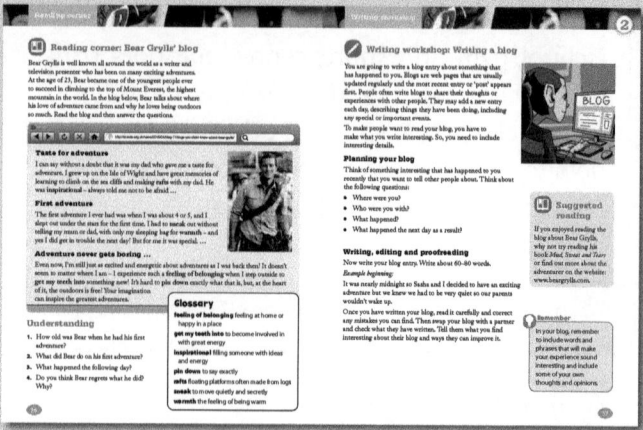

thoughts and ideas. Tell them that they are usually written in the first person (with the use of the word 'I'). Bear Grylls is addressing the reader, so we feel as though he is talking directly to us. This helps to make the reader interested in what they are reading.

Student Book answers

Understanding

Ask students to read the blog again and then answer the questions that follow.

Answers:

1. Bear was four or five when he had his first adventure.
2. He slept out under the stars on his own.
3. He got into trouble with his parents – perhaps they told him off and told him not to do it again.
4. Accept answers such as: No, I don't think Bear regrets what he did, as he says the adventure was special and he still finds adventures exciting now.

Writing workshop

Writing workshop

✏️ Writing a blog

Tell the students that they are now going to plan and write a blog entry of their own.

Planning

Remind them about the features of Bear Grylls' blog that they discussed (first person, opinions and personal thoughts and ideas). Explain that blogs are often updated regularly so that bloggers can share their experiences and thoughts with the readers, so each blog entry needs to include interesting details. This will make the readers want to read the blog again next time it is updated.

Ask the students to think of something interesting or exciting that has happened to them recently that they want to share with other people. They should then use the bullet points on page 37 of the Student Book to help them plan their blog.

Writing, editing and proofreading

When the students have finished planning, ask them to read the example beginning on page 37 of the Student Book. The time sets the scene and we know there are two people involved (Sasha and I) so the reader is immediately interested in knowing what Sasha and I will be doing at midnight. Remind students that the event they describe in their blog needs to be interesting and setting the scene very briefly at the beginning helps to add interest for the reader.

When students have written their blog, ask them to read it through, checking carefully for any mistakes in spelling, punctuation and grammar. Then they should swap it with a partner who will tell them what they find interesting in the blog and if there is anything that could be improved.

📖 Suggested reading

If the students found the blog about Bear Grylls interesting, suggest that they could find out more about him on his website (www.beargrylls.com) or by reading his book *Mud, Sweat and Tears*.

Workbook page 16: Writing a blog

Page 16 of the Workbook is a writing workshop for students to complete on their own as homework or in class. You may want to go through the exercise in class first to make sure students understand.

Students first pick a sport or activity to write about and make some notes, for example:

Scuba diving

- need a wetsuit, snorkel, air tank
- go and dive on a reef
- there will be many fish and maybe even a shark.

Then students will write their blog. When they have completed the blog, check that they have used the features of a blog (first person, opinions, and personal thoughts and ideas) and powerful adjectives to make their blog more interesting. Here is an example:

Hi everyone. I have had such an exciting week – there is so much to tell you about. I have discovered an exciting new sport called scuba diving. You have to go on a boat into the sea and pull on a wetsuit. You also need an air tank on your back. Don't worry though, you will be given training how to use it.

Why should you try it? Well, it is really exciting. You feel like you are flying through the water along the bottom of the sea. The colours of the fish are incredible. Watch out for any sharks though!

✏️ Blog entry

Extension

Ask the students to imagine that they are a well-known professional sports person who has many fans. When they have decided who they are, they should now imagine that the person is going to write their first ever blog entry. Remind the students that they should write the blog in the first person, using 'I', as if they are the sports person themselves. Ask them to explain what they have achieved in sport, how they have been helping others in their local community and how the readers can join in with what they have been doing. Remind them to include some opinions and personal thoughts and details that will be interesting for the reader.

Progress assessment

Progress check

Student Book answers

Progress check

1. One mark. b Athletes from all over the world take part in the Youth Olympic Games. [1]

2. One mark. a over 3,500 [1]

3. One mark each:
   a Would you like <u>anything</u> else?
   b <u>Someone</u> in the gym was listening to music.
   c Only <u>a few</u> of my friends like swimming. [3]

4. Two marks each:
   a <u>Everyone</u> should try to stay fit and healthy.
   b I have learned a lot about Bear Grylls but I want to find out <u>more</u>. [2]

5. Two marks each. Sample responses:
   • Can someone open the window?
   • If you are hungry you should have something to eat.
   • I heard the doorbell but there was nobody there. [4]

6. One mark each:
   a I <u>have read</u> a good book which I think you will like.
   b He <u>has fallen</u> off his bicycle. [2]

7. One mark each:
   a I <u>have listened</u> to everything you have said.
   b Jake <u>has played</u> the piano since he was five. [2]

8. Two marks each. Sample responses:
   • I have finished my homework.
   • It has just stopped raining.
   • They have lived in Italy since last year. [4]

9. One mark. b They are always supportive and mean a lot to me. [1]

10. Five marks. Students' own answers. Check for use of first person, interesting details, opinions. [5]

Total marks: 25

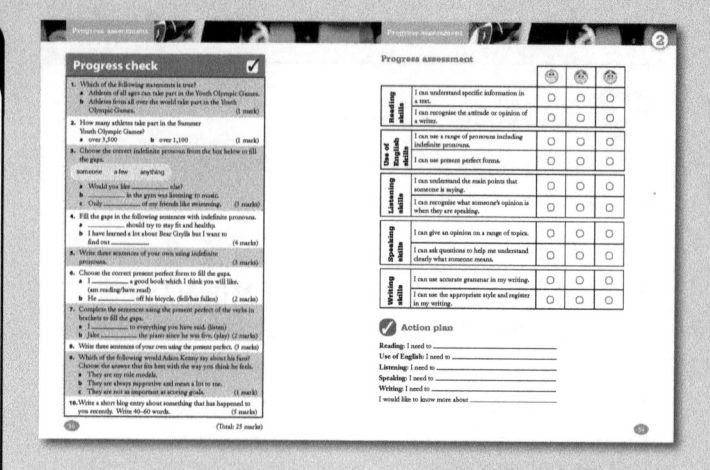

End-of-unit quiz

Workbook page 17: Fit for life quiz

The end-of-unit quiz on page 17 of the Workbook is a summary of the content you have covered in the unit. You can set this as homework or to complete in class. Go through the answers in class, and check that there are no gaps in students' understanding.

Answers:

1. C five days a week
2. He won a competition to design the medal.
3. <u>No one/Nobody</u> was coming to my Mum's shop, so I put up posters around the village. In no time at all, <u>everyone</u> in the whole village had come to her shop and they all bought something to take home.
4. Kai wanted to buy a surfboard, but the shop didn't have <u>any</u>.
5. Example: A good sporting role model can inspire people to take up sport, which will make them healthier.
6. B It is Monday, so I have brought my PE kit with me.
7. Jean <u>has played</u> football every day this week, but Zack and Mikal <u>have chosen</u> to play basketball.
8. The sentence uses language for giving opinions.

Progress assessment

Reflection

Reflecting on your learning

Have a discussion with the class about how they will continue to use the different skills they have covered in this unit. Students should then work independently on the progress assessment task. For each of the skills, ask them to tick the box that they think most fits how well they are doing. Now move on to the action plan. The aim is to encourage students to identify which skills they think they need more practice in, while reinforcing the skills they can do well. Give students the opportunity to practise the skills they have identified and revisit the action plan after a few weeks, encouraging students to compare later attempts with the first.

End-of-unit activity

Ask the students to complete this mini questionnaire about their learning in this unit. Put the questions on the board and they can discuss their answers with a partner.

1. What did you learn about the Youth Olympic Games?
2. What one piece of advice could you give someone who is about to write a report?
3. Give one fact about a sporting role model.
4. Name two sports you have not done before that you would like to try.
5. What did you learn about Bear Grylls?

Reflection

Teacher reflection

1. Which parts of the unit did the students enjoy most? Why was this?
2. Was there anything that the students found difficult in this unit? How can I make sure this is easier next time?
3. Considering the learning objectives and content, what did the students successfully learn while studying this unit?
4. Considering the learning objectives and content, what did the students struggle with while studying this unit? Why was this? What could I do to help them more?
5. Which parts of the unit did I teach well? How did I achieve this?
6. Which parts of the unit did I struggle to teach well? What can I do to improve this?
7. Next time I teach this unit, is there anything I can do to improve the learning experience for my students?

3 Work around the world

Learning objectives

In this unit, students will:

- Understand specific information in texts. **pages 36, 46** *7Re2*
- Understand the detail of an argument. **page 36** *7Re3*
- Deduce meaning from context. **page 36** *7Re6*
- Use familiar and some unfamiliar paper and digital resources to check meaning and extend understanding. **pages 37, 41** *7Re9*
- Develop coherent arguments, supported where necessary by reasons, examples and evidence. **pages 37, 41, 47** *7W4*
- Use, with some support, style and register appropriate to a limited range of written genres. **pages 37, 47** *7W5*
- Use appropriate layout for a range of written genres. **page 47** *7W6*
- Use a range of active and passive simple present and past forms; use a limited range of causative forms *have/get done*. **pages 38–39** *7Ug6*
- Use a growing range of present continuous forms and past continuous, including some passive forms. **pages 42–43** *7Ug7*
- Understand, with little or no support, most of the detail of an argument. **page 40** *7L3*
- Understand, with little or no support, most of the implied meaning in extended talk. **page 40** *7L4*
- Recognise, with little or no support, the opinion of the speaker(s) in extended talk. **page 40** *7L5*
- Deduce, with little or no support, meaning from context in extended talk. **page 40** *7L6*
- Link comments, with some flexibility, to what others say at sentence and discourse level in pair, group and whole class exchanges. **pages 44–45** *7S5*
- Interact with peers to negotiate classroom tasks. **page 45** *7S6*

Setting the scene

Work around the world

Write the unit title on the board and explain that this unit focuses on different kinds of jobs and careers. Ask the students to look at the pictures on page 40 of the Student Book and say what kinds of jobs are being done in the photos. Then read the three quotes out loud to the students and ask them what they think each one means. Explain that Elbert Hubbard was an American writer and artist who started out selling soap. Maya Angelou was an American writer and poet who also advocated equal rights for everyone. She started out as a singer before becoming a famous writer. Confucius was a Chinese teacher and philosopher whose ideas are still followed by many people today as a proper way to live life.

Thinking ahead

In this activity students think about different kinds of work: what work they would like to do, what they think they would be good at and what kinds of job members of their family have. Before the students focus on the questions, you could start by discussing the reasons why people work (for money, for satisfaction, to give purpose to their lives and so on). Then ask students to think about the many different kinds of work that people do around the world from manual work, such as being a builder, to professional work, such as being a teacher, lawyer or doctor. Now discuss each of the questions in turn and ask the students to give reasons for their opinions.

Work around the world

them to give reasons for their opinions and encourage them to listen to their partner's ideas and ask questions if they want to find out more.

Theme opener

Workbook page 18: Work around the world

Page 18 of the Workbook focuses on the theme of the unit. Students are encouraged to practise vocabulary that they have learned to think about different types of work, and a short reading activity tests their understanding.

Answers:

1. Example answer: I would like to be a rocket scientist because then I could spend the day mending rockets and could press the launch button.

2. Example answer:
   Q: What is the best part about your job?
   A: I love travelling all around the world.

3. The advertisement is for a teacher.

4. C   go into their office for a chat

5. 69 Warwick Road, London

6. Example answer: I would make a good teacher because I am patient when I have to explain something. Also, I am very hard working, which all teachers have to be.

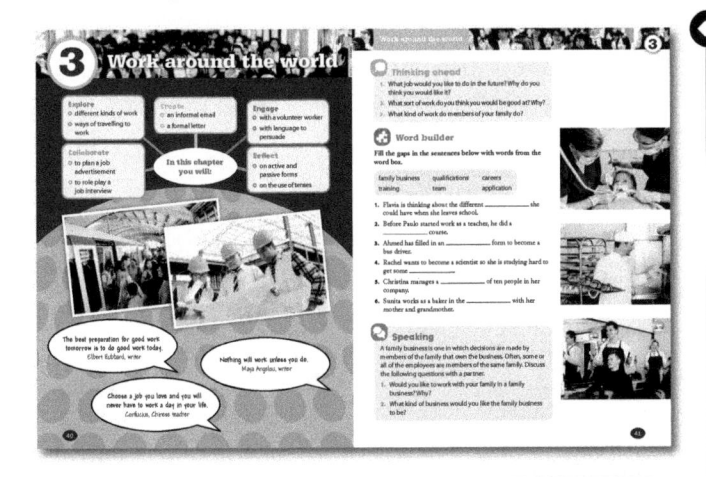

Vocabulary

Word builder

This section introduces students to some of the vocabulary that they will meet in the unit. Ask the students to read the sentences and then fill in the gaps in the sentences using words from the word box.

Answers:

1. Flavia is thinking about the different <u>careers</u> she could have when she leaves school.

2. Before Paulo started work as a teacher, he did a <u>training</u> course.

3. Ahmed has filled in an <u>application</u> form to become a bus driver.

4. Rachel wants to become a scientist so she is studying hard to get some <u>qualifications</u>.

5. Christina manages a <u>team</u> of ten people in her company.

6. Sunita works as a baker in the <u>family business</u> with her mother and grandmother.

Speaking

Speaking

In this activity students work with a partner to discuss questions relating to family businesses. Start by reading the explanation of what a family business is on page 41 of the Student Book. Ask the students to think of some examples of the kind of businesses that might be run by a family and whether they have any experience of family businesses, perhaps in their own family or in another family they know. Ask the students to discuss the questions with a partner. Remind

Extension

Joining the family business

Ask the students to imagine that their parents have just moved to a new country and want to start up a new business where they are now living. They should imagine that their father is a baker and wishes to open a shop selling local bakery goods. However, their mother is a dentist and wishes to start a dentistry practice in the town. They should imagine that both parents have asked them to join the family business but which one will they choose? Explain to the students that they should base their answer on the job they will be doing, not the person they will be working for. Tell the students to prepare for three minutes before telling their partner their decision and reasons for their choice.

Reading

Getting to work in Hong Kong

Prior knowledge

In this section students read an email about different forms of transport that people use to get to work in Hong Kong. First, ask the students how the adults in their family get to work. Discuss the meaning of the phrase 'public transport' and ask the students which forms of public transport they have used. Now check with the students that they know where on a map Hong Kong is. Tell them that Hong Kong is a small country but it has a large population. It has a total area of just over 1,100 square kilometres, and a total population of just over 7 million. This means that there are over 6,300 people living in each square kilometre. Give some other examples for comparison (examples: Denmark: 43,000 sq km, population just over 5.6 million, 332 people per square kilometre; New Zealand: just over 268,000 sq km, population just under 4.5 million, 17 people per square kilometre; Mexico: almost 2 million sq km, population 122.3 million, 65 people per square kilometre). Explain that because Hong Kong has so many people in a small space needing to get to work, it needs a good public transport system.

Reading

Getting to work in Hong Kong

Before the students read the email, read through the Glossary words and their definitions and ensure that the students understand their meaning. Then they can read through the text. Explain to the students that informal emails have a more relaxed tone than formal emails. The writer and the reader will know each other well and will probably have shared interests, hobbies and experiences. The writer uses the first name of the reader and not their surname; they sign the email using only their first name, not their surname; they might sign by using a nickname. Informal emails tend to tell the reader about one particular thing (an event, an experience, asking one question) and may briefly refer to a previous shared experience or email. Remind students that they can shorten words in informal emails (don't, can't, etc.) but they still need to avoid using slang.

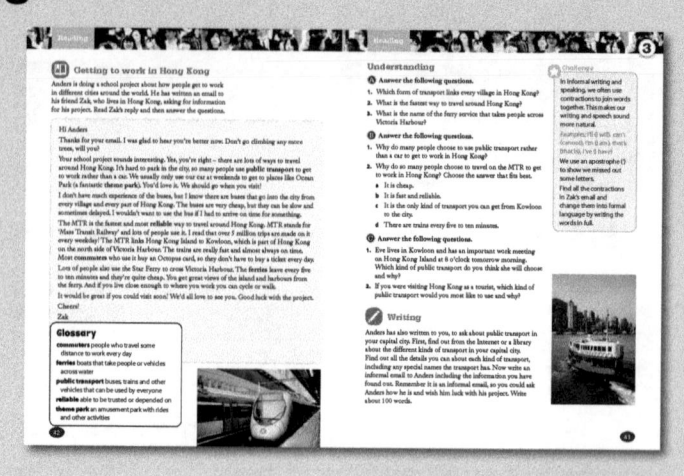

Student Book answers

Understanding

Ask the students to read through the email again and then answer the questions.

Answers:

A
1. the bus
2. the MTR
3. the Star Ferry service

B
1. Suggested response: They choose to travel to work by public transport rather than by car because it is hard to park in the city.
2. b It is fast and reliable.

C Suggested responses:
1. Eve will probably choose the MTR because it is reliable and fast. She needs to be certain of being there on time, so this is a likely choice.
2. If I visited Hong Kong as a tourist, I would like to use the Star Ferry because it would give me good views of Victoria Harbour and Hong Kong. Because I am on holiday it wouldn't matter if the journey was slow, or if I had to wait a few minutes for the ferry to come.

Reading

Writing

In this activity students research different kinds of transport in their capital city before writing an informal email describing them. Ask them to find out all the details they can about each kind of transport, including any special names the transport has. This section could be done in the school library during the lesson or as part of a homework task.

Now ask the students to write an informal email to Anders including the information they have found out. Remind the students that it is an informal email, so they need to start by using 'Dear Anders' and not using a surname. There are several acceptable ways to end an informal email so you could write these on the board for the students to choose:

- Hope to see you soon
- Hope this helps and see you soon!
- All the best
- Take care
- Best wishes
- Regards
- Good luck with the project and see you soon!

Challenge

Students may be familiar with contractions from primary level. Remind them that contractions are often used in informal speech and writing, but the words are often used in full in formal situations and in formal letters, such as application letters. Ask the students to read Zak's email again and make a note of all the contractions they can find. Then ask them to write the contractions out in full, adding the missing letters shown by the apostrophes.

Answers:

you're/you are
don't/do not
it's/it is
you'd/you would
wouldn't/would not
they're/they are
we'd/we would

Workbook page 19: Working in Hong Kong

On page 19 of the Workbook, students read a formal letter and answer some comprehension questions. Go through the answers in class, to check their understanding. Make sure to explain any difficult vocabulary.

Answers:

1. It is making some changes.
2. 11 a.m.
3. B 3
4. six weeks
5. Residents get a 30% discount when they buy their annual ticket.

Extension

Updating a transport system

Tell the students that the transport system in their capital city is adequate but with more and more commuters it needs updating. They have to think of a plan to update the system to make it faster and more reliable for the commuters. Firstly, give the students some examples of what might need to be done:

- new trains and/or buses (to replace out-of-date, old ones)
- more trains and/or buses (to improve waiting times and journey times)
- new kinds of ticket machine (online, chip and PIN/automatic payment)
- different kinds of ticket (monthly ticket, digital ticket, pre-paid tickets)
- new routes for areas which have few transport links.

Ask them to get into groups and plan what changes they are going to make. They need to explain their choices as well. Then they need to present their ideas to the class. Each class member will then vote on the best idea. If there is a tie at the end, you will have the casting vote.

Use of English

Active and passive

Grammar

Active and passive

In this section students develop their understanding of active and passive forms. Explain that the active form is used to say what the subject of a verb is doing. Write some examples on the board. (Farrah writes a blog every day. Martha designs buildings. Brad paints the bridge once a year.) Now read through the explanation in the language focus box on page 44 of the Student Book, explaining that the passive form is used to show what happens to the subject of the verb. Read through the explanation of how the passive is formed and explain that when we want to say who performed the action we use 'by'. Then ask the students to change the example sentences above into the passive. You may need to do the first one for them. (A blog is written every day by Farrah. Buildings are designed by Martha. The bridge is painted once a year by Brad.) Now ask the students to turn some present tense active and passive sentences into the past. (Examples: Farrah wrote a blog every day. A blog was written by Farrah every day. Martha designed buildings. Buildings were designed by Martha. Brad painted the bridge once a year. The bridge was painted once a year by Brad.)

Student Book answers

Using active and passive forms

Ask the students to complete the exercises on their own and then check their answers with a partner.

Answers:

A Jake usually <u>rides</u> his bike to work but sometimes he <u>catches</u> the train. He <u>makes</u> a snack before he leaves home and <u>eats</u> it during the morning.

B 1. The team <u>is managed</u> by Ted.
2. The offices <u>are cleaned</u> every Friday.
3. Lunch <u>is served</u> in the canteen.

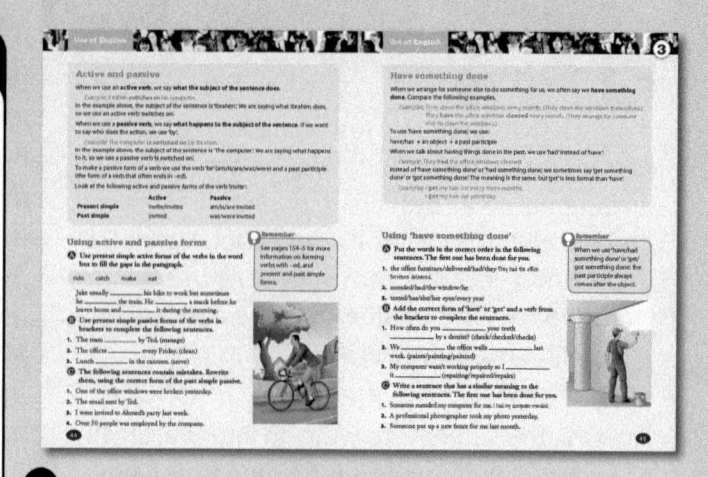

C Ask the students to rewrite the sentences using the correct form of the past simple passive.

1. One of the office windows <u>was</u> broken yesterday.
2. The email <u>was</u> sent by Ted.
3. I <u>was</u> invited to Ahmed's party last week.
4. Over 50 people <u>were</u> employed by the company.

Grammar

Have something done

In this section students develop their understanding of the use of the causative forms 'have/get done' to say that we have arranged for someone else to do something for us. Read through the language focus box on page 45 of the Student Book with the students and ensure they understand that we use 'has'/'have'/'had' with an object followed by the past participle. Write some more examples on the board. (Examples: I have my hair cut every few months. He has his teeth checked every six months. She had her car mended.) Explain that when we ask questions about things that have been arranged, we use 'do'/'does'/'did' with 'have' or 'has' (examples: How often do you have your hair cut? Does he have his teeth checked regularly? Did she have her car mended?).

Use of English

Student Book answers

Using 'have something done'

Answers:

A 2. He had the window mended.
   3. She has her eyes tested every year.

B 1. How often do you have/get your teeth checked by a dentist?
   2. We had/got the office walls painted last week.
   3. My computer wasn't working properly so I had/got it repaired.

C 2. I had my photograph taken professionally yesterday.
   3. I had a new fence put up last month.

Use of English

Workbook page 20: Active and passive

On page 20 of the Workbook, students practise using active and passive verbs. Go through the answers in class to check students' understanding.

Answers:

1. Most days, Chen takes the tram to get to work. Today, he is running late so he calls a taxi instead. On the way, he asks the driver to stop at a coffee shop and he buys a coffee and pastry for breakfast. Chen reaches his office on time, so he says thank you to the driver.
2. The timetable was written by Jake.
3. The ticket machines are used by thousands of commuters.
4. The red bicycle is ridden by Shania to work.
5. A newspaper is read by Mike each day.
6. Cars are driven onto the ferry by commuters each evening.
7. The streets of Hong Kong are mended by roadworkers.
8. We have just moved into our new house! One window was broken, but my mum got/had it mended before we moved in. She also had/got all the other windows cleaned. Now we are just waiting to have our furniture delivered.

Extension

Practising active and passive

In this activity students practise changing sentences from the active to the passive before writing four sentences about things they arranged to have done or got done this week. First ask the students to change the following sentences into the passive voice. Tell the students that they should change the present simple active into the present simple passive and the past simple active into the past simple passive (they should not change the tense, just change the active to the passive). Explain that when they change the sentences from active to passive, the subject of the verb will change. If the new subject is plural they will need to make sure they use a plural verb form.

1. Someone cleans the office every day.
2. The dentist checked my teeth.
3. The manager trains the new members of the team.
4. The chef made this delicious meal.

Answers:

1. The office is cleaned every day.
2. My teeth were checked by the dentist.
3. The new members of the team are trained by the manager.
4. This delicious meal was made by the chef.

Now ask the students to write four sentences about things they had done or got done for them this week.

Example answers:

I got my hair cut.
I had my homework marked.
I had my light fixed.
I got my shoes mended.

Listening

Working as a volunteer

Prior knowledge

In this section students will listen to an interview with a young person who has worked as a volunteer with Voluntary Service Overseas (VSO). They answer some questions on the recording before going on to speaking and writing activities relating to volunteer work. Begin by discussing the meaning of the verb 'volunteer' (to work for an organisation without being paid, often doing a task that will help people). Ask the students what kinds of projects people might volunteer for (examples: to build something in their local community or another community; to make something to raise money; to take something to people in need; to help their community or another community, and so on). Then ask the students why people might volunteer to do something (examples: to help their community or another community; to get experience; to make friends; to learn a specific skill).

Vocabulary

Word builder

This pre-listening Word builder activity introduces students to some vocabulary relating to volunteer work that they may find useful in the activities that follow. Ask the students to match the words on the left to the definitions on the right, then to fill in the gaps using the correct words.

Answers:

1. charities: organisations that help people in need

   volunteers: people who work for an organisation without being paid

   communities: groups of people living in the same area

   paid: receiving money

2. Some people work in organisations such as <u>charities</u> without being <u>paid</u> for their work. These people are called <u>volunteers</u>. The VSO (the Volunteer Service Overseas) is an organisation that arranges for volunteers to help in <u>communities</u> all around the world.

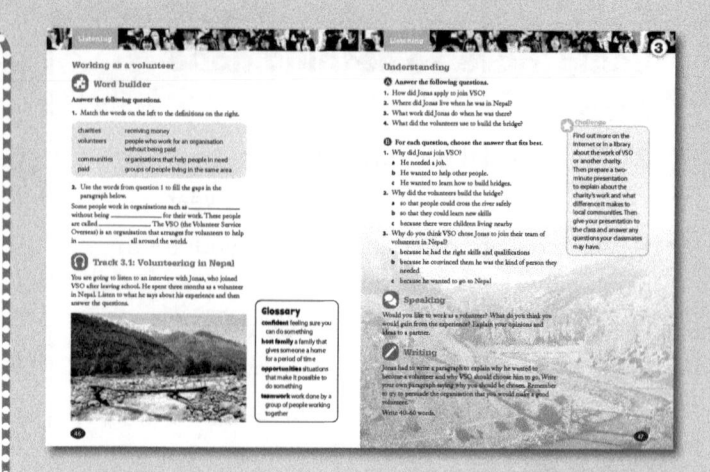

Listening

Track 3.1: Volunteering in Nepal

Before the students listen to Track 3.1, read through the words in the Glossary box on page 46 of the Student Book along with their definitions. Write one sentence for each word on the board. (Examples: If you work hard at school you will have many career opportunities. I decided to do a language course in Paris and stayed with a host family. I like working on my own but I enjoy teamwork even more. Sammy loves meeting new people and he is very confident.) Now listen to Track 3.1 together. A full transcript of this track is available on the CD.

Student Book answers

Understanding

Before they write their answers, ask the students to read through the questions. Then ask them to listen to the recording again and answer the questions.

Answers:

A 1. online/He completed an online application form.

2. with a host family/He lived with a host family in the local community he was working in.

3. He helped to build a bridge.

4. logs/They used logs from trees they had cut up.

B 1. b He wanted to help other people.

2. a so that people could cross the river safely

3. b because he convinced them he was the kind of person they needed

Listening

Speaking

This activity gives students the opportunity to discuss their opinions about whether they would like to work as a volunteer when they are older. Explain that this does not need to be a project that involves travelling to a different country. They could do volunteer work in their own community. Ask them to think about the benefits of volunteering both for the volunteer and for the people the volunteer is helping. Ask the students what they think they would gain from the experience. Ask them to work in pairs and explain their ideas to a partner, giving reasons for their opinions. Remind them to ask questions to find out more about what their partner thinks.

Writing

In this activity students write their own paragraph using persuasive language to convince VSO that they should be chosen to become a volunteer. Ask them to think about their discussions in the previous speaking activity when giving reasons why they want to become a volunteer, and remind them to use some of the vocabulary relating to volunteering that they have learned.

Example answer:

I would like the opportunity to become a volunteer because I want to help people. I enjoy teamwork and have taken part in events to raise money for charities and community projects. I play lots of sports and am very active. I would find being able to make a difference to other people's lives extremely rewarding.

Challenge

Ask the students to find out more on the Internet or in a library about the work of VSO or another charity. They then prepare a two-minute presentation to explain about the charity's work and what difference it makes to local communities. When they have prepared it, they should give their presentation to the class. They should then answer any questions their classmates may have.

Workbook page 21: Working as a volunteer

On page 21 of the Workbook, students listen to Beth giving a talk about volunteering overseas. You may choose to listen to the recording in class, stopping at any unfamiliar or difficult words. Check students' understanding by going through the answers in class.

Answers:

1. overseas: in or to another country
   rewarding: giving satisfaction or happiness
   foundations: the lowest part of a building
   periodic table: a table of chemical elements
2. **C** build a school
3. **B** Namibia
4. **C** on the day before it opened
5. **A** desks and seats
6. Beth's favourite poster told you how to write an exciting story.
7. Accept any one of: it is good fun/you make friends/you will remember it forever.

Extension

Volunteering overseas

Tell the students to imagine that they are going on a six-week trip overseas to help a community. Put them in groups and ask them to choose a country and a project, giving reasons why. You can put a list of countries and projects on the board to help them:

Namibia	work on a farm
Greenland	help to conserve wildlife
India	decorate the classrooms in a school
Indonesia	plant trees in a wood
Fiji	clean a beach

Use of English

The present and past continuous

Grammar

The present continuous

In this section students develop their understanding of the present continuous, which is made using the present form of 'be' (am/is/are) together with a present participle. Remind the students that they use 'am' with 'I'; 'is' with 'he', 'she' or 'it'; and 'are' with 'you', 'we' and 'they'. Write some more examples on the board. (Examples: I am talking to Ibrahim. Sophie is riding her horse. They are playing football.) Explain to the students that the present continuous is used to talk about actions that are happening now and have been going on for some time or will carry on for some time. Remind students of the difference between active and passive and explain how to form the passive form of the present continuous, using 'am', 'is' or 'are' with 'being' and the past participle. Give the students some more examples. (Examples: A bridge is being built over the river. My car is being mended. The office is being cleaned at the moment.)

Student Book answers

Using the present continuous

Ask the students to complete the exercises on their own and then check their answers with a partner.

Answers:

A 1. a   Alisha is eating her lunch.
       b   Jake is writing a letter.
       c   Ahmed is reading a good book.
    2. a   Jon is spending some time in Italy next month.
       b   The baker is making some bread.
       c   Mia is talking to her mother on the phone.

B 2. The rubbish is being collected.
   3. The old building is being knocked down.

C Students' own answers. Accept any four sentences that use the present continuous correctly.

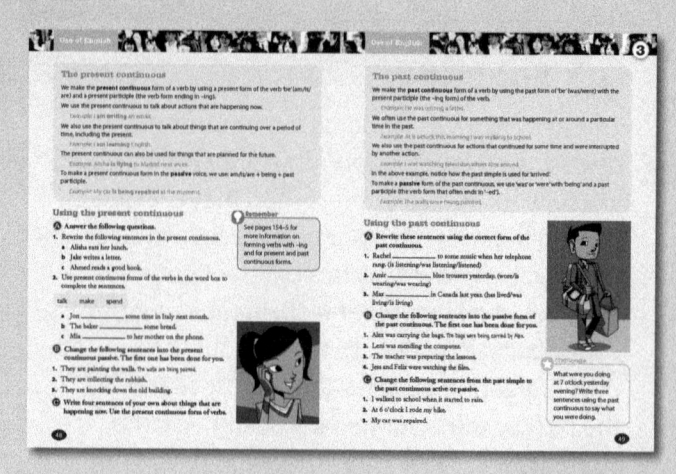

Grammar

The past continuous

In this section students develop their understanding of continuous forms by focusing on the past continuous. Tell them that the past continuous is formed in a similar way to the present continuous, except we use a past form of 'be' with a present participle. Remind students of the past forms of 'be' ('was' with 'I', 'he', 'she' and 'it' and 'were' with 'we', 'you' and 'they'). Write some examples of sentences in the past simple and past continuous on the board and compare their meanings. (Examples: It rained yesterday/It was raining when I walked home. She watched television/At 6 o'clock she was watching television. The children put on their coats/The children were putting on their coats when I arrived.) Read through the first three paragraphs of the language focus box on page 49 of the Student Book together before explaining the formation of the passive past continuous. Now remind students of the meaning of 'active' and 'passive' and read through the last paragraph. Write some examples of sentences in the past continuous active on the board, and then turn them into the passive. (Examples: The boy was reading the book/The book was being read by the boy. The chef was cooking the vegetables/The vegetables were being cooked by the chef.) Draw students' attention to how in the last example we change 'was' to 'were' because the subject is the plural 'vegetables'.

Use of English

Student Book answers

Using the past continuous

Ask the students to complete these questions on their own. Once they have finished, they may check their answers in pairs:

Answers:

A 1. Rachel <u>was listening</u> to some music when her telephone rang.
   2. Amir <u>was wearing</u> blue trousers yesterday.
   3. Max <u>was living</u> in Canada last year.

B 2. The computer was being mended by Leni.
   3. The lessons were being prepared by the teacher.
   4. The film was being watched by Jess and Felix.

C 1. I was walking to school when it started to rain.
   2. At 6 o'clock I was riding my bike.
   3. My car was being repaired.

⭐ Challenge

In this activity students write three sentences using the past continuous to say what they were doing at 7 o'clock yesterday evening. Explain that they should try to write interesting sentences and they can make things up if they wish. Remind students that they should use the present continuous in each sentence but they can also use the present simple if they are describing actions that interrupt another action.

Example sentences:

At 7 o'clock yesterday evening I was watching a football match on television with my brother. I was feeling very relaxed and sitting on a comfortable chair. I was enjoying the game when suddenly the television went off and the lights went out and we missed the rest of the game.

Use of English

Workbook page 22: Present continuous and past continuous

Page 22 of the Workbook gives students practise in using the present continuous and the past continuous. Go through the answers in class and make sure students are clear on the different uses of each.

Answers:

1. My older brother <u>is saving</u> his money to buy a new bike.
2. The hole in Ade's trousers <u>is being</u> <u>mended</u> at last.
3. My grandma <u>is cooking</u> a tasty stew for dinner.
4. We <u>are tidying</u> our bedrooms.
5. Example answer:
   I am really excited because my uncle and aunt <u>are spending</u> a week with us. Tomorrow, we <u>are seeing</u> a film at the cinema. Now, my mum <u>is calling</u> me because she <u>is waiting</u> in the kitchen for me to help her prepare dinner for my uncle and aunt.
6. Example: At 8 o'clock this morning, my dad <u>was walking</u> to work.
7. Example: Gina <u>was taking</u> some photographs when she noticed <u>it was getting dark</u>.
8. Example: The twins <u>were eating</u> their lunch when they heard <u>the bell ring</u>.
9. Example: The film <u>was playing</u> when my mother <u>arrived</u>.
10. Example: I <u>was playing football in the garden</u> when <u>I saw an amazing rainbow</u>.

Extension

Practising the past simple and past continuous

Ask the students to write a paragraph using the past simple and past continuous and some or all of the words from the list below.

| bicycle | ice cream | accident | pond |
| swim | police | walk | fall |

Speaking

Talking about jobs

Prior knowledge

The photos on page 50 of the Student Book serve as stimuli for the speaking tasks that follow. First students discuss what is involved in the jobs shown in the pictures and which of the jobs they would like to do. Ask the students to give a reason why they would like to do the job they have chosen. They then work with their peers to plan a job advertisement and role play a job interview. Begin by asking the students to look at the photos and identify what kinds of jobs are being done in each of the pictures. Do the students know anyone who has any of these jobs?

Then ask students what they know about how to apply for a job. Ask them whether they have ever seen an advertisement for a job and elicit examples of places where job advertisements appear (newspapers, magazines, radio, television, online). Ask them whether they have ever been for an interview for anything. Do they know anyone who has been for a job interview? Elicit some examples of the kind of questions that might be asked in a job interview. (Examples: Why would you like to do this job? What skills do you have to do this job? Do you like working as part of a team? How did you hear about the job?)

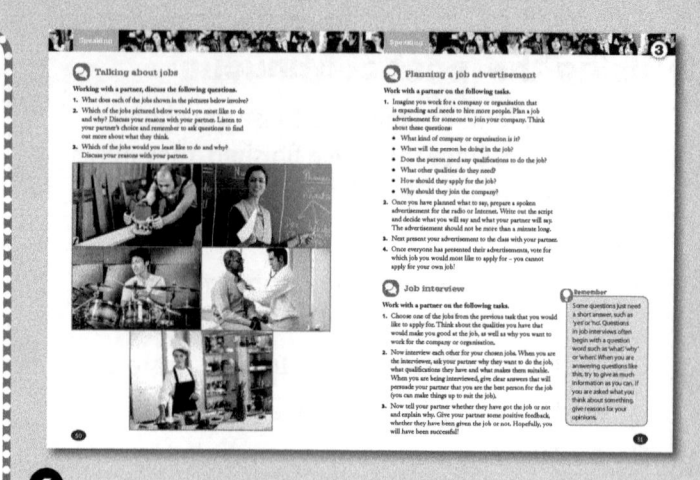

questions, discussing which of the jobs pictured they would most like to do and which they would least like to do. In both cases, they should give reasons for their choice.

Speaking

Talking about jobs

Ask the students to work in pairs for this activity. Before the students begin their discussions, remind them of the language they learned about in Unit 2 for giving and asking for opinions and reasons. Remind them that during their discussions, they should listen to their partner and ask questions if they want to find out more or do not understand.

When they discuss the first question, ask the students to talk about what a typical day would be like for someone with that job. Does the job involve helping people in some way? Does it involve making something? What time would a person doing that job need to get up for work? Can the job be done from home or would someone have to commute to a place of work? Is the job easy or does it need a lot of skill and years of training? Is it well-paid or low-paid work? They can now move on to the second and third

Speaking

Planning a job advertisement

In this activity students work in small groups to plan, write and present a script for a job advertisement for the radio. Draw students' attention to the bullet points on page 51 of the Student Book, which give ideas for the kind of information they can include in their advertisement. Tell the groups to think about the kind of language they can use to persuade people to apply for the job. How will they make the job sound appealing? What will they say about the company or organisation to make it sound like a good company to work for? Before they write the scripts for their radio advertisement, remind the students that a script includes the name of the speaker on the left, followed by the words that will be spoken. Explain that each student should be given a similar number of words to say.

When students have finished planning, they write out the script for their advertisement. Encourage them to include all the information they included in their plan and remind them that the advertisement should be about one minute long, not longer. Now the students can present the advertisement to the class. Remind them to speak clearly and not rush what they are saying because those listening will not have heard it before. At the end of the presentations, ask

Speaking

students which job they would like to apply for – they need to give reasons for their answers.

Speaking

💬 Job interview

In this activity students work in pairs to role-play an interview for a job, taking turns to be interviewer and interviewee. First they choose one of the jobs from the previous task that they would like to apply for (each member of the pair can choose a different job). Ask them to write down the qualities they have that make them well suited for the job, as well as reasons why they want to work for the company or organisation. Explain that they can make the things up, as in the role play they can pretend to be someone else. Qualities might include: hard-working, friendly, patient, clever, being a quick learner, calm, being a good team worker. Reasons to work for a company might include: good pay, good hours, flexible hours, chance of paid overtime, working for a well-known company, easy journey to work.

Before they conduct the interviews, write some examples of questions they can use on the board:

- What made you want to apply for this job?
- What qualifications do you have?
- What qualities do you have which make you suitable for this job?

Remind the students that when they are being interviewed, they need to give clear, confident answers that will convince their partner that they are the best person for the job. When they have finished their interviews, the students tell their partners whether they have got the job or not and explain why, giving some positive feedback whether their partner was successful or not.

Speaking

Workbook page 23: Job advertisement

On page 23 of the Workbook, students respond to a job advertisement. Students can start by completing the activity alone at home or in class. Then, go through their answers in class and encourage students to act out their questions in pairs. Circulate and listen to their conversations, checking for correctness.

Answers:

1. Example answers:

   Do you think I can do this job?

   Do you think it sounds interesting?

   Do you think I have enough time to do this job?

2. Students' own answers. Students can complete this in pairs in class or with someone they know at home.

3. Example answers:

   I am interested in the local community.

   I understand what interests young people.

   I would like to be a journalist in the future.

4. Example answers:

   Interviewer: What interests you about your local area?

   You: I think I am very lucky to live here because I love nature and the surrounding countryside is very beautiful.

   Interviewer: What changes would you like to see in the local area?

   You: There is not very much for young people to do. I would like to see more activities for teenagers.

   Interviewer: Why does your opinion matter?

   You: My opinion matters because it is important to listen to young people and there are many young people in the local community.

Extension

💬 Improving interview techniques

Tell the students to imagine that they did not get the job they were interviewed for in the task above, so they will need to apply for another job. Tell them to work in small groups and discuss how they can do better in their next interview. What could they improve? Why were they unsuccessful? Were they able to answer all the questions clearly and confidently? Did they give reasons for their answers? Ask them to get into different pairs and hold the interviews again. Then ask them to note down what they did better the second time.

Reading corner

Reading corner

Prior knowledge

In this section students read through a range of job advertisements before asking some questions. Remind students of the different places they might look if they want to find a job being advertised and write some examples on the board:

- online
- in a newspaper
- advertisement in a window
- word-of-mouth
- being asked to apply by the company

If possible, bring in some job advertisements in newspapers for the students to look at. Elicit examples of the kind of features included in job advertisements. (Examples: a brief heading, either 'wanted' or a one- or two-word job title; formal language; full sentences not always used; details about the job such as hours, salary, whether training will be given, qualifications and qualities needed and how to apply; abbreviations often used to save space.)

Reading

Job advertisements

Read through the job advertisements on page 52 of the Student Book with the students. Then ask them to think about the following questions for each advertisement:

- what is the title of the job?
- where will the job be done?
- does it involve working with a team?
- what does the job involve?
- what are the hours of work?
- how should someone apply?

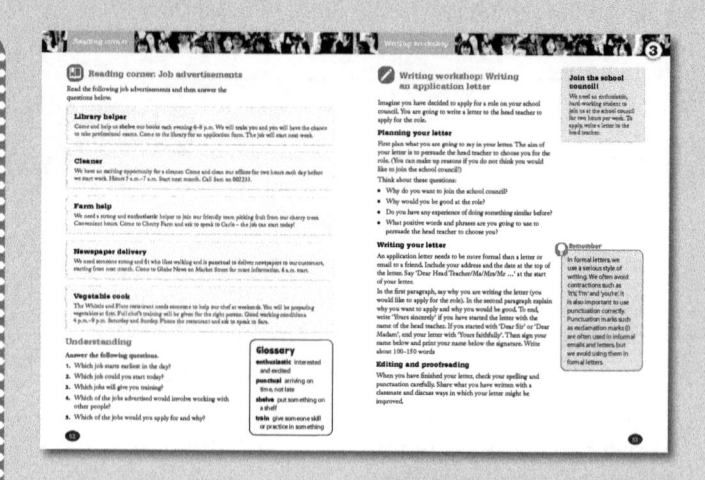

Student Book answers

Understanding

Answers:

1. The cleaner starts earliest in the day (5 a.m.).
2. You could start as the farm help today.
3. The library helper and vegetable cook jobs will give you training.
4. The library helper, farm help and vegetable cook jobs would involve working with other people.
5. Suggested response: I would apply to be the vegetable cook as I don't like getting up early in the mornings and I like working with a team because I am sociable. I would also like this job because it would give me training.

Writing workshop

Writing workshop

Writing an application letter

Planning

Tell the students they are going to plan and write an application letter for a position on the school council, and draw their attention to the 'Join the school council!' advertisement on page 53 of the Student Book. First ask the students to note down what they think a member of the school council has to do and what qualities they need to join the school council. They should have at least three ideas under each heading.

Writing

Explain that a letter of application should be formal and remind students of the features of formal letters: formal language, full sentences, full verb forms, no slang. Explain that they should include their address in the top right-hand corner of the page (they can make one up if they like) and the date underneath the address. Remind them that in formal letters if they don't know the person's name, they should start the letter with 'Dear Sir', 'Dear Madam' or 'Dear Sir or Madam' and finish with 'Yours faithfully'. If they do know the name, they should start the letter with 'Dear Mr …' or 'Dear Mrs …' and finish with 'Yours sincerely'. They also need to use persuasive vocabulary that will show their suitability for the job. They should use clear, simple English and the first paragraph should explain why they are writing. They can finish by saying what they would like to happen next, such as 'I hope to hear from you soon'. Remind them that they will need to use persuasive language to convince the head teacher they are the right person for the position.

Editing and proofreading

When the students have finished their letters, ask them to check their spelling and punctuation carefully and that they have written a letter which has a formal style. Tell them to share what they have written with a classmate and discuss ways in which their letter might be improved.

Workbook page 24: Writing a job application letter

On page 24 of the Workbook, students practise writing a job application letter. Students complete the work on their own in class or at home. Check their writing for formal style and persuasive language, as well as for correctness.

Example answer:

Dear Mrs Rose,

I am writing to ask to be chosen as your helper at the art club. I love art and am really interested in the history of art as well. I am reading a book about Van Gogh at the moment. In the evenings, when I have finished my homework, I like to draw or paint. I would love to be your helper, so hope you will choose me.

Yours sincerely,

Elle

Extension

Writing a formal letter

Ask the students to swap the letters they wrote in the Writing workshop activity with a partner. The partner will re-read the application letter before writing a letter back to the applicant telling them they have been given a place on the school council and explaining what their duties will be. Remind the students that this letter will also be a formal letter. They should write about 100 words for this formal reply letter.

Progress assessment

Progress check

Student Book answers

Progress check

1. Two marks. a the ferry; and

   c the bus [2]

2. Two marks. Example answer: The Star Ferry crosses Victoria Harbour every five or ten minutes and gives you great views. [2]

3. One mark. Jonas helped to build a bridge. [1]

4. One mark. b reasons why he wanted to become a volunteer [1]

5. One mark each.

   a The computer was mended yesterday.

   b The office was cleaned this morning. [2]

6. One mark each:

   a We had the windows cleaned yesterday.

   b I have my hair cut every two months.

   c They had the roof repaired last week. [3]

7. One mark each:

   a They are playing football.

   b She is leaving for the airport this evening.

   c I am reading an interesting book. [3]

8. Two marks. a The meeting was being held in the manager's office; and

   c The computer was being mended. [2]

9. Three marks. Example answers:
   - The name of the job.
   - Where the job will be located.
   - The hours of the job.
   - What you have to do in the job.
   - Any benefits given, for example, training.
   - How you apply and by when. [3]

10. Six marks. Example answer:

    Trainee chef

    Tasty Bites is a friendly, small family-run restaurant in the town centre. We need a new chef to come and help us from 5 p.m. until 10.30 p.m. six days a week. No experience needed as full training will be given, but you need to be hard-working and friendly. To apply call Sasha on 0112233 today. [6]

    Total marks: 25

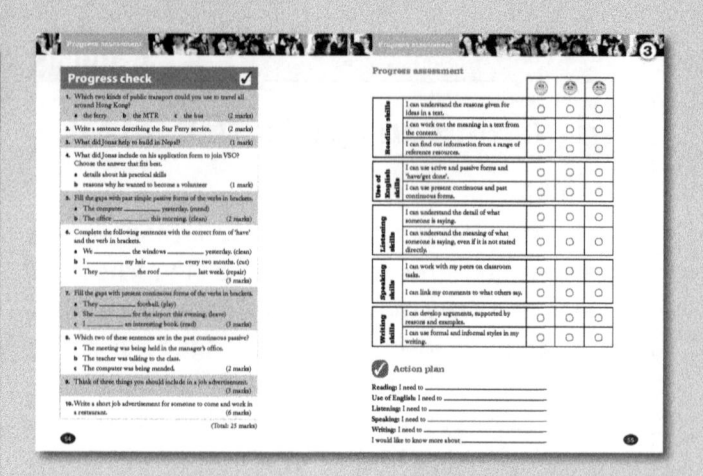

End-of-unit quiz

Workbook page 25: Work around the world quiz

The end-of-unit quiz on page 25 of the Workbook is a summary of the content you have covered in the unit. You can set this as homework or to complete in class. Go through the answers in class, and check that there are no gaps in students' understanding.

Answers:

1. every four minutes
2. passive
3. Luca had his teeth checked by the dentist.
4. There was nothing on the land when we arrived so we began by marking out where the four corners of the school would be. And then we started digging the foundations and building the walls.
5. Accept any answer that gives a choice with a reason for that choice. Example answer: I would choose to build a dam because it would help save water for the dry months of the year.
6. I am walking to school.
7. Example: My aunt was cycling to work when she saw the helicopter.
8. formal language

Progress assessment

③

Reflection
Reflecting on your learning
Have a discussion with the class about how they will continue to use the different skills they have covered in this unit. Students should then work independently on the progress assessment task. For each of the skills, ask them to tick the box that they think most fits how well they are doing. Now move on to the action plan questions. The aim is to encourage students to identify which skills they think they need more practice in, while reinforcing the skills they can do well. Give students the opportunity to practise the skills they have identified and revisit the action plan after a few weeks, encouraging students to compare later attempts with the first.

Speaking
💬 End-of-unit activity
Tell the students that sometimes we apply for a job because it is interesting, pays well or is in a convenient location. Tell them some jobs also have perks. Examples of perks might include:

- free lunch
- company car
- company telephone
- yearly bonus
- free education for your children
- an extra month's holiday every ten years
- an extra month's salary after every 12 months.

Ask the students to add some more perks to the list. Divide the class in half and ask half to stand in a circle with the other half then facing them in another circle around them. Students have to imagine they are being interviewed but this time the companies really want them and so rather than having to persuade the companies to offer them a job, it is the companies doing the persuading, offering perks. Each company is allowed to offer up to three perks. Students have to listen to the perks being offered and then rotate round to listen to some or all of the other companies (depending on how big the circle is and how much time you have). They then choose the 'company' they would like to work for, based on the perks being offered.

Reflection
Teacher reflection
1. Which parts of the unit did the students enjoy most? Why was this?
2. Was there anything that the students found difficult in this unit? How can I make sure this is easier next time?
3. Considering the learning objectives and content, what did the students successfully learn while studying this unit?
4. Considering the learning objectives and content, what did the students struggle with while studying this unit? Why was this? What could I do to help them more?
5. Which parts of the unit did I teach well? How did I achieve this?
6. Which parts of the unit did I struggle to teach well? What can I do to improve this?
7. Next time I teach this unit, is there anything I can do to improve the learning experience for my students?

4 Leisure

Learning objectives

In this unit, students will:

- Understand the main points in texts. **pages 52, 62** *7Re1*
- Understand specific information in texts. **pages 52, 62** *7Re2*
- Understand implied meaning. **pages 52, 62** *7Re4*
- Deduce meaning from context. **pages 52, 62** *7Re6*
- Compose, edit and proofread written work at text level, with some support. **pages 53, 56, 63** *7W2*
- Use appropriate layout. **page 63** *7W6*
- Use a limited range of comparative degree adverb structures *not as quickly as/far less quickly*; use a limited range of sentence adverbs including *too, either, also*; use a growing range of pre-verbal, post-verbal and end position adverbs. **pages 54–55, 58–59** *7Uw4*
- Understand, with little or no support, most specific information in extended talk. **page 56** *7L2*
- Understand, with little or no support, most of the implied meaning in extended talk. **page 56** *7L4*
- Recognise, with little or no support, the opinion of the speaker(s) in extended talk. **page 56** *7L5*
- Deduce, with little or no support, meaning from context in extended talk. **page 56** *7L6*
- Ask questions to clarify meaning. **pages 60–61** *7S2*
- Give an opinion, at discourse level. **pages 60–61** *7S3*
- Interact with peers to negotiate classroom tasks. **pages 60–61** *7S6*
- Use appropriate subject-specific vocabulary. **pages 51, 60–61** *7S7*

Setting the scene

Leisure

Explain to the students that in this unit they will be looking at leisure and how people spend their free time. Begin by introducing the word 'leisure' and ask the students what they think it means. Explain that leisure time is the free time we have when we can do what we like. Then focus on the photos on page 56 of the Student Book and discuss what each one shows. Ask the students what they think Angela Carter means in the quotation (you can use your imagination when you are reading and enter the world of the book). Ask the students what they think Michael Jordan means (he loves basketball and enjoys every game as much as he would his last game). Explain that Aesop was a famous storyteller. Elicit from students the meaning of 'adventure' (an exciting activity). Ask the students what they like doing in their leisure time. Do they like reading, playing sports, having adventures, or something else?

Thinking ahead

This section will help students to think about the theme of leisure. Read through the questions together and then ask the class to think of their answers by themselves, with a partner and then as a class. For each question, you can then brainstorm ideas on the board. This will enable students to extend their vocabulary and think of new ideas.

As a follow-up to this activity, you could ask the students to think of five questions to ask family and friends about what they do in their local area in their spare time. They could use the questions to create a questionnaire to carry out a survey. Example questions: What do you do in your leisure time? Where do you go? What can you do there? (Sports, shopping, cinema, etc.) When they have conducted the survey, they can present the results to one another, in pairs, groups or as a class.

Leisure

4

Theme opener

Workbook page 26: Leisure

Page 26 of the Workbook gives students practice in writing and speaking about the theme of the unit. Students will start by writing interview questions to ask a family member about how they spend their leisure time. They will then record (or write) their responses. Encourage students to practise interviewing family members or friends to practise speaking and listening. In class, students can pair up and ask each other their questions.

Answers:

1. Students may suggest questions such as:

    What kind of activities do you like to do in your spare time?

    Do you think you spend enough time on leisure activities?

    Would you like to do other activities? If so, what would you like to do?

    Do you ever go to the leisure centre? If so, how often?

    Can you think of other activities that could be started at your leisure centre?

2. Students' own answers.

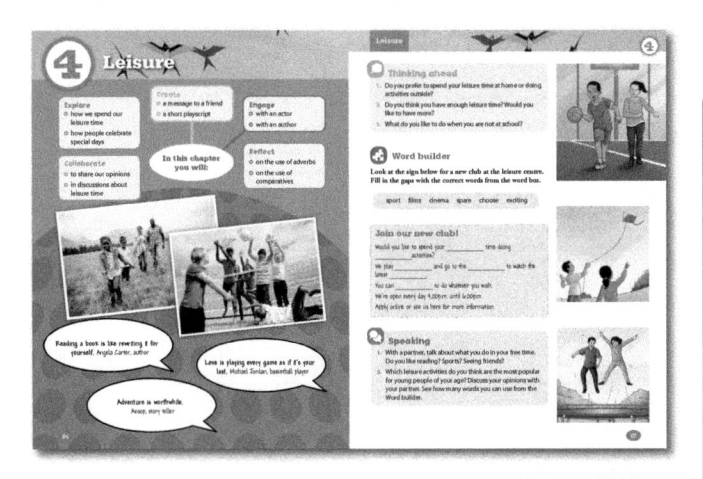

Vocabulary

🧩 Word builder

The questions in this section introduce students to some of the new vocabulary that they will find in the unit. They might know some of the words already but they may need extra support with more challenging vocabulary. Before they fill in the gaps, introduce the words and discuss their meaning. Then ask students to complete the activity, working on their own. Ask them to check their answers with a partner.

Answers:

Would you like to spend your <u>spare</u> time doing <u>exciting</u> activities?

We play <u>sport</u> and go to the <u>cinema</u> to watch the latest <u>films</u>.

You can <u>choose</u> to do whatever you wish.

Speaking

💬 Speaking

This speaking activity gives students an opportunity to use some of the leisure-related vocabulary they have learned in the Word builder activity.

Before the students discuss the questions in the activity, remind them about the words 'opinions' and 'reasons' and about the work they did in Unit 2 on the language they can use for giving and asking for opinions and reasons. Explain that we can also ask questions when we do not understand what someone means. For example, we can say 'I don't understand, please can you explain that?' Or we can say 'Can you give some examples to explain what you mean?' To encourage students to use different vocabulary, you could ask students to write the words from the Word builder in their books and tick the word every time they use it.

Extension

A poster for a new club

Ask the students what kind of club they would like to open in their local area. If they carried out the survey in the follow-up activity in the Thinking ahead section (see page 50), they can refer back to their results and decide whether there is a need for a club offering different activities in the area. What other activities could be introduced? Ask the more able students to create a poster for a new club at a leisure centre. Ask them to decide who the new club is for: for example, for children aged 4–6 or 7–12 or for teenagers aged 13–16.

Scaffold with questions such as:

- What kind of things will teenagers/children do at the club?
- When will the club open?
- How much will it cost to join or take part?
- When will it take place and where?
- How can people find out more?

51

Reading

Star chat

Prior knowledge

Explain to the students that they will read an online interview with a film actor and then answer some questions about it. Begin by asking them whether they enjoy watching films in their leisure time and which films they have watched at the cinema. Explain that the actor being interviewed is Daniel Huttlestone, who had a part in the film *Into the Woods*. Ask them what a musical film is and how it differs from other films.

Ask the students what an interview is (a meeting with someone to ask them questions or discuss something). Discuss when we might interview someone (examples: for a job, to find out more about something, for a magazine or newspaper article, for a television show).

Reading

Star Chat: *Into the Woods*

Before the students read the interview, remind students that in an interview, the interviewer asks the questions and the person being interviewed answers them, and they take turns to speak. Now either read the interview as a class, with two students reading the parts of Daniel Huttlestone and National Geographic Kids (NGK), or with each student reading with a partner.

When they have read the interview, ask the students what the purpose of the interview is (to find out more about the actor and the film). Focus students' attention on the layout of the interview, pointing out that the names of the people talking are on the left, with colons after the names. Speech marks are not needed. Remind students that we ask closed questions when we want a specific answer or specific details (examples: 'What is your name?', 'How old are you?'). We ask open questions to ask someone's opinion or if we want a longer answer (examples: 'Do you ever think …?' 'How do you …?'). Ask the students what kind of questions are asked by the NGK interviewer (open questions).

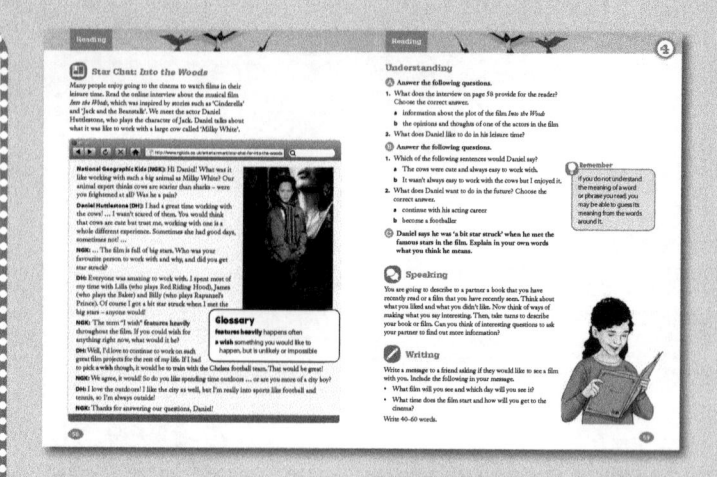

Student Book answers

Understanding

Ask the students to read the text again and then answer the questions on their own.

Answers:

A 1. b the opinions and thoughts of one of the actors in the film
   2. He likes to spend time outdoors playing sports such as football and tennis.

B 1. b It wasn't always easy to work with the cows but I enjoyed it.
   2. a continue with his acting career

C Example answer:
   He means he was very impressed by the famous actors and did not know what to say to them because he felt shy when he was around them.

Speaking

Speaking

This activity provides a good opportunity to develop students' understanding of how we can ask for and give opinions and how we can ask questions to clarify meaning. Suggest questions that they could ask each other such as:

- What did you enjoy most about the book/film?
- What was your favourite part in the book/film? Why?
- Who was your most/least favourite character? Why?
- Who would you recommend this book/film to?

Reading

Writing

Writing

In this activity, students write a message to a friend, asking the friend whether they would like to go and see a film. They could write the message directly in their exercise books, or they could draw a message bubble or box in their books. Before they write their messages, draw the students' attention to the bullet points on page 59 of the Student Book and explain that they need to make sure their message includes the information mentioned in these points. Remind students that the language used in written messages to friends can be informal and chatty and that we can use abbreviations and colloquial language.

Reading

Workbook page 27: *Tennis Shoes*

On page 27 of the Workbook, students read an extract from *Tennis Shoes*, by Noel Streatfeild. Comprehension questions test their understanding of the type of text and the content of the extract. They then practise writing opinions and descriptions.

Answers:

1 **B** a story
2. **A** at the beginning
3. Susan was in the year above at school as she was clever. Jimmy was a good swimmer, Nicky was 'ordinarily' intelligent, and David was a good singer.
4. She was lazy and not top of her class.
5. They were all good tennis players.
6. Students' own answers. Students should use language for giving opinions: 'I think that …', 'My view is that …' etc.
7. Students' own answers. Check that students have used a descriptive, narrative style.

Extension

Class magazine

Explain to the students that they are going to create a class magazine about films and books they have seen or read. Each student will contribute a description they have written of a film or book they have recently seen or read. Before they start writing, write the following suggestions on the board, or use the photocopiable sheet on the CD.

1. Name of book/film
2. Describe the book/film (funny, great, sad, interesting, disappointing, attractive, exciting)
3. What kind of book/film is it?
4. What I liked
5. My favourite character
6. My favourite part
7. What I disliked
8. Would I recommend it?
9. How many stars out of five?

Use of English

Adverbs

Adverbs
Grammar

Students may be familiar with adverbs from primary level. Remind them that we use adverbs to describe how, when, where or how often something happens or has happened. Read the examples in the language focus box on page 60 of the Student Book and write some other examples on the board. (Examples: how: well, softly; when: tomorrow, later; where: there, everywhere; how often: often, usually.)

Read through the Remember feature about adding '–ly' to an adjective that ends in 'y'. Explain that there are some other spelling rules for adding '–ly' and write the rules on the board or direct students to page 153 of their Student Books, for advice on spelling regular and irregular adverbs.

Tell students that some adverbs are irregular and do not follow any of the rules (example: the adverb of 'good' is 'well'). Read the examples of adverbs that have the same form as adjectives, and write some more examples on the board (examples: close, far, high, low, long).

Using adverbs
Student Book answers

Ask the students to complete the answers in pairs and then check their answers with another pair.

Answers:

A 1. when
   2. how
   3. how often
   4. where

B 1. I climbed the stairs <u>quietly</u> because my sister was asleep.
   2. I finished the puzzle <u>easily</u>.
   3. We arrived <u>late</u>, so we missed the beginning of the film.
   4. I don't want to be late. I would rather arrive <u>early</u>.

C Example answers:
   1. I <u>often</u> walk to school.
   2. I <u>always</u> eat healthy food.
   3. I <u>sometimes</u> go to the cinema on Friday evening.

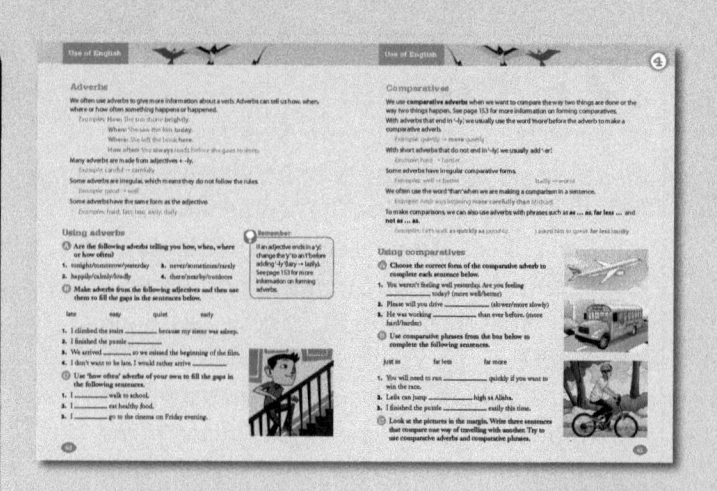

Comparatives
Grammar

In this section students build on what they have studied about adverbs to learn about comparative adverb structures. Remind the students about the work they did in Unit 1 on comparative adjectives. Explain that we use comparative adverbs to compare the way two things are done or happen. Read through the explanation on page 61 of the Student Book and give some examples of how the comparative adverbs can be used in sentences. (Examples: She was speaking more quietly than me. I see him more often than you do. It is raining harder now than it was. Alex can jump higher than me. He did better than expected in his exam; I did worse than I expected.) Focus on the final part of the language focus box about phrases such as 'as … as', 'far less … ' and 'not as … as'. Write some examples of how these phrases are used on the board. (Examples: I walked as quickly as I could; He plays tennis far less often than he used to; I can't run as fast as my brother.)

54

Use of English

Student Book answers

Using comparatives

Ask the students to complete the answers in pairs and then check their answers with another pair.

Answers:

A 1. You weren't feeling well yesterday. Are you feeling <u>better</u> today?
   2. Please will you drive <u>more slowly</u>.
   3. He was working <u>harder</u> than ever before.

B 1. You will need to run <u>far more</u> quickly if you want to win the race.
   2. Leila can jump <u>just as</u> high as Alisha.
   3. I finished the puzzle <u>far less/far more/just as</u> easily this time.

C Ensure the students are using comparative adverbs in their sentences rather than comparative adjectives. Example answers:

   A plane travels a lot faster than a bus.

   A bus can go much more quickly than a bicycle.

   I will get to where I am going a lot more quickly if I go by plane.

   If I go by bicycle, I will arrive later than if I go by bus.

   Buses get delayed by the traffic more often than bicycles.

   You travel faster in a plane than on a bus.

   When the traffic is heavy, it takes me a bit longer to get home by bus than by bicycle.

5. Sonia realised she was late for school, so she started to walk <u>more quickly</u>.
6. as quickly as a horse
   as slowly as a tortoise
   as carefully as an old man
   as happily as a child with an ice cream
   as quietly as a mouse
7. I can whisper <u>far more quietly</u> than you.
8. I can swim <u>far less quickly</u> than you.
9. She asked him to walk <u>far more carefully</u> as it was icy.
10. I found the race <u>far harder</u> this time.
11. The baby had fallen asleep, so Mum asked us to play <u>far more quietly</u>.

Extension

Using comparatives

Ask the students to work in a small group or with a partner and imagine they are creating a character for a game that will be played on a computer. They need to provide a short description of their character, using adverbs and comparative adverbs.

Provide word banks of words that the students can use.

Examples:

Verbs: swim, run, climb, walk, play, jump, dance

Adverbs: quickly, slowly, carelessly, gracefully, energetically, musically, noisily, softly, silently, loudly, kindly, nastily

Comparative phrases: far less than ..., not as ... as, a bit ... than, much ... than, a lot ... than

When they have completed the task, ask the students to swap their descriptions with another pair or group and compare their characters.

Use of English

Workbook page 28: Comparative adverbs

Page 28 of the Workbook tests students' understanding of comparative adverbs. Students can work alone at home or in class to complete the activities. Go through the answers in class, stopping at any difficulties.

Answers:

1. Hamza arrived <u>earlier</u> than Ruby.
2. Mia dances <u>more gracefully</u> now.
3. Louis was ill on Monday, but on Tuesday he felt <u>better</u>.
4. Ryu spoke <u>more confidently</u> in front of the class than before.

Listening

Interview with Jacqueline Wilson

Prior knowledge

Explain to the students that they are going to listen to an interview with the children's book author Jacqueline Wilson. As a pre-listening activity, ask the students whether they have read any of Jacqueline Wilson's books. If so, which ones have they read? Explain that Jacqueline Wilson has written many books for children and has won many awards. Give some examples of the titles of her books and some brief details about what they are about. (Examples: *Double Act*, which is about identical twins Garnet and Ruby, who look alike on the outside but are very different on the inside; *Best Friends*, which is about two friends, Alice and Gemma, whose friendship is at risk when Alice has to move a long way away.) In groups discuss what makes a good book. Write down ideas on the board. (Examples: It has a good plot, it has characters in it you want to know more about, it makes you laugh, you can't stop reading it, etc.)

Listening

Track 4.1: Interview with Jacqueline Wilson

Play the recording once and discuss the meaning of the Glossary words with the students. Ask the students to share three pieces of specific information about the author. (Examples: she has been writing stories since childhood; she came up with the name 'Tracy Beaker' in the bath; she didn't think the *Tracy Beaker* book would become a television show.) Remind the students of the features of interviews that they discussed earlier in the unit (see page 52). Explain that the same features are used in this interview, with the interviewer asking the questions and the person being interviewed (Jacqueline Wilson) answering them. A full transcript of this track is available on the CD.

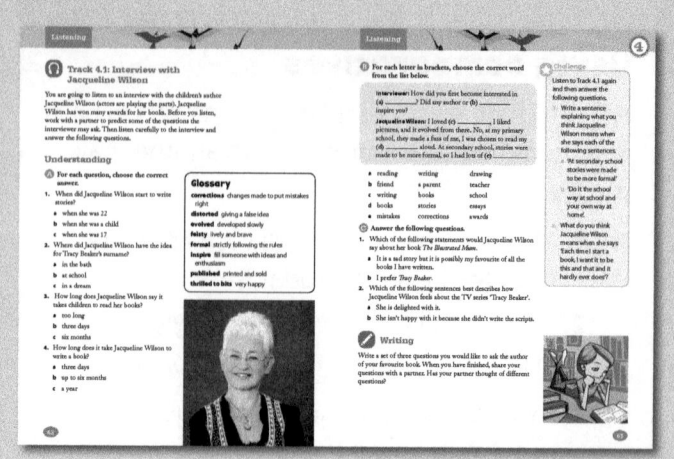

Student Book answers

Understanding

Ask the students to listen to the recording again and then answer the questions.

Answers:

A 1. a when she was 22
   2. a in the bath
   3. b three days
   4. b up to six months

B a writing
   b teacher
   c books
   d stories
   e corrections

C 1. a It is a sad story but it is possibly my favourite of all the books I have written.
   2. a She is delighted with it.

Writing

In this activity, students think of three questions they would like to ask the author of their favourite book. Discuss with the students the kind of questions they can ask. They might want to use open questions to find out more about the author and closed questions to find out specific facts.

Suggested questions:

Why do you write children's books?

Have you plans to carry on writing children's books?

What is your favourite part of writing and why?

Do you think reading is important?

Listening

Listening

Workbook page 29: Opinions

On page 29 of the Workbook, students listen to a recording of three friends talking about a film they have seen at the cinema. They are asked to identify each person's opinion about the film. Students can complete this alone at home or in class. You could listen to the recording again in class and go through the answers together, to check that students have correctly understood the different opinions of each of the friends.

Answers:

1. A enthusiastically
2. C a book
3. B Monica and Tia
4. A the mountain air
5. **Tia:** No! I thought it was very <u>complicated</u> and I didn't <u>understand</u> what happened at the end. It was really <u>confusing</u> and I nearly fell asleep in places. What about you, Monica?

   Monica: I didn't think it was that bad, but I <u>agree</u> with you that the ending was a little <u>confusing</u>.
6. Encourage students to use the information to give specific examples about their opinions. You could emphasise that this is important.

   Examples:

   George's opinion of the film was very enthusiastic. He enjoyed the film because he really liked the fact that the film is based on the book.

   Tia's opinion of the film was very bad. She found it very complicated and found it difficult to think of one part she enjoyed.

   Monica's opinion of the film was more mixed. She thought it was too long but liked the beginning of the film because it helped her understand more about the characters.

⭐ Challenge

In this Challenge activity students will write sentences to explain the meaning behind some of Jacqueline Wilson's statements in the interview. Remind the students that sometimes when people are speaking, they do not always say exactly what they mean openly or directly. We have to read between the lines or work out the meaning from other things that are said. Ask the students to read the questions and then listen to Track 4.1 again, listening for the sentences referred to in the questions.

Example answers:

1. a She means that when she was at secondary school her teachers wanted her to write stories with correct grammar and punctuation and other formal features.

   b She means that you can write as teachers want you to write, with correct punctuation and grammar at school, but when you write at home you are free to write stories in whatever way you like.
2. She means that when she starts to write a new book she has a plan in her head about what she wants it to be like, but in the end it is usually different.

Extension

Developing character

Ask the students to imagine they are a book author like Jacqueline Wilson and they are coming up with ideas for a book about a new character. Tell them to think about:

- What does the character look like?
- How does the character behave?
- What does the character like doing?
- How does the character dress?
- What are the character's characteristics?

Ask them to describe their character. They could write a paragraph, or write a character description and information around the side of a picture of their character (this could be one they have drawn or a picture or photograph they have found of someone who could be their character). Then ask the students to work in small groups and share information about their character.

Use of English

Adverbs in sentences

Grammar

Adverbs in sentences

In this section students will develop their knowledge of adverbs by focusing on the position of adverbs in sentences. Explain that sometimes adverbs come at the beginning of a sentence, sometimes at the end and sometimes in the middle. Read through the first paragraph of the language focus box on page 64 of the Student Book together. Give some further examples of adverbs used after a verb (examples: He ran quickly around the track; He jumped higher than me). Note that although adverbs often come after verbs, if a verb is made up of an auxiliary and a main verb, the adverb goes after the auxiliary (examples: I have always liked football; I don't often go to the cinema).

Now remind students of the meaning of the word 'object' in a sentence and read the second paragraph of the language focus box. Ask the students to identify the object in the example given (the door) and point out the position of the adverb after the object. Read through the rest of the language focus box and give more examples of adverbs used in each position (examples: I arrived early; I often watch films at the weekend; I am usually on time for school; Unfortunately, I have forgotten my book).

Student Book answers

Using adverbs in sentences

Answers:

A 1. He read the book quickly.
   2. He was speaking loudly.
   3. I often play tennis on Fridays.

B 1. a Did you see the film <u>last night</u>?
      b He plays the piano <u>well</u>.
      c They <u>usually</u> listen to music in the evening.
   2. a I <u>often</u> go to the cinema with my friend.
      b The football team are playing <u>well</u>.
      c He listened <u>carefully</u>.

C Students' own answers. Ask the students to check each other's sentences.

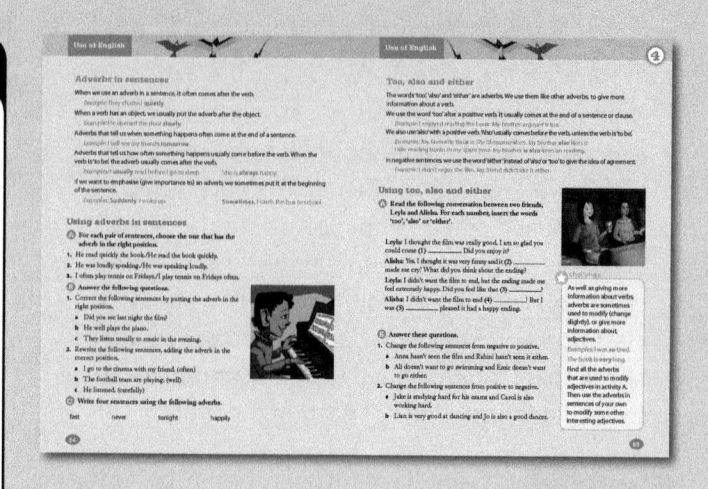

Grammar

Too, also and either

In this section students build on their knowledge of adverbs, focusing on the use of 'too', 'also' and 'either'. Explain that like other adverbs these words are used to add extra information in a sentence. Read through the examples in the language focus box on page 65 of the Student Book, explaining that 'too' and 'also' have very similar meanings and they are both used in positive sentences. We use 'either' in negative sentences. Focus on the position of 'too' and 'either' at the end of the example sentences. Explain that 'also' is usually used before a verb, although it comes after the verb 'to be'. Give some more examples (examples: I like swimming and I also like football; I like swimming and I like football too; I don't like swimming and I don't like football either. I am hungry and I am also very tired; I am hungry and I am very tired too; I am not hungry and I am not tired either).

Student Book answers

Using too, also and either

Answers:

A 1. too   2. also   3. too
   4. either 5. also

B 1. a Anna has seen the film and Rahini has also seen it/Rahini has seen it too.
      b Ali wants to go swimming and Emir wants to go too/Emir also wants to go.
   2. a Jake isn't studying hard for his exams and Carol isn't working hard either.
      b Lian isn't very good at dancing and Jo isn't a good dancer either.

Use of English

⭐ Challenge

In this Challenge activity students will practise using adverbs of degree to modify adjectives. Students may not be familiar with adverbs of degree or adverbs used to modify adjectives, so students may need guidance before they start the activity. Write some examples on the board (for example, 'too', 'quite', 'very', 'terribly', 'fairly'), as well as examples of how these adverbs are used before adjectives in sentences. When they have found all the adjectives in the conversation, tell them to think of some interesting adjectives to use in sentences with the adverbs.

Answers:

really (good), so (glad), very (funny), extremely (happy)

Students' own sentences. Accept any sentences that use the adverbs correctly to modify adjectives.

11.

Aleksy: Where shall we go?

Sam: We could go to the cinema, but I don't want to see the film that's on.

Aleksy: No, I don't want to see it <u>either</u>. What about the beach?

Sam: That sounds good. Then we could go swimming <u>too</u>.

Aleksy: I'd <u>also</u> like to look around the shops. Do you need to buy anything?

Sam: No.

Aleksy: I don't <u>either</u>. What about the park?

Sam: OK, we can go to the park <u>too</u>. Then let's get an ice cream on the way home.

In class, encourage students to come up with more ideas to extend this conversation. They could role play this activity in groups or with a partner.

Use of English

Workbook page 30: Adverbs in sentences

On page 30 of the Workbook, students will practise placing adverbs correctly in sentences. They will also practise using 'too', 'also' and 'either' correctly. Set as homework or as an in-class exercise and go through the answers in class, stopping at any difficulties.

Answers:

1. Ali walked <u>slowly</u> because he felt so tired.
2. He was speaking <u>quietly</u> as he had lost his voice.
3. Alicia was working <u>hard</u> as she wanted to pass the exam.
4. I <u>often</u> go shopping at the weekend.
5. The party preparations are going <u>well</u>.
6. Dai was reading the book <u>fast</u>, so he had nearly got to the end.
7. I <u>never</u> go there.
8. What are you doing <u>tonight</u>?
9. <u>Unluckily</u>, it rained as soon as we got to the skatepark.
10. Mr Rana always drove his car <u>carefully</u>.

Extension

Practising too, also and either

This task will give students some extra practice in using too, also and either. Write the following words on the board. Then ask the students to work in pairs and write a sentence for each pair of words using 'too', 'also' or 'either'.

1. theatre/cinema
2. football/shopping
3. reading/writing
4. travel/visit

Example sentences:

1. We can go to the cinema and also go to the theatre next week.
2. I love playing football and I like shopping too.
3. He doesn't like reading and he doesn't like writing either.
4. We can travel to Italy and also visit Maria.

Speaking

New places and special days

Prior knowledge

In this section students will discuss what they like doing in their leisure time and where they would like to visit.

You may want to ask the class to research their dream destination and bring in leaflets, photographs or information about places or countries. Divide the class into groups of four and look at a map of the world. Ask the students to locate where they are on the map, and then ask whether they have visited any other countries and where they would like to visit. If possible, supply pictures of different cities or countries. Look at tourist guides, leaflets or information online for the chosen country/countries.

Speaking

Look at the pictures on page 66 of the Student Book and discuss as a class what the people in the pictures are doing. Write vocabulary connected to new places on the board. Then ask the students to work in pairs to answer the questions in the speaking activity. Remind them to listen to each other's ideas and give reasons for their opinions.

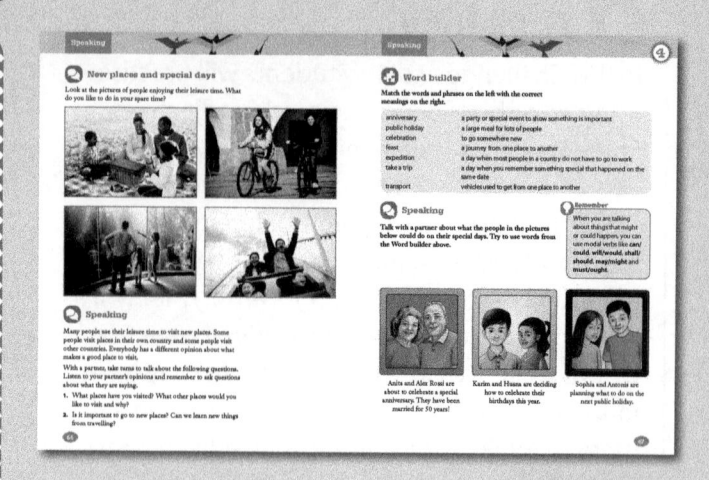

Vocabulary

Word builder

This activity will help students to learn some new vocabulary that they can use in their discussions about leisure. Ask students to match the words in the left-hand column to the meanings on the right, working on their own. When they have finished, ask them to check their answers with a partner.

Answers:

anniversary: a day when you remember something special that happened on the same date

public holiday: a day when most people in a country do not have to go to work

celebration: a party or special event to show something is important

feast: a large meal for lots of people

expedition: a journey from one place to another

take a trip: to go somewhere new

transport: vehicles used to get from one place to another

Speaking

Speaking

In this activity students work with a partner to discuss what the people in the pictures on page 67 of the Student Book could do on their special days. Ask the students to read the captions to the pictures carefully and discuss the kinds of things that would be appropriate for each occasion. What would each pair enjoy and would any other people be involved? Encourage students to use words from the Word builder and to use some modal verbs mentioned in the Remember feature. Students may be familiar with the use of some modal verbs from primary level. They will learn more about them in Unit 6.

Example responses:

Anita and Alex could go to a restaurant to celebrate their special anniversary.

Anita and Alex might take a trip to celebrate their special anniversary.

Karim and Husna might have a feast to celebrate their birthdays.

Karim and Husna ought to have a party to celebrate their birthdays.

Sophia and Antonis should go on an expedition to the mountains on the next public holiday.

Sophia and Antonis could go to Greece on the public holiday.

Workbook page 31: Visiting new places

The speaking exercise on page 31 of the Workbook will give students practise in using comparative adverbs and 'too', 'also' and 'either' in spoken language. You may choose to go through the activity in class first, and explain to students that modal verbs can be used to talk about something that might happen and include: can/could, will/would, shall/should, may/might, must/ought.

Example answer:

Mr Harris: When we get home, we must book the transport to the hotel.

Mrs Harris: Yes, we also need to pack our clothes.

Mr H: Do you think it will be hot there?

Mrs H: Yes, it will certainly feel warmer than it does here.

Mr H: We should buy some sun-cream too.

Mrs H: Remember it's a public holiday. What time do the shops close?

Mr H: Hmm … I'm not sure.

Mrs H: I'm not sure either. Is it 4 p.m.?

Mr H: They close much earlier than the other shops then. We should walk more quickly!

Mrs H: I don't think it will make any difference. It will only make me more tired than I already am …

Extension

Questions and answers

This task will give students an opportunity to use some of the vocabulary they have learned in this section. Ask them to think of five questions to ask a local person about activities that can be done in their area or places that can be visited. Ask them also to plan the five answers. When they have finished, ask them to exchange their questions and answers with a partner. As a follow-up activity, they could read out the questions and answers to one another and suggest ways to improve the answers.

Reading corner

Prior knowledge

Students read an extract from *The Lion, the Witch and the Wardrobe*, an adventure fantasy story by C.S. Lewis. They answer some questions about the text before writing their own playscript in which Edmund describes to his sister his walk through the woods. Before they read the text, elicit examples of other adventure or fantasy stories the students have read. You may want to discuss the meaning of the word 'fantasy'. Explain that fantasy stories are often set in imaginary worlds and explore themes of good against evil. Before they read the extract, give the students a brief introduction to the story. (Four siblings discover a wardrobe in a large house they are visiting. When they enter the wardrobe they pass through into an imaginary world where they have an adventure and meet talking animals and other strange characters.)

Reading

The Lion, the Witch and the Wardrobe

Read the extract with the class as well as the Glossary words and their definitions. Students may need support with other difficult vocabulary, so discuss the meaning of any other unfamiliar words (for example, delicious, struck, birch trees, branch, chattering). Can the students guess the meaning of the words from the context? You can then discuss the descriptive language used in the extract, ('robes of snow'), use of colour connotation ('white shapes', 'dark green of firs'), adverbs ('grew louder', 'suddenly chirped') and sensory description ('delicious sunlight', 'noise of water', 'wherever Edmund's eyes turned …').

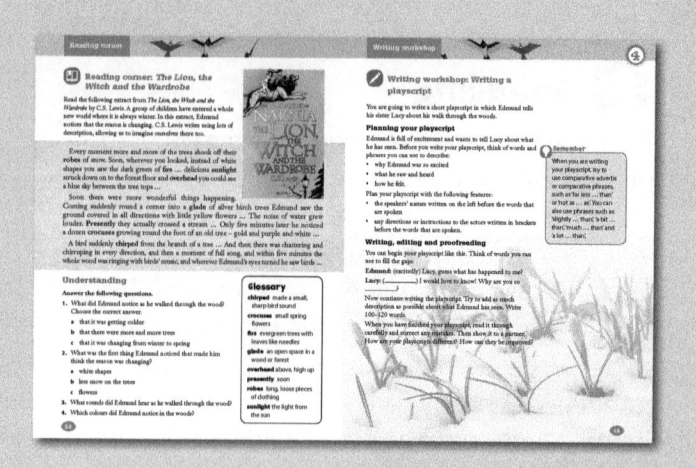

Student Book answers

Understanding

Ask students to answer the questions on their own.

Answers:

1. c that it was changing from winter to spring
2. b less snow on the trees
3. Edmund heard the sounds of water and birds. (The noise of water grew louder/A bird suddenly chirped/chattering and chirruping/ringing with birds' music.)
4. White, dark green, blue, silver, yellow, gold and purple.

Reading

Suggested reading

If the students liked reading the text from *The Lion, the Witch and the Wardrobe*, ask them to pick another fantasy book – they can either read it alone or you could choose it as your next class reading book. Examples: *Charlotte's Web* by E.B. White, *Stig of the Dump* by Clive King, *The Secret Garden* by Frances Hodgson Burnett.

Writing workshop

Writing a playscript

Planning

Tell the students that they are going to plan and write a short playscript. Remind them also about the powerful adverbs C.S. Lewis used to describe the fantasy world in the extract. Before they plan their script, remind them of how to lay out a script, with the speaker's name on the left and stage directions in brackets before the words that are spoken. Brainstorm as a class the answers to the prompts in the planning section on page 69 of the Student Book.

Suggestions:

- Edmund was so excited because he could see that winter was ending and spring was on its way.
- He could see new life, the snow leaving the trees, the blue sky, the yellow flowers, silver birch trees, crocuses, an old tree, birds and the sun. He could hear the birds singing and the noise of the water.
- Edmund felt excited, happy, hopeful, positive and encouraged, etc.

Writing, editing and proofreading

When they have finished their planning, ask the students to continue writing the playscript. Encourage them to add as much description about what Edmund has seen as possible. Ask them to work from their draft but to think about ways they could make it even better. Ask them to write 100–120 words. When they have finished their playscript, ask them to read it through carefully, correct any mistakes in spelling, punctuation or grammar and then show it to a partner. Can their partner suggest any ways in which the script can be improved?

Workbook page 32: Writing a playscript

On page 32 of the Workbook, students will practise writing a playscript. In class, you might want to suggest students think of suitable adverbs that can be placed in the playscript as directions. For example: happily, enthusiastically, impatiently, indifferently, sadly, gloomily, miserably, cheerfully.

The playscript might start like this:

Alex: (excitedly) Eric, I've had an idea. Why don't we go to see a football match on Saturday afternoon?

Eric: (quietly) I'm not too sure … Why are you so happy?

Here is an example of how you might continue the playscript:

Alex: (loudly) I want to go to the game!

Eric: (sadly) I'm not sure I do. I thought we agreed that we were going to go the cinema.

Alex: (carefully) But that was before I knew about the football game …

Eric: (patiently) I know you love football, Alex, and you know I like going to the cinema. Can't we find a way to do both?

Alex: (quickly) We could easily do both. Why don't we go to the football game and on the way back go to the cinema? That way we can relax after the game.

Eric: (eagerly) That's a great idea, Alex. I can't believe you came up with it so quickly.

Alex: You know I think fast.

Eric: You think correctly.

Alex: Are you OK with that then? On Saturday, we will watch the game and then go to the cinema?

Eric: (loudly) I can't wait.

Continuing the playscript

Ask the class to imagine that Edmund carries on telling Lucy about his adventure. Ask them to continue their script by adding six more lines. You can ask the class the following questions: What happens next? Did Edmund meet somebody? What was happening around him? Did he see something happen? How did he get home?

Divide the class into groups of four and ask them to read out their scripts to each other. They should then choose one script to perform to the whole class. Before performing the playscript, tell them to practise reading it aloud, adding as much expression as they can and emphasising any stage directions (such as 'enthusiastically' or 'excitedly', etc.).

Progress assessment

Progress check

Student Book answers

Progress check

1. One mark. Example answer:
   He likes to spend time outdoors and plays tennis and football. [1]

2. One mark. **b** I would love to train with the Chelsea football team. [1]

3. One mark. **b** over 80 [1]

4. One mark. **a** I don't know exactly where my ideas come from. [1]

5. One mark each:
   - more easily
   - more often
   - better
   - later [4]

6. One mark for each sentence. [4]

7. One mark each:
   a I saw the film <u>yesterday</u>.
   b I <u>rarely</u> have time to watch TV. [2]

8. One mark for each sentence. [2]

9. One mark each:
   I love swimming and my brother loves to swim <u>too</u>. I <u>also</u> love tennis. I am not very fast at running and my brother isn't <u>either</u>. [3]

10. Six marks. One mark each for three comparative adverbs and three marks for the rest of the sentences. [6]

Total marks: 25

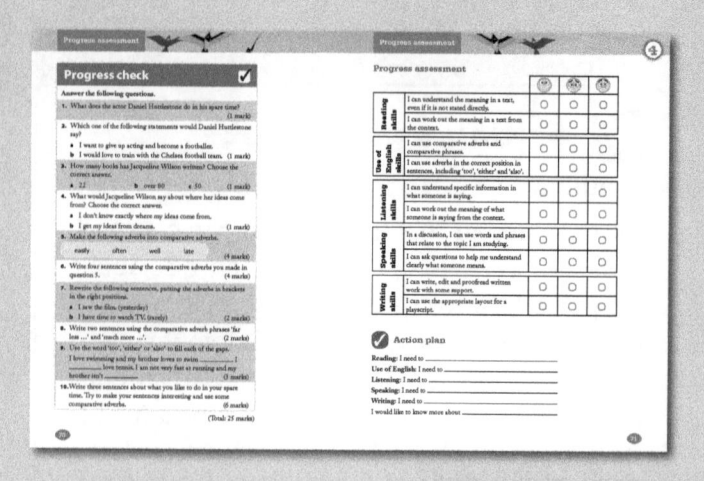

End-of-unit quiz

Workbook page 33: Leisure quiz

The end-of-unit quiz on page 33 of the Workbook is a summary of the content you have covered in the unit. You can set this as homework or to complete in class. Go through the answers in class, and check that there are no gaps in students' understanding.

Answers:

1. **C** the characters
2. **B** a novel
3. A beetle does not move as quickly as a rabbit. Travelling by bus is sometimes just as slow as walking.
4. Sunita: Let's go to the park early. Then we'll have time to visit the museum <u>too</u>.
   Chloe: Great, and we can <u>also</u> eat in the museum café.
5. **C** She understood where the characters came from and what their lives were like.
6. **A** She disagreed with Monica.
7. Examples:
   Hamza: (<u>excitedly</u>) Did you see that film they showed on television last night? Wasn't it funny? I loved it!
   Kara: (<u>doubtfully</u>) Really? I didn't laugh once.
8. Example:
   Leo: (<u>thoughtfully</u>) Hmmm . . . it was OK. I thought the beginning was very funny, but I was a bit confused by the end.

Progress assessment

Reflection
Reflecting on your learning
Have a discussion with the class about how they will continue to use the different skills they have covered in this unit. Students should then work independently on the progress assessment task. For each of the skills, ask them to tick the box that they think most fits how well they are doing. Now move on to the action plan. The aim is to encourage students to identify which skills they think they need more practice in, while reinforcing the skills they can do well. Give students the opportunity to practise the skills they have identified and revisit the action plan after a few weeks, encouraging students to compare later attempts with the first.

Listening
🎧 End-of-unit activity
This activity will allow students to evaluate the unit and to reflect on their learning.

Explain to the students that they will hear a conversation between Maria and Costas about the topics in this unit. Ask the students to listen to Track TB4.1 twice and then answer the following questions (see the photocopiable sheet on the CD).

1. What did Costas find hard to believe in the interview with Daniel?
2. What did Costas find interesting about the Jacqueline Wilson interview?
3. What comparative adverbs are used?
4. What was the name of Jacqueline Wilson's favourite book?

Answers:
1. That he had to work with a cow.
2. How Jacqueline Wilson began writing and how she came up with the name for the book *Tracy Beaker*.
3. really, today, later
4. *The Illustrated Mum*

When they have answered the questions, ask them to write down everything they have learned about interviews. You can recap on use of questions, opinions and specific points.

Reflection
Teacher reflection
1. Which parts of the unit did the students enjoy most? Why was this?
2. Was there anything that the students found difficult in this unit? How can I make sure this is easier next time?
3. Considering the learning objectives and content, what did the students successfully learn while studying this unit?
4. Considering the learning objectives and content, what did the students struggle with while studying this unit? Why was this? What could I do to help them more?
5. Which parts of the unit did I teach well? How did I achieve this?
6. Which parts of the unit did I struggle to teach well? What can I do to improve this?
7. Next time I teach this unit, is there anything I can do to improve the learning experience for my students?

5 Friends

Learning objectives

In this unit, students will:

- Understand implied meaning. **pages 68, 78** *7Re4*
- Recognise the attitude or opinion of the writer. **page 68** *7Re5*
- Recognise typical features at word, sentence and text level. **page 78** *7Re7*
- Use, with some support, style and register appropriate to a limited range of written genres. **page 79** *7W5*
- Spell a growing range of high-frequency vocabulary accurately. **pages 69, 79** *7W7*
- Punctuate, with accuracy. **page 79** *7W8*
- Use a growing range of abstract nouns and compound nouns; use a limited range of gerunds as subjects and objects; use a limited range of complex noun phrases. **pages 70–71, 74–75** *7Uw1*
- Use a range of determiners including *all, half, both [of]*. **pages 74–75** *7Ug1*
- Understand, with little or no support, the main points in extended talk. **pages 72–73** *7L1*
- Understand, with little or no support, most of the detail of an argument in extended talk. **pages 72–73** *7L3*
- Understand extended narratives on a range of general and curricular topics. **pages 72–73** *7L8*
- Give an opinion, at discourse level. **pages 76–77** *7S3*
- Link comments, with some flexibility, to what others say at sentence and discourse level in pair, group and whole class exchanges. **page 77** *7S5*
- Use appropriate subject-specific vocabulary and syntax to talk about a limited range of curricular topics. **pages 76–77** *7S7*

Setting the scene

Friends

Write the unit title on the board. Explain that this unit will explore the theme of friends. Ask the students to study the photographs on page 72 of the Student Book and ask them how they can tell that the people are friends. What do they think is happening in the photos? Now read the quotations and discuss what each one means. Explain that a proverb is a short, well-known saying that states a truth or gives advice. Discuss the meaning of 'A friend in need is a friend indeed' (a true friend is the one who is there to help when you are in trouble) and Thomas Aquinas's quotation 'There is nothing on this earth more prized than true friendship' (real friendship is more precious than anything else). Ralph Waldo Emerson's quotation comes from an essay he wrote on friendship. Ask students to put it into their own words (example: 'If you want to have friends you must be friendly yourself').

Thinking ahead

Now focus the students' attention on the Thinking ahead questions on page 73 of the Student Book. Ask them to list as many words and phrases as they can to do with friendship. By writing down the words and phrases they think of, they will start to build a personal bank of words for their work on the unit. Suggest that they continue to collect vocabulary for their personal list throughout the unit. When students have compared their list with their neighbour, ask them to share their lists as a class. You may wish to write some other helpful words and phrases on the board for them (examples: reliable, good company, trustworthy, always there, dependable). Spend some time discussing the meaning of the words.

Friends

Theme opener

Workbook page 34: Friends

Page 34 of the Workbook gives students practice in writing about the theme of the unit. If using in class, students can discuss their answers in pairs for additional speaking practice.

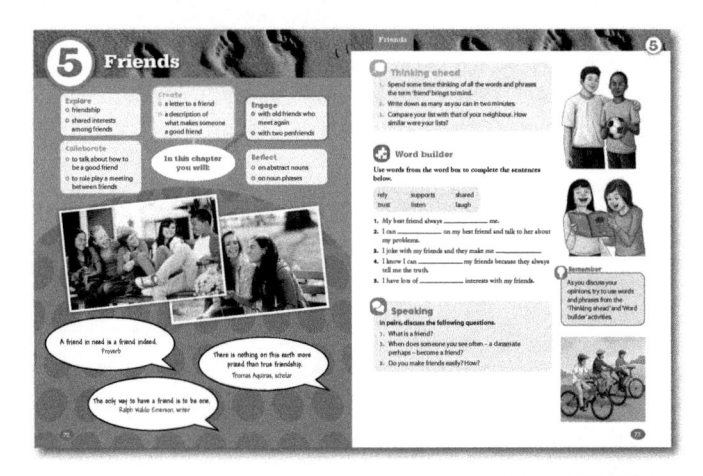

Vocabulary

Word builder

This activity helps students to extend their vocabulary and prepare them for new words they may find in the unit. Ask students to fill the gaps in the sentences, working on their own. When they have finished, ask them to check their answers with a partner.

Answers:

1. My best friend always <u>supports</u> me.
2. I can <u>rely</u> on my best friend and talk to her about my problems.
3. I joke with my friends and they make me <u>laugh</u>.
4. I know I can <u>trust</u> my friends because they always tell me the truth.
5. I have lots of <u>shared</u> interests with my friends.

Extension

A story about friendship

The students are going to work together in small groups on the possible story behind one of the quotations on page 72 of the Student Book.

First, ask the students to discuss which quotation they want to work on. Next they should agree on a story outline. Possible stories might include:

- 'A friend in need is a friend indeed': A famous person starts to have difficulties and all their friends disappear, except for one. That friend saves the other from some danger and the situation changes.
- 'There is nothing on this earth more prized than true friendship': A friend supports someone through a very difficult time in their life.
- 'The only way to have a friend is to be one': A selfish person with no friends sees someone else with lots of friends. They try to become less selfish and more friendly and make more friends.

When the students have their story worked out, they should discuss how they are going to present it: for example, as an acted out scene, a mime or a group story-telling.

Speaking

Speaking

This is an exercise which provides conversation practice. Begin by reading the questions to the students and explain that there is no right or wrong answer to these questions but an opportunity for them to exchange ideas and opinions. Before they start to work in pairs, ask the students to look through their vocabulary list and think about the words and phrases they might want to use in their conversations. Remind them to use words from the Word builder activity. In their conversations, encourage them always to try to think of an example to show what they mean.

Reading

What makes a good friend?

Prior knowledge

Students read two informal emails in which two friends change their arrangements to meet up. In the process, they show that they are good friends. Elicit from the students how they would greet or address a friend at the start of an email and how they would end an email to a friend. (Examples: Hi, Hello, See you soon!, Speak soon, All the best, Love, etc.) Ask them what kind of language they would use in an email to a teacher, another adult they didn't know very well or someone they didn't know. (Examples: Dear, Regards, Best wishes, etc.) Explain that informal emails to friends are written in a friendly, chatty style using informal words, phrases and expressions. They often make references to past experiences the friends have shared, and they might include some jokes and questions.

Reading

📖 What makes a good friend?

Read the emails with the class before they start on the Understanding section. Ask the students to find the particular features of informal emails that have been discussed. As you read through the emails with the students, stop at any unfamiliar words and phrases (for example: appointment, awful jokes). Explain that in informal writing words can have a different, less precise meaning than when used more formally. Example: awful jokes means 'not very funny jokes'.

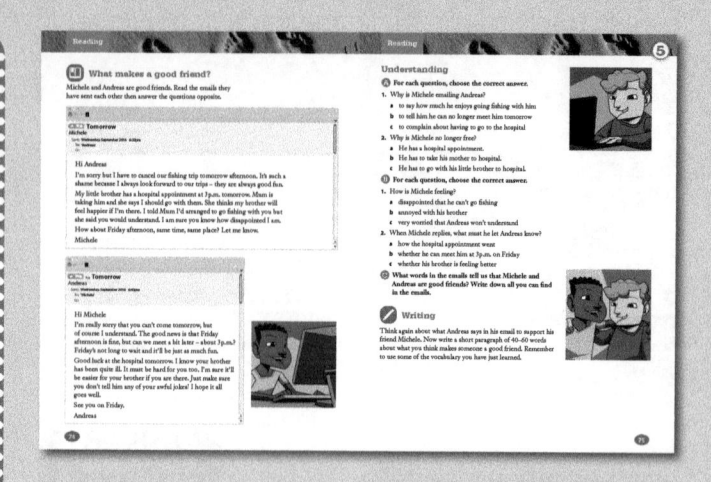

Student Book answers

Understanding

Ask students to read the emails again and then answer the questions on their own.

Answers:

A 1. b to tell him he can no longer meet him tomorrow
   2. c He has to go with his little brother to hospital.

B 1. a disappointed that he can't go fishing
   2. b whether he can meet him at 3 p.m. on Friday

C Allow all reasonable suggestions, including references to overall tone.

Example answers: I always look forward, always good fun, Mum, you would understand, I am sure you know, how disappointed, I understand, Good luck, I know, It must be hard for you, Just make sure you don't tell him any of your awful jokes!, I hope it all goes well.

Ask the students to explain each one. (Example: 'I always look forward' – the use of 'always' gives evidence of friendship: 'if we're together it's always fun'.)

Reading

Writing

Writing

In this activity, students will write a short paragraph about what makes someone a good friend. They will pull together all their thoughts about friendship, especially considering the example of Andreas and Michele. Ask them to discuss briefly in pairs what it is that Andreas has done for Michele (provided support, encouragement, shown understanding, been amusing) before doing the writing task on their own. Remind them to check the lists of words and phrases to do with friendship that they have made. Go through the words and their meanings again as a class before they start the writing activity. When they have finished, ask the students to share their paragraph with their neighbour. Then ask for volunteers to read their paragraph to the whole class.

Reading

Workbook page 35: What makes a good friend?

On page 35 of the Workbook, students practise reading and answer questions to check their understanding. Students also write an email to a friend. Check that they have correctly used the features of informal emails (friendly, chatty style, informal words, phrases and expressions, informal start and end).

Answers:

1. **B** Andreas
2. **A** a fishing trip
3. we went to last time/let's try it again
4. Accept any answer saying he would like to go.

Extension

Wall display and research

Explain to the students that this is an opportunity to take the Writing project one step further by creating a wall display featuring the paragraphs they have produced and incorporating pictures and drawings to illustrate them.

This provides an opportunity for students to explore different ways of presenting what they have written. Ask the students to work in small groups and decide what their display might be like. What will the artwork be like (for example, original drawings or newspaper/magazine cut-outs)?

For stronger students there is scope here for some library or Internet research on famous friends. Invite them to explore famous friends in history and in fiction. Encourage the exploration of examples from their own heritage and culture. They should then choose one example and write a short piece about them. These can then be added to the wall displays.

Use of English

Nouns

Grammar

Nouns

In this section students develop their knowledge of nouns, focusing on compound nouns, concrete nouns and abstract nouns. They will then move on to gerunds (–ing forms of verbs used as nouns).

Start by reminding students of the work they did in Unit 1 on countable and uncountable nouns. Students may be familiar with the idea of 'compound words' and 'compound sentences' from primary level. Remind students that a compound noun is made up of two or more words. Write some examples on the board (whiteboard, toothpaste, full moon, notebook, saucepan, birthday, post office, capital letter, passer-by) and ask the students to split each of the words up into the separate words that make them up.

Read through the section on compound nouns in the language focus box on page 76 of the Student Book together. Work through the examples together.

Now go through the second part of the language focus box on concrete and abstract nouns. Ask students to give examples of each. For concrete nouns, take each sense in turn and see how many examples they can come up with. Then do the same with abstract nouns conveying 'thoughts', 'feelings', 'ideas' and 'character'. Write the two headings 'Concrete' and 'Abstract' on the board and write some examples below each heading (examples: school, email, hospital/advice, illness, trust). Ask the students whether they can see a difference between the two kinds of nouns. Explain that concrete nouns name things we see, feel, hear, touch or smell. Look at the examples on the board and ask the students to say which of the senses they relate to. Ask the students to think of examples for each sense. Now explain that abstract nouns name things we cannot detect with our senses. Instead, they name things to do with thoughts, feelings, ideas and qualities. Elicit further examples from the students.

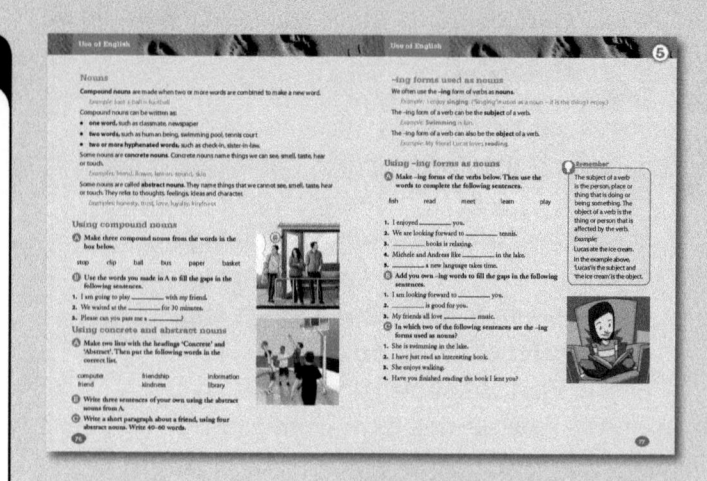

Student Book answers

Using compound nouns

Answers:

A   paper clip
    basketball
    bus stop

B   1. I am going to play <u>basketball</u> with my friend.
    2. We waited at the <u>bus stop</u> for 30 minutes.
    3. Can you pass me a <u>paper clip</u>?

Student Book answers

Using concrete and abstract nouns

Ask the students to complete the answers in pairs and then check their answers with another pair.

Answers:

A | Concrete | Abstract |
    |----------|----------|
    | computer | friendship |
    | friend | information |
    | library | kindness |

B   Accept any sentences using the abstract nouns 'friendship', 'information' and 'kindness' correctly.

C   Students' own answers. Accept any paragraphs that use four abstract nouns correctly.

Use of English

Grammar

–ing forms used as nouns

In this section students are given practice in the use of gerunds. Students may be familiar with –ing forms of verbs as present participles in continuous forms of verbs (examples: I am swimming. He was reading), and when used as adjectives (examples: interesting, boring). Remind students of these uses and then explain that –ing forms of verbs are also used as nouns in sentences. When they are used in this way, they are known as 'gerunds'.

Work through the language focus box and remind students of the subject/verb/object sentence structure. One way to do this is to write two very simple sentences on the board: I like apples. I like swimming. Ask the students to identify the subject of each sentence ('I'), the verb (like) and the object (apples/swimming). (What do I like? apples/swimming.) Explain that the word 'swimming' is used as a noun and the object of 'like'. Give some further examples of gerunds used as the subject of sentences (Reading is an essential skill. Eating is important too).

Use of English

Workbook page 36: Nouns

On page 36 of the Workbook, students practise using compound nouns, concrete and abstract nouns, and gerunds (–ing verbs as nouns). Set as homework or as an in-class exercise and go through the answers together, making sure to stop at any difficulties.

Answers:

1. There are six compound nouns: tennis court, takeaway, park bench, railway line, sunset, school friends.
2. a Walking is great exercise. (*accept* gardening)
   b The old couple loved flowers and so really enjoyed gardening.
   c Reading and writing are basic skills.
3. friendship   honesty   sympathy   trust
4. Accept any answer using two of the above nouns.

Student Book answers

Using –ing forms as nouns

Answers:

A 1. I enjoyed meeting you.
   2. We are looking forward to playing tennis.
   3. Reading books is relaxing.
   4. Michele and Andreas like fishing in the lake.
   5. Learning a new language takes time.

B 1. Example answers: meeting/playing with/seeing
   2. Example answers: Eating healthy food/Doing lots of sport/Keeping fit
   3. Example answers: listening to/playing/dancing to

C 3 and 4

Extension

More practice with gerunds

The object of this activity is to give more practice in the identification and use of gerunds. Quickly revise the information in the language focus box. Then ask students to identify the gerunds in the following sentences.

1. He finished reading his book.
2. Painting is one of his hobbies.
3. Would you mind closing the door?
4. Dancing is fun.
5. She suggested going to see a film.
6. Learning another language is useful.

Now ask the students to identify whether the gerunds are used as subjects or objects in the sentences.

Listening

Old friends meet again

Prior knowledge

Explain to the students that they are going to hear two old friends, Marianna and Lucia, talking about their schooldays as they are brought together after 60 years. In preparation, ask the students to imagine meeting up with a school friend sometime in the future. What might they talk about? What would they remember? What aspects of their present school time would be likely to stick in their memories?

Warm-up exercise – role play

Ask the students to imagine the following scene.

It is 10 years into the future. You are alone and sitting in a café when someone comes up to you. You think you may have seen the person before and are wondering where you might have met when they say: 'You're [your name], aren't you? We were at school together!' The conversation would then continue as you share memories.

Ask students independently to put themselves in that situation and to reflect. Ask them what they might remember. For example:

- about other classmates, teachers and lessons
- what did they especially enjoy or dislike?
- is there an amusing incident that they might remember?

Ask them to note down their answers and share them with their neighbour. Then, in pairs, discuss their memories and continue the conversation as a role play, making use of the memories they have shared.

Vocabulary

Word builder

The words introduced here are all used in the listening exercise in this section. Ask students to match the words on the left with the correct definition on the right, working on their own. When they have finished, ask them to check their answers with a partner.

Answers:

twins: two children born at the same time from the same mother

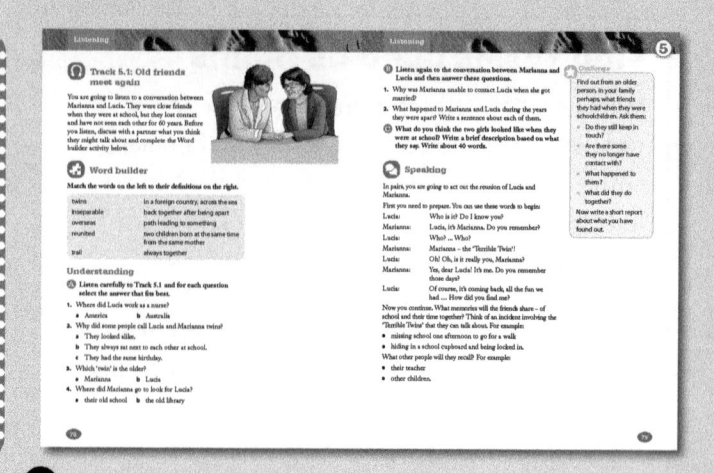

inseparable: always together

overseas: in a foreign country, across the sea

reunited: back together after being apart

trail: path leading to something

Listening

Track 5.1: Old friends meet again

Now play Track 5.1. Ask the students what the reactions of the two friends were as they met. What did they talk about? Play the recording a second time and ask the students to answer the questions. A full transcript of Track 5.1 can be found on the CD.

Student Book answers

Understanding

Answers:

A 1. a America
   2. a They looked alike.
   3. a Marianna
   4. b the old library

B 1. Example answers: because Lucia had moved overseas/because Lucia was in America
   2. Example answers:
      Marianna moved several times, married Franco and lived in Australia for 45 years.
      Lucia lived in America for several years working as a nurse.

C Accept any descriptions that describe their appearance as referred to in the recording, including that they looked like each other, dressed the same and had the same hairstyle.

Listening

⭐ Challenge

In this activity students gather information from an older person such as a parent or grandparent about the friends they had when they were at school. Tell them to ask what school friends the person had, what they recall about them and whether they still keep in touch. When they have gathered the information ask the students to write a short report.

The report might be something like this:

My father's best friend was a boy called Stefan. Last time he heard, Stefan was a pilot flying passenger planes. They do not keep in touch. The only school friend he still sees is Radu who works in town. All the others have moved away. My father was a good boy at school, but Stefan sometimes did naughty things. He took a snake to school one day. They used to explore the countryside together.

💬 Speaking

Explain to the students that they are going to continue the conversation between Marianna and Lucia. First, play the recording again and ask the students to listen to see what differences they can distinguish between the two friends. For example, Marianna is older but has more to say than Lucia; Lucia lived in America for several years and worked as a nurse and Marianna married Franco and moved to Australia. Ask them to prepare in pairs by reading through the beginning of the conversation together. Then they should agree how the conversation should continue. They need to choose an incident to talk about and work out what that incident involved. If they do not have a clear idea of what the incident might be, tell them to use one of the suggestions on page 79 of the Student Book. They also need to agree in advance on the classmates and teachers they will refer to. Refer them back to the warm-up exercise for ideas.

Listening

Workbook page 37: Anka the athlete

On page 37 of the Workbook, students listen to two recordings: a sports commentator and an interview with the friend of an athlete.

Students then answer questions to check their understanding. When students have completed the work on their own (at home or in class), listen to the recordings again together, making sure to explain any difficult words. Check students' understanding by going through the answers together.

Answers:

1. stadium: a sports arena
   orphan: a child whose parents have died
   deprived: poor, lacking basic facilities
   success: doing well
2. B Anka
3. C everyone's hearts
4. A running
5. Anka grew up in a very <u>poor</u> area.
6. She <u>lost</u> her parents when a young child.
7. She became a <u>national</u> athlete.
8. A at school
9. C She was smiling and strong.
10. C She always ran everywhere.

Extension

TV interview

Ask the students to imagine that they are television reporters given the task of interviewing the 'Terrible Twins'. The interview will be a short presentation in which the two friends are asked about their reunion, their memories and what has happened to them in between. The students' job is to prepare and present the interview. It would perhaps be a short (2–3 minute) feature in a news magazine programme. Play Track 5.1 once more and as they listen ask students to make notes about the things they want to talk about with the two friends and the questions they want to ask. Ask them to write out a draft of their interview before moving to work in small groups.

In these groups they are going to create the scene in which the two old friends appear before television cameras. Next they should decide which role each one is going to take – taking turns perhaps. Finally, they should act out the role play, based on the interview questions and comments they had drafted earlier.

73

Use of English

Noun phrases

Grammar

Noun phrases

In this section students build on their understanding of nouns, focusing on noun phrases. Remind students about the work they did earlier in the unit on compound, abstract and concrete nouns. Remind them that a noun is a word that names a person, animal, place, thing or idea and ask them to give some examples. Write their examples on the board, with some of your own. Explain how the limited information contained in the noun itself (book – which book?) is extended by the formation of noun phrases. Explain that these are groups of words that include the noun and other words that tell us more about it. Give some examples – my book, that chair, the boy. Explain that 'my', 'that' and 'the' are examples of a group of words called determiners. Other determiners include: this, a, an, all, half, both (of). Determiners are either specific (my book) or general (a book). Read through the language focus box with the students, giving them further examples and asking them to supply some of their own. When they are secure in their understanding ask them to do the questions independently before comparing answers with their neighbour.

Student Book answers

Using noun phrases

Answers:

A 1. a Do you know <u>my</u> brother?
       b I will come to <u>your</u> house after school.
       c Please could you pass me <u>that</u> blue pen?
    2. a my brother
       b your house
       c that blue pen

B 1. I wanted to meet up with <u>my friends</u> after school.
    2. It's cold outside. You will need to wear <u>a warm coat</u>.
    3. I have only eaten <u>half of the apple</u>.

C Accept any noun phrases that use the nouns with determiners and adjectives correctly.

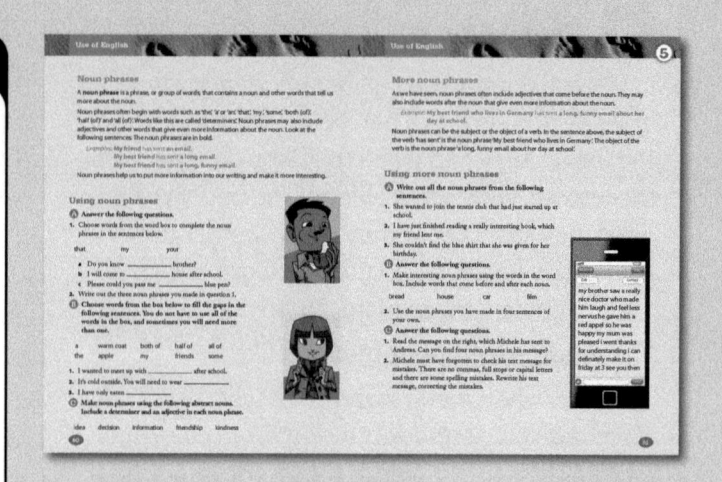

Grammar

More noun phrases

This section focuses on more complex noun phrases. Explain to the students that words can be added before or after the noun to give more information about a noun. Introduce this by writing a noun on the board. Add a determiner, then an adjective and then add a clause after the noun. Then ask for suggestions from the class to see how long and complex a noun phrase they can make. For example:

apple

my apple

my red apple

my red apple that I brought to school

my red apple that I brought to school in my coat pocket

my red apple that I brought to school in my coat pocket this morning

Explain to the students that noun phrases can function as subjects and objects in sentences. You could start with a simple sentence such as 'I am reading a book'. Explain that 'a book' is a noun phrase and the object of 'I am reading'. (What am I reading? A book.) Then move on to 'I am reading a book about animals'. Can they find the noun phrase? (a book about animals.) Is it the subject or object? (object.) Then go on to noun phrases as subjects. Read the language focus box together. When the students are secure in their understanding, ask them to complete the exercise that follows.

74

Use of English

⑤

Student Book answers

Using more noun phrases

Answers:

A 1. the tennis club that had just started up at school
  2. a really interesting book, which my friend lent me
  3. the blue shirt that she was given for her birthday

B 1. Accept answers that are interesting noun phrases using the nouns given.
  2. Accept any sentences that use the noun phrases the students made in question 1 correctly.

C 1. my brother, a really nice doctor who made him laugh and feel less nervous, a red apple, my mum
  2. My brother saw a really nice doctor who made him laugh and feel less nervous. He gave him a red apple, so he was happy. My mum was pleased I went. Thanks for understanding. I can definitely make it on Friday at 3. See you then.

Extension

Practising noun phrases

Students are going to write a short paragraph using noun phrases to extend their understanding of noun phrases and make their writing more interesting. Ask them to read through the section on noun phrases once more before writing some sentences of their own. Tell them they are going to write a description of their classroom. They should try to make the classroom sound interesting by their choice of noun phrases. Give some examples to get them started (the teacher's desk stacked high with books, a half-open window that looked out on the entrance to the building). Preparation: ask them what objects/people they might include. How can they make their description special? After they have written their paragraph, ask them to share what they have written with their neighbour.

Use of English

Workbook page 38: Noun phrases

Page 38 of the Workbook gives students additional practice in using complex noun phrases. Students can complete the work on their own at home or in class. Go through the answers together, stopping at any difficulties.

Answers:

1. How much is that chocolate cake, please?
2. I had walked miles and my tired feet were hurting.
3. He ate his delicious lunch quickly and left.
4. Her friend sat at the table that was nearest the door.
5. The man in a blue jacket with bright buttons spoke first.
6. The little girl who spoke quietly was my friend's sister.
7. Accept any sentences that have correct noun phrases.

Speaking

Friends together

Prior knowledge

In this section students are going to discuss how friends often share interests. They will consider independently the kind of person they are and characteristics they might share with a friend before going on to make use of their findings in discussion in pairs. They also interact with peers to negotiate a classroom task as they go on to discuss meeting a new student and then act out the meeting as a role play. In preparation for this, ask the students to look at the pictures on page 82 of the Student Book and say what they show and discuss with them briefly different kinds of activities (indoor/outdoor/sporty, etc.) and which ones they enjoy.

Speaking

As an introduction to this speaking task, ask students independently to make brief notes about one person from each of the pictures on page 82 of the Student Book. The aim is for them to think about the kind of person that would be involved in such an activity and, in the process, to build up a vocabulary that they can use in any discussion of personality and characteristics.

Ask them to think about:

- who the person is
- what they are doing
- what that might include (what they are playing/reading/etc.)
- what words they might use to describe them.

Now ask them to discuss the questions in the speaking activity with a partner. When they have finished their discussions, ask them to make a list of any words they thought of in answer to question 2. Then compare lists as a class. Write any suitable words on the board and ask students to add any new words to their lists. (Examples: lively, outgoing, thoughtful, quiet, creative, fun, humorous, athletic.)

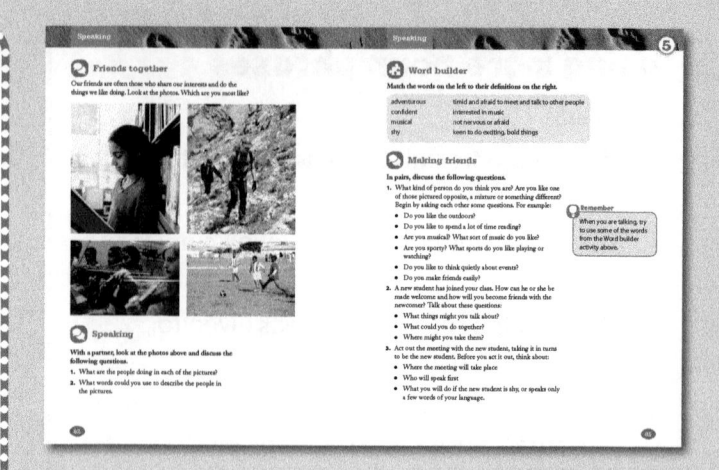

Vocabulary

Word builder

Ask students to match the words on the left with their definitions on the right.

Answers:

adventurous: keen to do exciting, bold things

confident: not nervous or afraid

musical: interested in music

shy: timid and afraid to meet and talk to other people

Speaking

Speaking

💬 Making friends

The speaking activities here give practice in specific objectives but they are designed so that one can lead on to the next.

1. In this exercise, students practise giving opinions and asking each other questions to clarify meaning. Ask the students to discuss their answers to the questions in pairs. Suggest that they take it in turns to be interviewer/interviewed, asking or answering the questions, adding questions of their own if they like. Remind them that an interviewer's job is to gain as much information from the person they are interviewing as they can, so extra questions following up an initial answer will be helpful. Direct students' attention to the Remember feature in the margin and encourage the use of the appropriate words in their conversation. For example, someone who enjoys the outdoors will talk about their adventurous life, while someone who admits to not being very confident is likely to be shy.

2. This activity is an opportunity for students to interact with their peers and practise linking comments with some flexibility. Ask students to work in pairs or in small groups. They should prepare by agreeing some basic 'facts' about the new student, such as where they are from (are they local/from a different region/from another country?). Remind them that the object of the discussion is to devise strategies for befriending the newcomer.

3. Following on from the second exercise, students now act out a meeting between themselves and the new student. Remind the students that the secret of role playing is to plan what you will be doing and saying and think about the character you are playing.

Speaking

Workbook page 39: Getting to know you

On page 39 of the Workbook, students imagine and write a conversation that might take place between themselves and a new member of the class. One way to check this is to ask students to go through the conversation with you in class. Give them warning of this, as they will need a few minutes to gather their thoughts and weaker students may need further help. You could guide them through the examples suggested (interests, likes and dislikes, and so on) and then arrange for them to work in pairs on the conversation.

Extension

Research project

The students are going to carry out a survey of the class to find out how their classmates spend their spare time. This will involve group interaction as they plan, execute and follow-up the survey. Ask them to think of some questions for the survey, working on their own. Explain that these questions will be different from those they were asking as 'interviewers'. An interviewer needs to ask leading questions, but the questions on a survey should elicit one word answers.

Allow students five minutes to prepare some questions. Next ask them in pairs to compare lists and agree a revised set. Finally, in small groups they should select the best questions for the survey. In their groups they then need to decide how they might carry out the survey – you will need to advise them what options are available – and what they are going to do with the results.

Reading corner

Prior knowledge

In this section students are going to read a letter sent from one penfriend to another. Begin by asking if any of them know what a penfriend is (a friend whose friendship you develop by writing letters to them, although you will probably never have met). Ask students if they have, or have had, such a friend – to whom they send emails perhaps. If so, where does that friend live and what kind of things did they write about? Did it help them with their written English? Ask them how modern technology has helped communications with penfriends.

Reading

📖 Letter to a friend

Before reading through the letter to a friend with the students explain that this is an informal letter, so the language is friendly and more like a spoken conversation. Ask them to be ready to spot examples of the informality, especially in the choice of vocabulary (and use of exclamation marks!). Read the letter with them and ask them independently to answer the questions and then check their answers with their neighbour.

Student Book answers

Understanding

Answers:

1. c Leon
2. b Leon and Anna are going to Myra's house.
3. b that her mother was ill and she had a new teacher

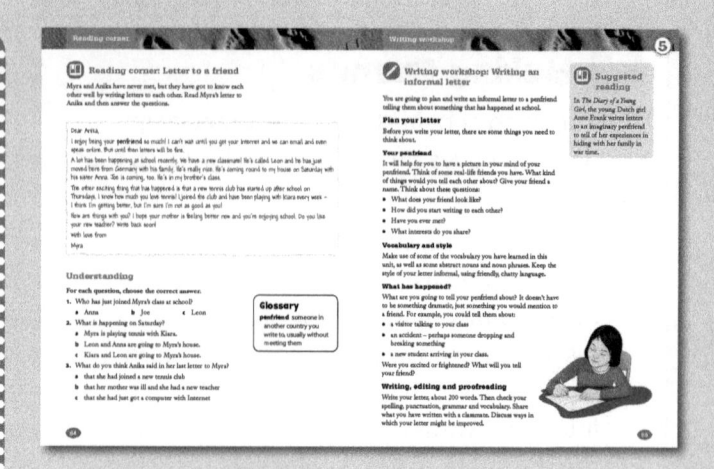

Extension

✏️ Writing a diary entry

In *Artichoke Hearts* by Sita Brahmachari, twelve-year-old Mira Levenson keeps a diary. It helps her relax and express her feelings, especially about her family. Her grandmother is unwell and everyone seems so busy … and to have secrets, as well. Mira begins to have secrets of her own. Explain this background to the students and read the extract from this book that is available on the CD. Encourage the students to listen for ways in which Mira expresses her thoughts, feelings and opinions. Ask the students to write a similar diary entry, recording not so much what happened on a particular day as who they met, how they got on together and how they felt. Explain that they should be honest and that you will not ask them to read their entry out loud, though they can share it with their neighbour if they wish. Do not ask them to read their diary entry out, but do ask them how they felt putting their thoughts into words.

Writing workshop

Writing an informal letter

Planning

Explain to the students that they are going to plan and write a letter to a penfriend telling them about something that has happened at school. Remind them that they will be concentrating on the content and form of the letter, which should be similar in style to the letter from Myra to Anika. Go through Myra's letter with them again, pointing out the way the content is structured. Draw students' attention to the way Myra begins. She says how much she enjoys writing to her penfriend but with no wasted words. Ask them to say what the other paragraphs are about (para 2 – the new classmate; para 3 – the tennis club; para 4 – questions for Anika). Ask them what they notice about how the letter begins and ends (Dear Anika … With love from, Myra). How would these differ if it were a letter to an adult – their teacher, perhaps? Do they notice any other features of informality? (Lots of exclamation marks, all the names are informal.) Before they start writing, work through the planning instructions on page 85 of the Student Book with the students. Give them five minutes to brainstorm ideas in pairs under each of the headings: Your penfriend; Vocabulary and style; What has happened?

Writing, editing and proofreading

Ask the students independently to produce the first draft of their letter on their own. Encourage them to think how they might make their letter interesting and relevant and how they can include words and ideas from the unit. Remind students to check punctuation and spelling, especially of new words they have learned in this unit. Then ask them to share their drafts with a neighbour. When they have read through each other's letters, they should discuss how the letters might be improved.

Questions they might ask themselves about the letters include:
- Is the spelling and punctuation correct?
- Is that the right word to describe x? (Is there a better one?)
- Is the content clear? (what happened? who was involved? etc.)
- Is the letter overall an interesting (lively) read?

When they have finished checking their letters, ask them to write out the final version.

Workbook page 40: Writing a letter

On page 40 of the Workbook, students write a letter to a relative (informal). Good answers will make use of the framework provided and, in continuing the letter, answer the questions their grandma asks. Refer students to the Student Book teaching on informal letter writing on page 85.

Progress assessment

Progress check

Student Book answers

Progress check

1. One mark each:
   a My best friend is someone I can <u>rely</u> on.
   b My friend <u>listens</u> to me when I talk about my problems.
   c He always sticks up for me and <u>supports</u> me. [3]
2. One mark. a to tell him he couldn't go fishing tomorrow [1]
3. One mark. a same time but on Friday [1]
4. One mark each:
   a birthday
   b washing machine
   c passer-by [3]
5. One mark each:
   - happiness
   - peace
   - honesty [3]
6. One mark. a Franco [1]
7. One mark. She was a nurse. [1]
8. One mark. a Walking is good for your health. [1]
9. Two marks each:
   a playing tennis with my friends
   b my old friend Jenny who moved to France
   c That bread that you have just baked [6]
10. Five marks. Students' own answers. Check all information is included. [5]

Total marks: 25

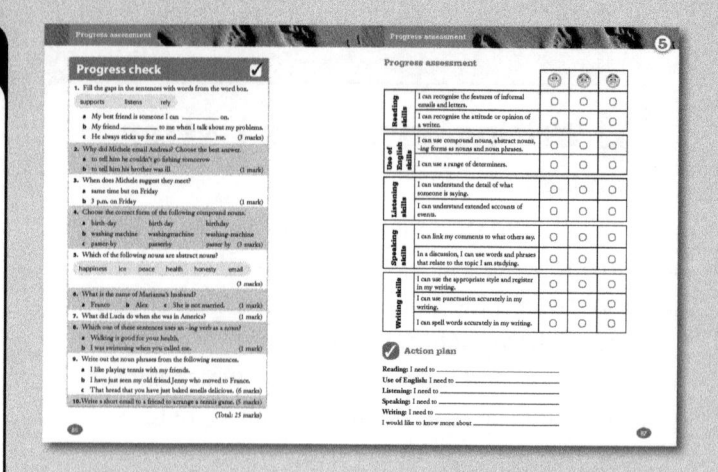

End-of-unit quiz

Workbook page 41: Friends quiz

The end-of-unit quiz on page 41 of the Workbook is a summary of the content you have covered in the unit. You can set this as homework or to complete in class. Go through the answers in class, and check that there are no gaps in students' understanding.

Answers:

1. B it is in the school holidays
2. A the same place as last time
3. Compound nouns: grandparents; New Year's Day; schooldays
   Abstract noun: schooldays; New Year's Day
4. A I love running.
5. a athlete
   b Taquara
   c first
   d represent
   e parents
   f coach
6. B Daniela
7. B With love

Progress assessment

Reflection

Reflecting on your learning

Have a discussion with the class about how they will continue to use the different skills they have covered in this unit. Students should then work independently on the progress assessment task. For each of the skills, ask them to tick the box that they think most fits how well they are doing. Now move on to the action plan questions. The aim is to encourage students to identify which skills they think they need more practice in, while reinforcing the skills they can do well. Give students the opportunity to practise the skills they have identified and revisit the action plan after a few weeks, encouraging students to compare later attempts with the first.

Listening

End-of-unit activity

This activity will allow students to reflect on the unit and to evaluate what they have found easy and interesting in the unit. Explain that you are going to read an email in which Anders explains to a friend that he can't see him till next week. Tell students that they should listen to the email and answer the questions. Read the email through twice and then ask them to answer the questions.

Hi Yusuf

I can't manage tonight – our term doesn't end till next week. I'm still trying to sort out abstract nouns and noun phrases. Could do with your help. We've been looking at friends. I now have lots more words to call you and I think I now know why you're loyal (look it up, it's one of the words we learned last week). It's the music! We are inseparable because you play the drums to my bass guitar. See you next week.

Anders

Questions:
1. Why is Anders not free to meet Yusuf?
2. What has Anders found difficult?
3. What interest do they share?
4. Anders has learned the word 'loyal'. What other word about friendship has he learned?

Answers:
1. his school term hasn't finished
2. abstract nouns and noun phrases
3. music
4. inseparable

Reflection

Teacher reflection

1. Which parts of the unit did the students enjoy the most? Why was this?
2. Was there anything that the students found difficult in this unit? How can I make sure this is easier next time?
3. Considering the learning objectives and content, what did the students successfully learn while studying this unit?
4. Considering the learning objectives and content, what did the students struggle with while studying this unit? Why was this? What could I do to help them more?
5. Which parts of the unit did I teach well? How did I achieve this?
6. Which parts of the unit did I struggle to teach well? What can I do to improve this?
7. Next time I teach this unit, is there anything I can do to improve the learning experience for my students?

6 Where we learn

Learning objectives

In this unit, students will:

- Read a limited range of extended non-fiction texts. **page 84, 94** *7Re8*
- Begin to recognise inconsistencies in argument in short texts. **page 84** *7Re10*
- Develop coherent arguments, supported when necessary by reasons, examples and evidence, for a limited range of written genres on general and curricular topics. **page 95** *7W4*
- Use appropriate layout for a range of written genres. **page 95** *7W6*
- Use a range of modal forms for a range of functions: obligation, necessity, possibility, permission, requests, suggestions, prohibition. **pages 86–87, 90** *7Uf1*
- Use a range of questions using a range of different tense and modal forms. **page 90** *7Ug2*
- Use a growing range of conjunctions including *since, as* to explain reasons and the structures *so … that, such a/… that* in giving explanations. **pages 90–91** *7Ug10*
- Understand, with little or no support, most of the detail of an argument. **pages 88–89** *7L3*
- Recognise, with little or no support, the opinion of the speaker(s) in extended talk. **pages 88–89** *7L5*
- Recognise typical features at word, sentence and text level in a limited range of spoken genres. **88–89** *7L7*
- Use formal and informal registers in talk. **pages 92–93** *7S1*
- Respond, with some flexibility, at both sentence and text level, to unexpected comments. **pages 88, 93** *7S4*

Setting the scene

Where we learn

Write the unit title on the board and explain that this unit will focus on the different places where we learn and different ways of learning. Focus students' attention on the pictures on page 88 of the Student Book and ask them to describe what each one shows. Read Einstein's quotation and ask the students what they think it means. Discuss the difference in the meaning of 'know' and 'understand' and elicit examples from their own experience of things they might know but not quite understand (examples: poems they know by heart but do not understand the meaning of, mathematical rules or formulae they can follow to get a right answer but do not understand why). Now read Franklin's quotation and explain the meaning of 'involved' in this context (affected by or included in an activity or event, actively participating). Ask the students whether they agree with the quotation and elicit reasons and examples from the students' own experience. Then read Stoker's quotation and ask the students to think of a time when they have learned something from not succeeding.

Thinking ahead

The purpose of the Thinking ahead activity on page 89 of the Student Book is to encourage students to think about the theme of the unit before they begin more specific exercises. The questions can be discussed in mixed ability groups. When the groups have discussed the questions, ask them to choose a spokesperson to present their opinions to the class.

Suggested responses:

1. We do not just learn in schools and traditional classrooms. We can learn things anywhere and from everything and everyone in the world.
2. How to behave with different people, skills, sports and talents.
3. Not always. Sometimes we learn by ourselves or by making mistakes.

Where we learn

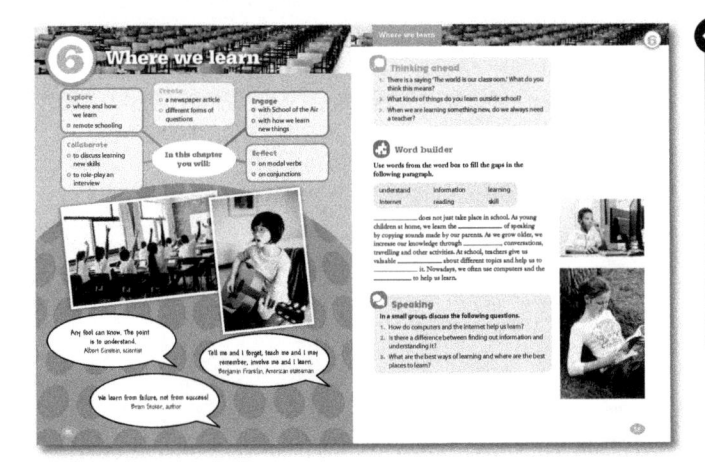

Ask what other ways there are to learn something (examples: by being told/taught by someone/by teaching oneself; by doing research; by copying someone else; by doing, practising and applying skills – for practical and technical skills). Ask the groups to discuss the questions in pairs and remind them to listen to each other's opinions and ask each other questions.

Theme opener

Workbook page 42: Where we learn

Page 42 of the Workbook focuses on the theme of the unit. This is a good opportunity to encourage students to use new vocabulary such as 'education', 'knowledge', 'subjects', 'Internet', 'library' and 'college'. In class, you could divide students into small groups to discuss their ideas on future schools. Ask the students to compare their ideas of what a future school will look like. Each group is to feed back their ideas to the class through a spokesperson.

Vocabulary

Word builder

The Word builder activity on page 89 of the Student Book introduces students to some of the new vocabulary that they will find in the unit.

Answers:

<u>Learning</u> does not just take place in school. As young children at home, we learn the <u>skill</u> of speaking by copying sounds made by our parents. As we grow older, we increase our knowledge through <u>reading</u>, conversations, travelling and other activities. At school, teachers give us valuable <u>information</u> about different topics and help us to <u>understand</u> it. Nowadays, we often use computers and the <u>Internet</u> to help us learn.

Extension

Presentation

Ask the students to work in groups of four or five to prepare and give a short presentation on the different places where we learn. Explain that each person in the group should speak for about one minute. Ask them to include an example of one thing they can learn best in each of the following places:

- a school classroom
- the Internet
- a library
- home
- outside.

Speaking

Speaking

This speaking activity provides an opportunity for students to use some of the vocabulary they have used in the Word builder activity and to collaborate with their peers in a group discussion. To prepare students for the discussion, give them some examples of things they might wish to learn (examples: when the bicycle was invented; how a bicycle works; how to ride a bicycle; the meaning of the word 'technology'; how a computer works; how to play a new computer game). Ask them which of these they would be able to find out about on the Internet and which they would not. Ask them whether they always understand what they read on the Internet and what they do if they do not understand something they have read.

83

Reading

School of the Air

Prior knowledge

Students read an informative text about School of the Air in Australia before answering some questions about the text. Read the title to the students 'School of the Air: the world's largest classroom!' and find Australia on a world map or a globe. Ask the students whether they have heard of School of the Air and what they think it is. Explain that School of the Air is a kind of distance learning that enables students in remote areas in Australia to receive an education while living at home. Explain that students who attend School of the Air learn the same subjects as other children in Australia and have teachers who they speak to every day. Elicit from the students what they think are the main differences between traditional schools and School of the Air.

Reading

School of the Air

Before reading the text with the class, read through the Glossary box on page 90 of the Student Book along with the definitions. Then read the text and discuss the meaning of any other unfamiliar words (for example, operating, technology, organises). Can the students guess the meaning of these words from the context? Ask the students what kind of writing this is (factual non-fiction). Remind them of the features of this kind of text: facts rather than opinions; technical language and subheadings that reflect the content of each paragraph. Draw students' attention to the title of the text and ask them why they think the writer describes School of the Air as 'the world's largest classroom'. Ask them to find the subheadings in the text and one fact from each paragraph.

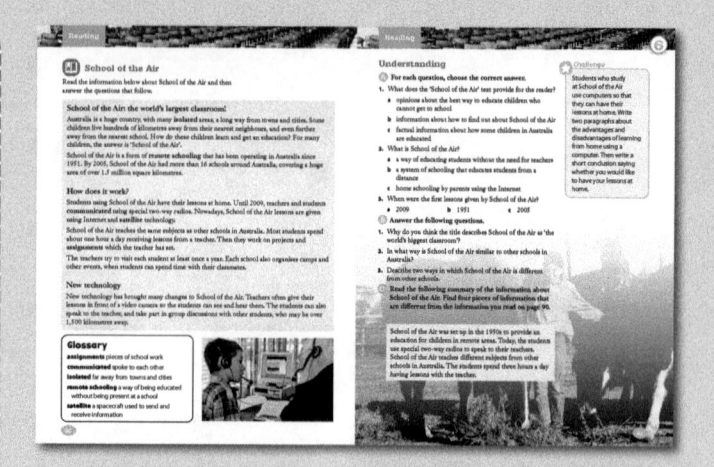

Student Book answers

Understanding

Ask the students to read the text again and then answer the questions on their own.

Answers:

A 1. c factual information about how some children in Australia are educated

2. b a system of schooling that educates students from a distance

3. b 1951

B 1. Example answer: because it covers over 1.5 million square kilometres

2. It teaches the same subjects as other schools in Australia.

3. Example answers: The students have their lessons at home via the Internet. The students spend one hour a day having lessons. The students don't see their teachers every day. The students only see their classmates at camp.

C 1. School of the Air was set up in the 1960s. (text says 1951)

2. Today, the students use special two-way radios. (text says now use Internet and satellite technology)

3. School of the Air teaches different subjects from other schools in Australia. (text says students learn the same subjects)

4. The students spend three hours a day having lessons with the teacher. (text says one hour)

Reading

⭐ Challenge

In this writing activity students will consider the advantages and disadvantages of learning from home. Before they start writing their paragraphs, ask them to make notes listing the good things and bad things about learning from home under two headings, 'Advantages' and 'Disadvantages'. Ask them to consider both lists and decide which list they think is stronger. They then write their ideas in two paragraphs, with a short conclusion stating whether they would like to have their lessons at home.

Reading

Workbook page 43: Learning from instructions

On page 43 of the Workbook, students read an instructional text and answer questions about the text type and their understanding of the text. They also practise using modal verbs to write their own instructions.

Answers:

1. B on a sunny window behind a blind
2. Natural light is sunlight – light from the sun and not from an artificial light.
3. You must not get the leaves of an orchid wet when you water it.
4. You should cut the orchid halfway down the stem.
5. We know this is writing to give information as it is a list of instructions that use commands such as 'Do not' (the imperative).
6. Accept answers that use information from the extract and which use modal forms such as 'should/can/could/must/ought [to] …'

Extension

✏️ Writing an email and a diary entry

This activity will give students the opportunity to use some of the vocabulary they have learned about School of the Air and also to practise different writing styles. Ask the students to imagine that they are students of School of the Air. Tell them to write an email to a friend who lives in another country about the school and how they are taught. Tell them to include the following information in their email:

- what School of the Air is
- how it works
- how they are taught
- where they learn
- what their day is like.

When they have finished their emails, ask them to check and edit them with the help of a partner.

As a second part of this activity, ask the class to write a diary entry about School of the Air. Ask them to include what they have studied today, as well as some other thoughts and ideas that a student of School of the Air might include in their diary entry. For example:

- if they like being a student of School of the Air
- what they studied today and whether they enjoyed their lessons
- if they like their teacher
- whether they are finding anything difficult
- whether they are looking forward to going to camp.

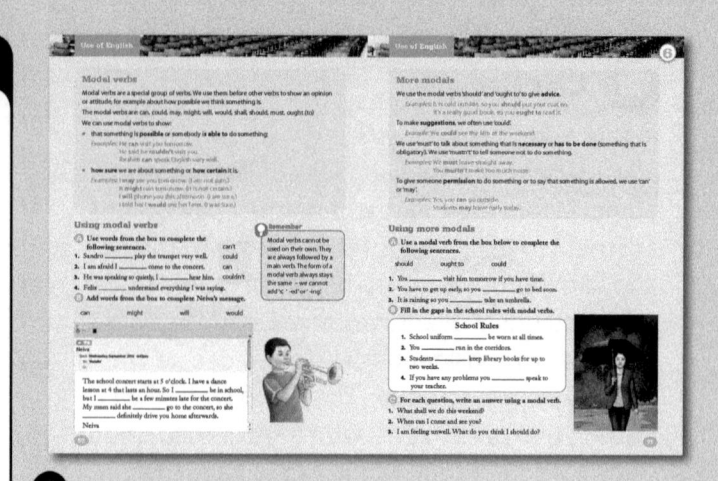

Use of English

Modal verbs

Grammar

Modal verbs

In this section students develop their knowledge of modal verbs. First, write the modal verbs on the board: can/could, may/might, will/would, shall/should, must, ought to. Explain that a modal verb adds different meaning to the main verb in a sentence. Ensure that students also know the negative forms (can't/cannot/couldn't, may not/might not, will not/won't/wouldn't, shall not/shan't/shouldn't, must not/mustn't, ought not/oughtn't). Read through the explanation of modal verbs that refer to ability, possibility, likelihood and certainty on page 92 of the Student Book. Then focus the students' attention on the Remember feature in the margin, explaining that modal verbs do not change their form. Point out that modal verbs come before the main verb. Write on the board some more examples of sentences that use modals in the senses described on page 92 and ask the students to identify the modal and the main verb in each sentence. (Examples: She can't swim/He told me he could come to my party/She said she might come to my party/He will pick you up from the airport/She might leave school early.)

B From: Neiva

To: Natalia

The school concert starts at 5 o'clock. I have a dance lesson at 4 that lasts an hour. So I <u>will</u> be in school, but I <u>might</u> be a few minutes late for the concert. My mum said she <u>would</u> go to the concert, so she <u>can</u> definitely drive you home afterwards.

Neiva

Student Book answers

Using modal verbs

Ask the students to complete the answers in pairs and then check their answers with another pair.

Answers:

A 1. Sandro <u>can</u> play the trumpet very well.
   2. I am afraid I <u>can't</u> come to the concert.
   3. He was speaking so quietly, I <u>couldn't</u> hear him
   4. Felix <u>could</u> understand everything I was saying.

Grammar

More modals

In this section students focus on modal verbs that are used to give advice and suggestions, as well as to express obligation and necessity, permission and prohibition. Read through the explanation on page 93 of the Student Book and work through the examples together. Explain that unlike other modal verbs 'ought' is used with the 'to' infinitive of the main verb (rather than the base form of the main verb). Write on the board some more examples of sentences using modal verbs in the senses described to ensure understanding before the students work through the exercises independently. (Examples: You should leave now if you want to arrive on time./You ought to clean your teeth every morning./We could play football after school if you have time./You must finish your homework before you watch television./You mustn't be late./Yes, you can borrow my phone./No, you may not have an ice cream.)

Use of English

(6)

Student Book answers

Using more modals

Ask the students to complete the answers in pairs and then check their answers with another pair.

Answers:

A 1. You <u>could</u> visit him tomorrow if you have time.
   2. You have to get up early, so you <u>ought to</u> go to bed soon.
   3. It is raining so you <u>should</u> take an umbrella.

B Example answers:
   1. School uniform <u>must</u> be worn at all times.
   2. You <u>mustn't</u> run in the corridors.
   3. Students <u>can</u> keep library books for up to two weeks.
   4. If you have any problems you <u>should</u> speak to your teacher.

C Students' own answers. Accept any answers to the questions that include modal verbs used correctly.

   Example answers:
   1. We could go to the cinema on Saturday.
   2. You can/could come tomorrow.
   3. You should/ought to see a doctor.

Use of English

Workbook page 44: Modal verbs

Page 44 of the Workbook gives students practice using modal verbs. Go through their answers in class, checking their understanding and correct use of the verbs.

Answers:

1. Would you like some pizza?
2. Can I help you?
3. Could we leave now?
4. May I have a tissue please?
5. Should I reserve a table?
6. Will you go on Friday?
7. Shall I book a ticket?
8. Luisa: Karima just phoned. She said perhaps we <u>could</u> go to the park today.
   Mum: Maybe later, but you absolutely <u>must</u> tidy up all your books first.
   Luisa: I've done that. <u>Can/May</u> I go?
   Mum: In a minute. It looks like it might rain, so I think you <u>ought to</u> wear your coat.
   Luisa: I will. So <u>can/may</u> I go to the park now?
   Mum: Yes, you <u>can/may</u>. Have fun!
9.

Advice	Suggestion	Necessary	Permission
ought to	could	must	can/may

10. Students' own answers but make sure that students include a number of modal verbs.

Extension

Practising modal verbs

This task gives students more practice using modal verbs. Ask the students to write a message to a friend about their plans for the weekend using as many modal verbs as they can. They can write their own message or you can use the example below as a gap filling exercise.

Hi Katia

I <u>may</u> see you after all! I <u>might</u> be able to come to your house after school. <u>Should</u> I come at about 6? <u>Will</u> you be back? Mum says I <u>can't</u> stay for long and I <u>ought to</u> be home by 7.30. <u>Could</u> your Mum give me a lift home?

Hope so. See you later.

Zara

Listening

School of the Air

Prior knowledge

Remind students about the information they read earlier in the unit about remote schooling and explain that they are now going to listen to an interview with Christina, a student of School of the Air. Remind students of the difference between open and closed questions and explain that in an interview, an interviewer will often ask a mixture of open and closed questions. As a pre-listening activity, ask the class to think of some open and closed questions that they would like to ask Christina. Write the questions on the board as the class share them.

- What time do you start your lessons?
- How far do you live from the nearest ordinary school?
- Have you made friends?
- What are the advantages and the disadvantages of School of the Air?
- What is your day like?
- How do you communicate with other students of School of the Air?

Listening

Track 6.1: School of the Air

Play Track 6.1 once and ask the students to listen to the language that is used by the interviewer and by Christina. Is it formal or informal? (Quite formal. Christina's language is slightly less formal than that of the interviewer, as she uses phrases such as 'kind of'.) Ask the students whether the interviewer asks open or closed questions (a mixture; closed: 'How old are you and where do you live?' open: 'What's the best thing about School of the Air?') Discuss the meaning of difficult vocabulary, such as cattle, remote, disadvantages. Play the track a second time and ask the students to answer the questions. A transcript for Track 6.1 can be found on the CD.

Student Book answers

Understanding

Ask the students to listen to Track 6.1 again and answer the questions.

Answers:

A 1. c over 300 kilometres
 2. b because she lives too far away to travel to an ordinary school
 3. c a computer

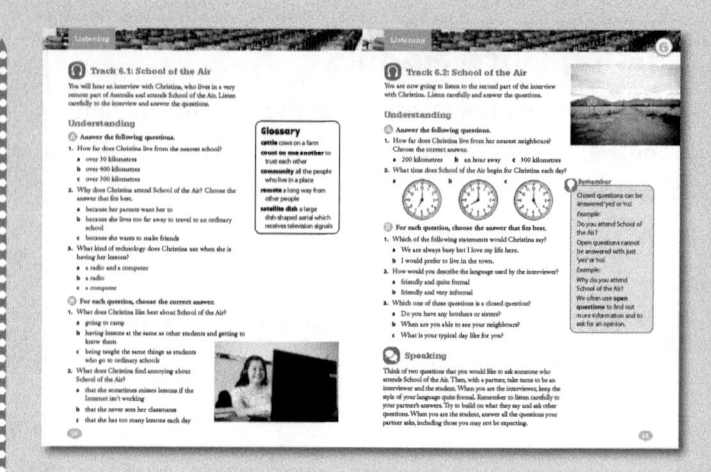

B 1. b having lessons at the same time as other students and getting to know them
 2. a that she sometimes misses lessons if the Internet isn't working

Listening

Track 6.2: School of the Air

Now listen to Track 6.2 with the students in which Christina gives more information about School of the Air and her life on the cattle station. Remind the students to listen for examples of open and closed questions and to think about Christina's opinions and feelings. Remind the students to pay particular attention to the details of Christina's day and to listen for any clues she gives about her opinions and feelings. A transcript for Track 6.2 can be found on the CD.

Student Book answers

Understanding

Ask the students to listen to Track 6.2 again and answer the questions.

Answers:

A 1. b an hour away
 2. b 8 o'clock

B 1. a We are always busy but I love my life here.
 2. a friendly and quite formal
 3. a Do you have any brothers or sisters?

Listening

Speaking

Speaking

In this activity students think of two questions they would like to ask someone who attends School of the Air before role playing an interview with a partner. Tell the students to include one closed question and one open question. Then tell the students to take turns to be the interviewer and interviewee. Remind them that they should use fairly formal language, as in the interview with Christina. The interviewer should listen carefully to the answers and build on them to ask further questions as the interview goes on. The interviewee should respond to all the questions, including those they may not be expecting.

Extension

Writing a blog

Ask the students to imagine that they are a student who attends School of the Air. Ask them to write a blog for a website that looks at different ways children are educated. Remind the students about the features of blogs that they learned about in Unit 2. Encourage them to include some or all of the following details in their blog:

- Where do they live and why are they educated at home?
- What is a typical day like for them? What time do they get up? What do they do before and after school?
- Would they recommend home schooling? What are the good things about it? What are the bad things?

Listening

Workbook page 45: Conversations with Melina

On page 45 of the Workbook, students listen to two conversations: one formal and one informal. You may choose to listen to the recordings in class, stopping at any unfamiliar or difficult words. Go through the answers in class, checking students' understanding.

Answers:

1. **C** to discuss her progress and how she has been helped to learn
2. **A** completing homework
3. **B** ballet, swimming and Greek school
4. **B** It is good because it can bring so much to your life.
5. **C** friendly but quite formal
6. **B** She says, "actually".
7. She wants to go to university.
8. Fab

Use of English

Questions and requests

Grammar

Questions and requests

In this section students develop their knowledge of how to form questions using a range of different tense and modal forms. Explain the meaning of 'auxiliary verb' and write some examples of sentences containing auxiliary verbs on the board (examples: He has finished his homework/It is raining). Ask the students to identify the auxiliary verbs in these sentences (has/is) and which forms are used (present perfect/present continuous). Now explain that to turn these sentences into questions, we move the auxiliary verb to the front of the clause, so it comes before the subject. Write the questions on the board (Has he finished his homework? Is it raining?). Remind students that modal verbs are a type of auxiliary verb and explain that when we use them in questions, they come at the beginning of the clause. Write some examples on the board (examples: Will she see her friend tomorrow? Can he play football after school?). Explain that in the present and past simple there is no auxiliary verb, so we use 'does' or 'do' in the present and 'did' in the past. Read through the language focus box on page 96 of the Student Book together and ensure that the students understand before they work through the exercises independently.

Draw the students' attention to the Remember box and the seven question words:

What? Where? Which? Who? When? Why? How? Explain that these need to be placed at the front of the question (example: Where is your school?).

Student Book answers

Using questions and requests

Answers:

A 1. Was she hungry?
   2. Do you like listening to music?
   3. May I have another glass of water?
   4. Would you like to play basketball after school?

B 2. Does he like playing tennis?
   3. Did she work hard at school?
   4. Is she eating her lunch?
   5. Can he have another apple?

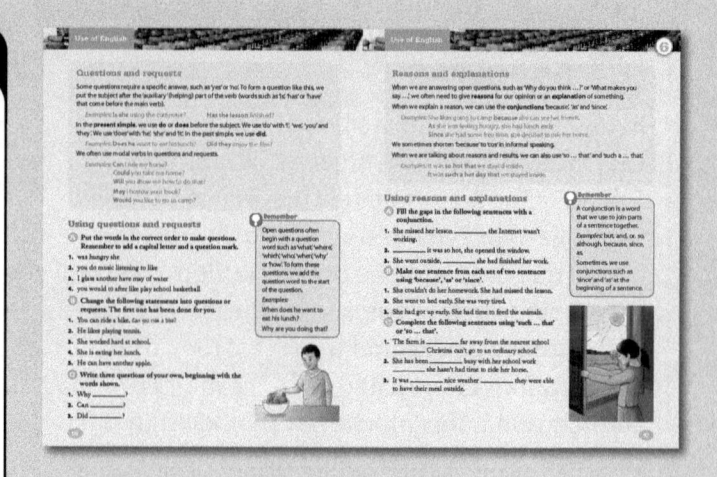

C Example answers:
   1. Why do you think that?
   2. Can you speak English?
   3. Did you hear the news today?

Grammar

Reasons and explanations

In this section students focus on ways to give reasons and explanations using conjunctions and the structures 'so … that' and 'such a … that'. Read through the Remember feature on page 97 of the Student Book, and remind students that conjunctions are used to join words, phrases or clauses together. Explain that when we want to give a reason or explanation for something, we often use the conjunctions 'because', 'since' or 'as'. Now read through the language focus box on page 97 together. Draw students' attention to the last section, which focuses on 'so … that' and 'such a … that'. Write some more examples of sentences that use these structures on the board. (Examples: I was so tired that I almost fell asleep. It was such a windy day that we had to stay inside.) Students may wonder when to use 'so' and when to use 'such a'. Explain that 'so' can be used before an adjective or adverb that is not followed by a noun (examples: so tired that/so quickly that), and 'such a' is used before an adjective and a noun (examples: such a windy day that; such a long game that).

90

Use of English

Student Book answers

Using reasons and explanations

Answers:

A 1. She missed her lesson <u>because</u> the Internet wasn't working.

2. <u>Since/As</u> it was so hot, she opened the window.

3. She went outside, <u>as/since</u> she had finished her work.

B 1. She couldn't do her homework <u>because</u> she had missed the lesson.

2. She went to bed early <u>because/as/since</u> she was very tired.

3. <u>Since/As</u> she had got up early, she had time to feed the animals.

C 1. The farm is <u>so</u> far away from the nearest school <u>that</u> Christina can't go to an ordinary school.

2. She has been <u>so</u> busy with her school work <u>that</u> she hasn't had time to ride her horse.

3. It was <u>such</u> nice weather <u>that</u> they were able to have their meal outside.

Extension

Practising reasons and explanations

Write the conjunctions 'because', 'since' and 'as', and the structures 'so … that' and 'such a … that' on the board. Ask students to work in pairs and write five sentences about School of the Air using each of the conjunctions and structures to give explanations or reasons.

Example sentences:

The students attend School of the Air <u>because</u> they live too far away from ordinary schools.

<u>Since</u> there are camps and other events, the students can spend time with each other.

It is easier for students to use School of the Air now, <u>as</u> they have computers and the Internet.

Some homes in Australia are <u>so</u> remote <u>that</u> they may be hundreds of kilometres from the nearest town.

Christina lives in <u>such a</u> remote place <u>that</u> her nearest neighbours are over an hour away.

Use of English

Workbook page 46: Conjunctions

Page 46 of the Workbook gives students practice using conjunctions. Students complete the work alone in class or at home. Go through the answers in class to check their understanding.

Answers:

1. Antoinette had no reason to drive to school <u>because</u> the school was near enough to walk to.

2. <u>Since</u> he hardly used it, Mr Hussain decided to sell the car.

3. We took <u>so</u> many books <u>that</u> we found all the answers.

4. That was <u>such a</u> great holiday <u>that</u> I can't believe it's over.

5. Bori loved tennis and so she played <u>until</u> it got dark.

6. I worked <u>so</u> hard all day <u>that</u> I fell asleep immediately.

7. Example answers:

On Monday, I learned my spellings quickly <u>because</u> I had ballet class in the afternoon.

<u>Since</u> I am going to Nisha's birthday on Friday, I will finish my book chapter on Thursday.

<u>As</u> I have already done my research project, I can spend all day at the beach.

I danced <u>so</u> quickly <u>that</u> I was tired, but we did swim later.

I have <u>such a</u> long essay to write <u>that</u> I hope I won't be late for the party.

Speaking

Learning new skills

Prior knowledge

In this section students use the pictures on page 98 of the Student Book as stimuli for speaking tasks in which they discuss learning new skills. Begin by discussing the meaning of the word 'skill' (the ability to do something well). Discuss how we learn new skills such as tying our shoelaces, riding a bike or speaking a new language. Do we always need help to learn new skills or are there any skills we can teach ourselves? Discuss the idea that to become very good at something often takes a lot of practice. Some skills, such as how to play the piano, might take years of practice. Elicit some other examples of skills one can learn and ask the students whether they have recently learned any new skills. Did they teach themselves or did someone teach them? Are they still learning and practising? Before the students begin the speaking activity, remind them of the language they learned in Unit 2 for asking and giving opinions and reasons.

Speaking

Organise the students into small groups for this activity. First they look at each picture and discuss what kind of skill is being learned in each. Ask them to discuss whether they have learned any of these skills themselves. They then discuss how we learn new skills and whether we always need someone to help us. Finally they discuss whether they enjoy the process of learning a new skill that takes a lot of practice. Encourage the students to give reasons for their opinions and also to ask each other both open and closed questions to find out more.

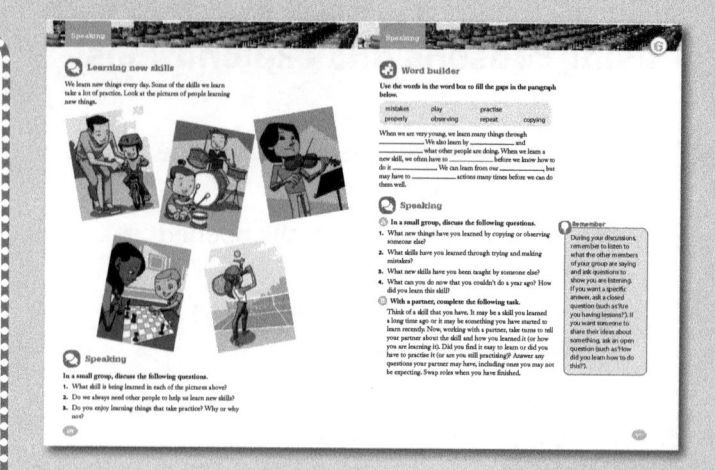

Vocabulary

Word builder

This activity will help students to learn some new vocabulary that they can use in their discussions about learning new skills. Ask students to use the words in the word box to fill the gaps in the sentences, working on their own. When they have finished, ask them to check their answers with a partner.

Answers:

When we are very young, we learn many things through play. We also learn by copying and observing what other people are doing. When we learn a new skill, we often have to practise before we know how to do it properly. We can learn from our mistakes, but may have to repeat actions many times before we can do them well.

Speaking

Speaking

A This activity is designed to encourage students to use new vocabulary related to learning. Organise the students into small groups for this activity and ask them to consider each of the four questions. Draw attention to the importance of providing full answers and including vocabulary connected to learning. Discuss the importance of working together and taking turns to listen and respond to questions. Stress the importance of experimenting with words and structures such as conjunctions (for example, 'because', 'since' and 'as') in their sentences.

B In the second part of the activity students discuss a skill they have learned with a partner, answering any questions their partner may have. Explain that their partner may make comments or ask questions they were not expecting and they will need to find ways of answering these questions and responding to the comments. Introduce the task and allow each student to have some thinking time to consider his or her new skill. Write some key questions on the board to help weaker students (examples: What is your new skill? How did you learn to do it? Did you find it easy or was it difficult? How did you practise?). Divide the class into pairs: A tells B about the new skill, B asks three questions to A after hearing about the new skills and vice versa. Stress the importance of asking both closed and open questions and ask for an example of each to be included in the three questions.

Workbook page 47: Using questions

On page 47 of the Workbook, students practise using closed and open questions. Students can complete the work at home or in class. In class, encourage students to role play the activity in pairs, reading their questions to their partner and getting answers. If you can, you may also want to arrange a call to a student of a remote school as a class activity.

Example answers:

1. What is the most interesting part of your day?
2. How do you meet other children?
3. Where do you meet them?
4. How do you spend your day?
5. What do you like learning about?
6. How do you study?
7. What do you find most difficult about being a remote student?
8. Do you like learning through the Internet? Why, or why not?
9. What are your plans for the future?
10. Would you like to go to university?

Extension

Presentation

To encourage further collaboration and practice with responding to unexpected comments, ask the class to think of as many skills they have learned as they can. Brainstorm all ideas and write in a spider diagram. Divide the class into small groups, and ask them to prepare a presentation to give to the class on a new skill they have learned. Each member of the group should have a role. Each group should leave time at the end of the presentation for questions from the class. Ask each student to write one question as they are listening to each presentation and use this as an opportunity to encourage the more hesitant speakers to ask a question.

Reading corner

Reading corner

Prior knowledge

Students read a newspaper article about a study that suggests that healthy breakfasts can improve performance in school tests before answering some questions about the article. They then write a short newspaper article of their own, using the article they have read as a model. Before they read the article, ask the students whether they ever read newspaper articles themselves, either in print or online. What kind of things would they expect to read in a newspaper article? Are newspaper articles fact or fiction? (They should be factual.) Is their purpose to inform or persuade? (The purpose of news articles should be to inform; some other articles may present the opinion of the writer and may be designed to persuade the reader.)

Reading

📖 Healthy breakfasts

Before reading the newspaper article on page 100 of the Student Book together, read through the Glossary words and their definitions. Then read through the article and discuss the meaning of any other difficult vocabulary. When you have finished reading, discuss the purpose of the article (to inform readers about a study that suggests a link between healthy breakfasts and better performance at school). Ask the students to identify: the headline (A healthy breakfast: the secret to success at school?); the bullet points (Eating breakfast can help you learn; Students who eat a healthy breakfast do better in tests); the introduction (paragraph one); answers to questions beginning 'who' (scientists/5,000 students), 'when' (2015), 'why' (to find out if students who eat healthy breakfasts do better at school), 'where' (at over 100 schools) and 'how' (scientists looked at what students ate for breakfast and their scores in tests); a reference to what someone has said (Hannah Littlecott said "strongest evidence …"); and the conclusion (final paragraph).

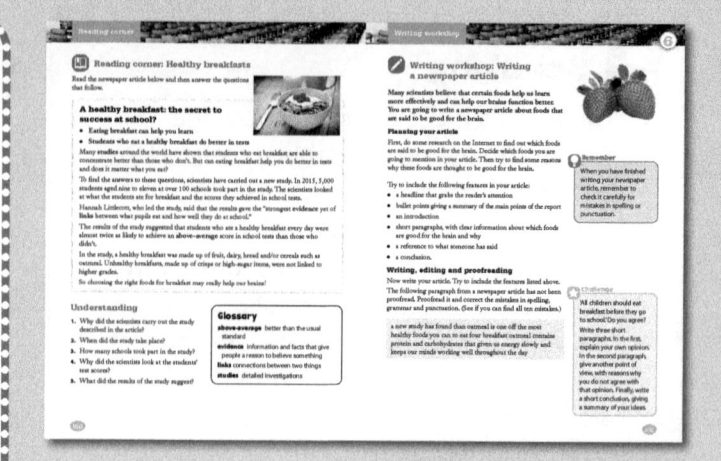

Student Book answers

Understanding

Ask students to answer the questions on their own.

Answers:

1. to find out if breakfast really does help students to perform better in tests
2. 2015
3. 100 schools
4. Example answer: To see if students who had eaten a healthy breakfast did better than those who hadn't.
5. Example answer: Students who ate a healthy breakfast were almost twice as likely to achieve an above average score in school tests than those who didn't.

94

Writing workshop

✏️ Writing a newspaper article

Tell the students that they are going to plan and write a newspaper article about healthy foods.

Planning

Divide the class into small groups and ask each group to research different kinds of healthy foods. You may want to make some suggestions of foods they can research, such as whole grains, oily fish, berries such as blueberries and blackcurrants, nuts, avocados, etc. Ask them to find out why the foods are healthy and whether any studies have been done that link them to health and performance in school.

When the students have finished their research, ask them to decide which foods they are going to write about in their article. Then read the list on page 101 of the Student Book together, reminding them of the features they should include. Students can then write their reports independently, using the suggested structure on page 101.

Writing, editing and proofreading

When they have finished their reports encourage students to check them carefully for mistakes in spelling, punctuation and grammar. Ask the students to work with a partner to find the ten mistakes and then rewrite the paragraph correctly.

Answers:

<u>A</u> new study has found <u>that</u> oatmeal is one <u>of</u> the most healthy foods you can <u>have</u> to eat <u>for</u> breakfast<u>.</u> <u>O</u>atmeal contains protein and carbohydrates that <u>give</u> us energy slowly and <u>keep</u> our minds working well throughout the day<u>.</u>

Workbook page 48: Writing a newspaper article

On page 48 of the Workbook, students plan and write a newspaper article on their own, in class or as homework. Take in their work, and check that they have followed the prompts (headline, summary, paragraphs explaining the '5ws', opinion and conclusion).

⭐ Challenge

In this writing activity students will begin to develop coherent arguments in their writing by considering another point of view other than their own, and by giving reasons for their own opinions. Ask the students to write three paragraphs in response to the question 'All children should eat breakfast before they go to school. Do you agree?' In the first paragraph they explain their own opinion. In the second they consider a different point of view, and give reasons why they disagree with that opinion. Finally they write a short conclusion giving a summary of their ideas. When they have finished, ask them to check that they have given clear reasons for their opinions.

💬 Presentation

Extension

This activity will encourage students to apply their learning from this unit and focus on the use of questions and answers.

Each student researches a current topic, news story or global issue online and reports back to the class. Each student will then prepare a two-minute presentation, which will then be followed with a short question and answer session.

Progress assessment

Progress check

Student Book answers

Progress check

1. One mark. **b** to provide an education for children living in remote areas of Australia [1]
2. One mark. **b** at least once a year [1]
3. One mark. **a** to help her family feed the animals on the farm [1]
4. One mark. **a** I am lucky to attend School of the Air. [1]
5. One mark each:
   a   It is very late, so you <u>should</u> go to bed.
   b   Of course you <u>can</u> borrow my phone. [2]
6. One mark for each question. [4]
7. One mark each:
   It was <u>so</u> cold outside <u>that</u> I stayed indoors.
   <u>As/since</u> Tina had a warm coat, she went for a walk. [3]
8. One mark for each correction:
   The <u>study</u> found that a <u>healthy</u> breakfast <u>can</u> make a <u>difference</u> to how well we learn. [5]
9. One mark. Accept any one of: short paragraphs, a reference to what someone has said, an introduction, a conclusion, answers to questions that begin 'what', 'where', 'why', 'when', 'who' and 'how'. [1]
10. Six marks. Three marks for a headline that grabs the attention and one mark for each bullet point. [6]

Total marks: 25

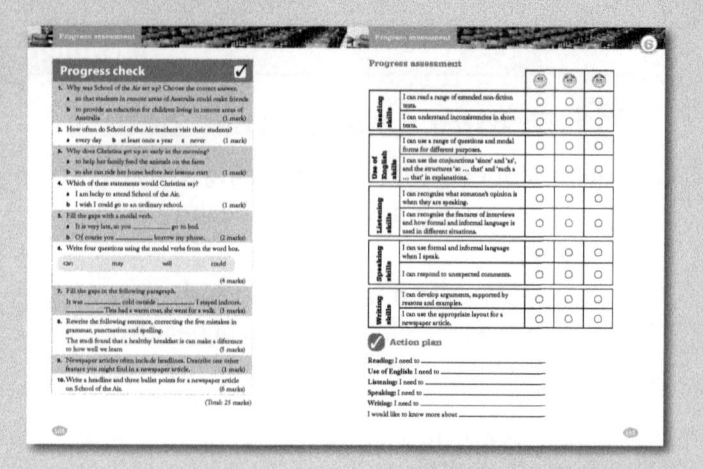

End-of-unit quiz

Workbook page 49: Where we learn quiz

The end-of-unit quiz on page 49 of the Workbook is a summary of the content you have covered in the unit. You can set this as homework or to complete in class. Go through the answers in class, and check that there are no gaps in students' understanding.

Answers:

1. **A**   It is a set of instructions.
2. **C**   It is not good for orchids to stand in water.
3. Example answers:
   A   Shall I meet you tonight?
   Should I see Miss too?
   B   May I go now?
   How might you achieve the targets?
   C   How can you improve?
   How could you find more time to finish your homework?
4. I feel lucky to have received such a great <u>education</u>. I have developed my <u>knowledge</u> on so many things and I feel like I have made really good progress in lots of <u>subjects</u>, particularly English.
5. **C**   to improve her subject knowledge
6. English
7. **B**   My aunty's cheesecake was so delicious that I asked her for the recipe.
8. **C**   a fictional story

Progress assessment

Reflection
Reflecting on your learning
Have a discussion with the class about how they will continue to use the different skills they have covered in this unit. Students should then work independently on the progress assessment task. For each of the skills, ask them to tick the box that they think most fits how well they are doing. Now move on to the action plan questions. The aim is to encourage students to identify which skills they think they need more practice in, while reinforcing the skills they can do well. Give students the opportunity to practise the skills they have identified and revisit the action plan after a few weeks, encouraging students to compare later attempts with the first.

Listening
End-of-unit activity
This activity will allow students to evaluate the unit and to reflect on their learning.

Explain to the students that they will hear a conversation between Ben and Dan about what they have learned about remote schooling. Ask the students to listen to Track TB6.1 twice and then answer the questions on the photocopiable sheet (see CD). A full transcript of the track is available on the CD.

Answers:
1. Accept any three of: can, can't, would, might, and could.
2. Accept any two of: since, because, as.
3. Ben thinks School of the Air is a great idea and he would love it.
4. Dan is not sure he would like to go to School of the Air, but he would like to talk to someone who is educated at home about their experience.
5. Ben would enjoy it more. He says he might never come back if he visited. Dan says he would miss everyone at home.

Reflection
Teacher reflection
1. Which parts of the unit did the students enjoy most? Why was this?
2. Was there anything that the students found difficult in this unit? How can I make sure this is easier next time?
3. Considering the learning objectives and content, what did the students successfully learn while studying this unit?
4. Considering the learning objectives and content, what did the students struggle with while studying this unit? Why was this? What could I do to help them more?
5. Which parts of the unit did I teach well? How did I achieve this?
6. Which parts of the unit did I struggle to teach well? What can I do to improve this?
7. Next time I teach this unit, is there anything I can do to improve the learning experience for my students?

7 Culture and customs

Learning objectives

In this unit, students will:

- Understand specific information in texts. **pages 100, 110** *7Re2*
- Understand implied meaning. **pages 100, 110** *7Re4*
- Deduce meaning from context. **pages 100, 110** *7Re6*
- Brainstorm, plan and draft written work at text level, with some support. **pages 101, 111** *7W1*
- Compose, edit and proofread written work at text level, with some support. **pages 101, 111** *7W2*
- Use, with some support, style and register appropriate to a limited range of written genres. **pages 101, 111** *7W5*
- Use a range of prepositions preceding nouns and adjectives in prepositional phrases; use prepositions *as*, *like* to indicate manner; use a growing range of dependent prepositions following adjectives. **pages 102–103** *7Uw5*
- Use *if/unless/if only* in second conditional clauses and *wish [that]* clauses [present reference]. **pages 106–107** *7Ug11*
- Understand, with little or no support, most specific information in extended talk. **pages 104–105** *7L2*
- Understand, with little or no support, most of the implied meaning in extended talk. **pages 104–105** *7L4*
- Ask questions to clarify meaning. **pages 99, 105, 108–109, 110** *7S2*
- Give an opinion, at discourse level. **pages 99, 105, 108–109, 110** *7S3*

Setting the scene

Culture and customs

Write the heading 'Culture and customs' on the board and explain that in this unit various aspects of culture and customs will be explored, including examples of customs in different parts of the world, and there will be opportunities for students to talk and write about their own culture. Ask the students to look at the photographs on page 104 of the Student Book and say what they think is happening in each. Where do they think the events might be taking place? What do they think the people might be celebrating?

Direct the students' attention to the quotations and discuss their meaning (see the Challenge panel on page 99). Ask the students to consider what might come under the general heading 'culture' (the things people do and why; customs; traditions; festivals celebrated).

Thinking ahead

Direct students' attention to the Thinking ahead questions. Begin by asking them to supply as many words and phrases about customs and culture as they can. This is probably best introduced by asking what events they celebrate, how and why. Then divide the class into groups of four or five to discuss local customs and celebrations. They may need some initial prompting here – you could tell them something from your own experience, or what you have observed of local culture. (For example, 'I always remember the Spring carnival in our home town … what about you?' or 'Last summer I enjoyed watching the dances celebrating xx, did any of you go?') Ask the students about traditional costume. Does their region have one and if so, what is it like? Ask them whether they would wear special clothes for a local or family occasion.

Culture and customs

Challenge

Students will have discussed the meaning of the quotations during the 'Setting the scene' discussions. In this writing activity they write the meaning of the quotations in their own words. Before they write their sentences, ask them to check in a dictionary to find out the meaning of words they are unsure of (example: ritual).

Example answers:

J. Martin Cohe: People from different countries all around the world can be friends even though they are different in many ways.

Miller Williams: Ceremonies and traditions that stay the same are important because they connect us with the past.

Aaron Hill: The way that people behave and think is affected by the customs of the place they live in.

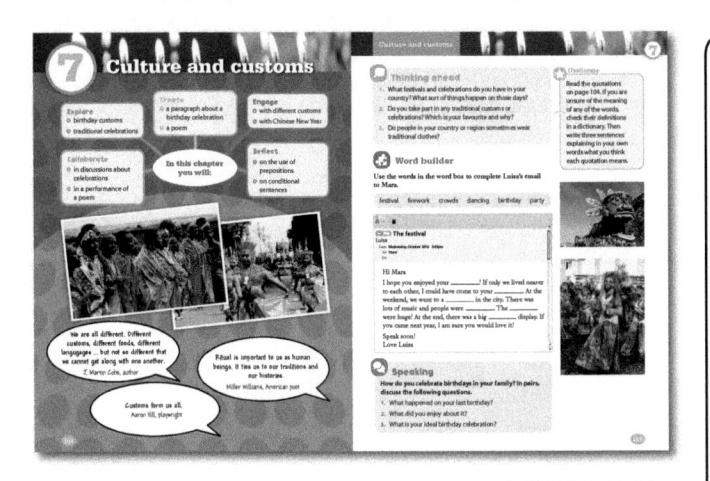

Vocabulary

Word builder

This exercise gives students practice in extending their vocabulary and prepares them for new words they may find in the unit. Ask students to fill the gaps in the email, working on their own. When they have finished, tell them to check their answers with a partner.

Answers:

Hi Mara

I hope you enjoyed your <u>birthday</u>! If only we lived nearer to each other, I could have come to your <u>party</u>. At the weekend, we went to a <u>festival</u> in the city. There was lots of music and people were <u>dancing</u>. The <u>crowds</u> were huge! At the end, there was a big <u>firework</u> display. If you came next year, I am sure you would love it!

Speak soon!

Love Luisa

Theme opener

Workbook page 50: Culture and customs

Page 50 of the Workbook focuses on the theme of the unit. Students are encouraged to practise vocabulary that they have learned to talk about festivals and customs around the world. Check students' answers for correctness, and ensure that they have followed the prompts, such as 'On my birthday, I …', 'When we celebrate, we …' and 'Other festivals in my country are …'.

Extension

Writing a postcard

Ask students to imagine that they were present at one of the celebrations shown in the pictures on pages 104 and 105 of the Student Book. Ask them to write a postcard briefly describing what happened or what they saw. First they will need to choose their picture, decide what it shows and who they will send their postcard to. Remind them to make use of the vocabulary they have been learning.

Their cards might be something like this:

We went to an amazing festival like the one on this postcard yesterday. There were lots of people there. Some people were dancing in the street and there were fireworks at the end. You would have loved it.

Lots of love Alex

Speaking

Speaking

This activity prepares students for the reading exercise that follows on page 106 of the Student Book. Begin by referring to Luisa's email and asking the students how they celebrate birthdays. Has anyone had a birthday recently? Did they have a party?

Ask the students to discuss the questions in pairs. After five minutes ask the pairs to share their answers with the class.

Reading

Birthday celebrations around the world

Prior knowledge

In this section students read about different ways in which people celebrate birthdays around the world before answering questions about the information they have read. Some of the birthday celebrations described involve special treats; in others there are unusual rituals to be observed. Before reading the text, ask the students if they know of any unusual ways in which birthdays are celebrated. (Perhaps a relative of theirs celebrates in an unusual way, or maybe they have heard of different customs elsewhere.)

Reading

📖 Birthday celebrations around the world

Read the information with the students, pausing after each entry to check that there are no major problems of understanding. Make sure that the difference between treats and rituals is understood and direct students' attention to the Glossary terms and their definitions.

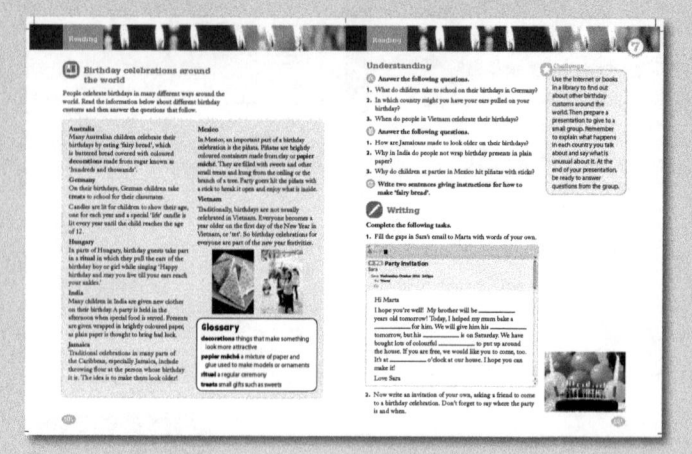

Student Book answers

Understanding

Ask students to read the text again and then answer the questions on their own.

Answers:

A 1. treats
   2. Hungary
   3. on the first day of the New Year

B 1. Flour is thrown at them./They are covered in flour.
   2. Plain paper is thought to bring bad luck/be unlucky.
   3. They hit them to break them open so they can get to the sweets inside.

C Students' own answers. Accept any answers that are consistent with the description of fairy bread in the text. For example: Butter a slice of bread. Cover with a thick layer of hundreds and thousands.

Reading

Writing

In this activity students complete an invitation email before going on to write an invitation of their own. Before they fill the gaps in the paragraph and write their own invitations, give them the opportunity to read through the text 'Birthday celebrations around the world' again, so they can draw on some of the information provided in the text. Ask them what kind of information they need to include in their invitation to a birthday celebration (what the celebration is, what will happen, where it will take place, on which day and at what time).

Answers:

1. Accept any reasonable answers but look especially for ones that draw on the vocabulary and information students have gathered from the unit.

   Example answer:

   Hi Marta

   I hope you're well! My brother will be <u>ten</u> years old tomorrow! Today, I helped my mum bake a <u>cake</u> for him. We will give him his <u>presents</u> tomorrow, but his <u>party</u> is on Saturday. We have bought lots of colourful <u>decorations</u> to put up around the house. If you are free, we would like you to come, too. It's at <u>3</u> o'clock at our house. I hope you can make it!

   Love Sara

2. Students' own emails. Accept any invitation that includes the necessary information.

Challenge

In this activity students use the Internet or a library to find out about other birthday customs around the world. They then prepare a presentation to give to a small group. Explain that there are four stages to this activity:

- search/reading about the customs
- writing down information
- preparation/presentation of the talk
- answering questions.

Tell them to find three examples that they think unusual. (There are more in the Workbook.)

Their presentation should include a brief description of each custom and what they thought was unusual about it.

Workbook page 51: Birthday customs around the world

On page 51 of the Workbook, students read about how different cultures celebrate birthdays. They then answer comprehension questions and share their opinion regarding these customs.

Answers:

1. **B** butter or grease
2. **C** at the front of the house
3. **A** with a paper hat
4. Canada
5. Accept any answer that gives a custom and explains why the student finds that custom unusual.

Party planning (Extension)

This task provides students with an opportunity to collaborate with their peers and explore birthday celebrations in a different culture from their own in a slightly different way. Ask the students to plan a birthday party following the customs of one of the countries described in the text on page 106 of the Student Book. Arrange the students in small groups of five or six and ask them to select one of the birthday customs described. In their groups they should agree exactly what the celebration will involve (for example, where it will be held, what will happen, who will be invited, whether games will be played, whether special food will be prepared, whether decorations will be needed, and so on). There is scope here for the students to do some research to see if there are additional things that can be included. When they have made their plans, ask the students to act out the celebration as a role play. This can then be performed to the whole class.

Use of English

Prepositions

Grammar

Prepositions

In this section students build on their knowledge of prepositions and prepositional phrases.

Begin by reminding them that prepositions are words that are used before other words (nouns, pronouns and noun phrases) to show location (over, under, before, behind), time (before, after, at, during), direction (to, from, across, near) and manner (with, without, of, against). Read through the section on prepositions and prepositional phrases in the language focus box on page 108 of the Student Book together. Explain that a prepositional phrase is made up of a preposition and the words that follow it (noun, pronoun or noun phrase). The noun, pronoun or noun phrase that follows the preposition is the object of the preposition. When a preposition is used in a sentence it always has an object. Ensure understanding by going through the examples in the Student Book and asking the students to identify the preposition and object in each case. Then ask them to complete the exercise independently.

Student Book answers

Using prepositions

Answers:

A after the birthday party

outside the new building

under the bed

over the garden fence

Explain that, while some of the prepositions and nouns can be joined up differently and make sense (for example, under the new building, outside the garden fence), only the set of answers given above makes use of all of them.

B Accept any three sentences that use prepositional phrases from A correctly.

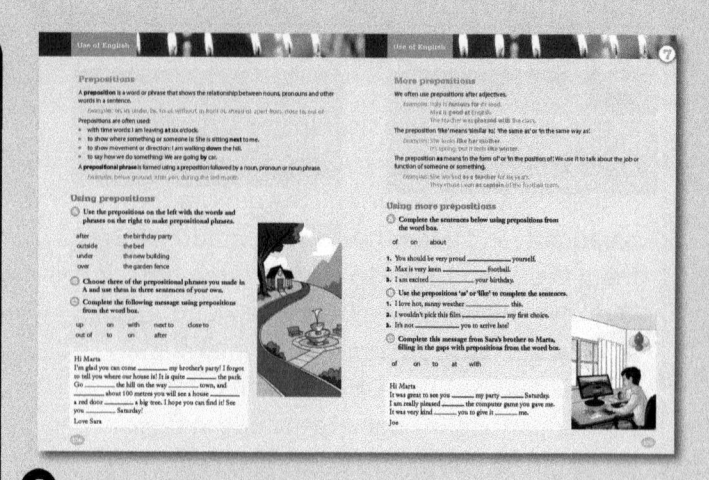

C Hi Marta

I'm glad you can come <u>to</u> my brother's party! I forgot to tell you where our house is! It is quite <u>close to</u> the park. Go <u>up</u> the hill on the way <u>out of</u> town, and <u>after</u> about 100 metres you will see a house <u>with</u> a red door <u>next to</u> a big tree. I hope you can find it! See you <u>on</u> Saturday!

Love Sara

Grammar

More prepositions

The students now consider the use of prepositions after adjectives and the use of 'as' and 'like' to indicate manner. Explain that certain adjectives are followed by particular prepositions, but there is no set rule for which prepositions should be used with which adjective: they have to be learned. Read through the examples on page 109 of the Student Book together and ask students to think of some more examples (examples: nice of you/nice to me/ angry about/angry with, and so on).

Guide the students through the uses of 'like' and 'as' as prepositions. Write the following two sentences on the board: 'He spoke like a teacher' and 'He spoke as a teacher' and point out the difference in meaning (the first: He wasn't a teacher but he spoke in a similar way to a teacher; the second: He was a teacher and he spoke in his role as a teacher). Give some more examples (examples: As your mother, I will help you. Like your mother, I will help you).

Use of English

Student Book answers

Using more prepositions

Ask students to work through the questions independently and then compare answers in pairs.

Answers:

A 1. You should be very proud <u>of</u> yourself.
   2. Max is very keen <u>on</u> football.
   3. I am excited <u>about</u> your birthday.

B 1. I love hot, sunny weather <u>like</u> this.
   2. I wouldn't pick this film <u>as</u> my first choice.
   3. It's not <u>like</u> you to arrive late!

C Hi Marta

   It was great to see you <u>at</u> my party <u>on</u> Saturday. I am really pleased <u>with</u> the computer game you gave me. It was very kind <u>of</u> you to give it <u>to</u> me.

   Joe

Example starters:

11. My brother was pleased <u>with</u> … (accept <u>about</u>)
12. They were sorry <u>about</u> … (accept <u>for</u>)
13. Jim is a good swimmer but is not keen <u>on</u> …
14. As leader he was responsible <u>for</u> …

Extension

More practice with 'like' and 'as'

This task will give students more practice with using 'like' and 'as', which are often confused. Remind students of the different meanings of the prepositions 'as' and 'like' and then ask them to fill the gaps in the following sentences with 'like' or 'as'.

1. He looked _____ his brother.
2. She got a job _____ a nurse when she left school.
3. We need some more decorations _____ these.
4. The word 'dance' can be used _____ a verb or a noun.
5. The news came _____ a nice surprise.
6. There were lots of people dancing. It was _____ a party.

Answers:

1. He looked <u>like</u> his brother.
2. She got a job <u>as</u> a nurse when she left school.
3. We need some more decorations <u>like</u> these.
4. The word 'dance' can be used <u>as</u> a verb or a noun.
5. The news came <u>as</u> a nice surprise.
6. There were lots of people dancing. It was <u>like</u> a party.

Use of English

Workbook page 52: Prepositions

Page 52 of the Workbook gives students practice in using prepositions. Students complete the work on their own in class or at home. Go through the answers in class, to check students' understanding.

Answers:

1. <u>After</u> the party he went <u>to</u> his room and wrote <u>about</u> it <u>in</u> his diary. He also sent thank you notes <u>to</u> everyone <u>apart from</u> his parents, who he had thanked <u>in</u> person.
2. Jemima bought balloons because her birthday was <u>on</u> Saturday.
3. The path ran <u>under</u> the bridge and <u>across</u> the field.
4. Omar went for a walk <u>before</u> lunch.
5. The thief left <u>without</u> taking anything when he heard the alarm.
6. Joe spent his holidays working <u>as</u> a messenger boy.
7. Let me, <u>as</u> a friend, ask you why you did that.
8. The bird looked <u>like</u> an eagle, though it was rather small.
9. Sunita did well at school <u>like</u> her brother before her.

Listening

Chinese New Year

Prior knowledge

Explain to the students that they are going to hear two recordings about Chinese New Year, or Spring Festival as it is sometimes called.

In the first one a Chinese girl talks about her family's preparations for the celebration, and in the second two people are interviewed about the New Year celebrations they are watching in Hong Kong.

As a pre-listening activity, ask students to brainstorm what they know about New Year celebrations around the world. Ask them how they celebrate New Year and whether it is an important time for their family. Ask them to write down words and phrases they would use in conversation about the celebrations. Write key vocabulary on the board.

Listening

🎧 Track 7.1: Preparations for New Year

Play Track 7.1 to the students. Explain that Mu Lan is describing events in her family at New Year. Ask them how they would describe Mu Lan's mood. Is she excited or bored? What things sound most important in what she describes? Play the track a second time and ask the students to complete the listening exercise. A transcript of Track 7.1 can be found on the CD.

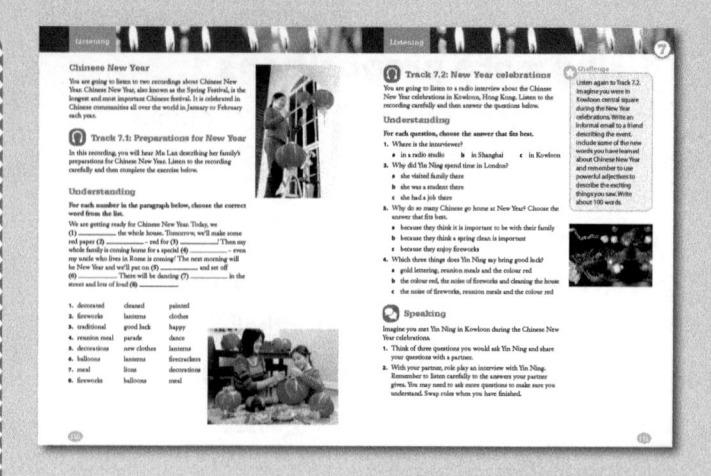

Student Book answers

Understanding

Answers:

1. cleaned
2. lanterns
3. good luck
4. reunion meal
5. new clothes
6. firecrackers
7. lions
8. fireworks

Listening

🎧 Track 7.2: New Year celebrations

In preparation for this ask students to imagine that they are taking part in a street celebration. Ask them for words and phrases describing what the atmosphere would be like. Build up a vocabulary list on the board. (Your list might include: noisy, crowded, exciting, lively, full of expectation.) Play the recording through and ask the students to describe what is happening. Now play the recording a second time and tell the students to complete the questions. Play it a third time if necessary. A transcript of Track 7.2 can be found on the CD.

Listening

Student Book answers

Understanding

Answers:
1. c in Kowloon
2. b she was a student there
3. a because they think it is important to be with their family
4. b the colour red, the noise of fireworks and cleaning the house

Speaking

💬 Speaking

Give students the opportunity to listen to the radio interview again. This time they need to be thinking of the questions they want to ask Yin Ning. This is a role play exercise for pairs, so it is important that the questions open up suitable areas for conversation. Explain that they should be looking to ask straightforward questions that can readily be answered from the information in the radio presentation. (Examples: Why is New Year such an important time for you? What do you most enjoy about New Year? What do the fireworks and the cleaning represent?) Ask the students in pairs to agree questions and practise their answers, taking turns to be interviewer. Give them time to practise before asking them to present their role play to the class.

⭐ Challenge

In this writing activity students write an informal email to a friend. They imagine they were in Kowloon central square during the New Year celebrations and write an email describing what they saw. Before they start writing, ask the students to listen to Track 7.2 again and make notes about the things the interviewer and Yin Ning could see and hear during the celebrations. Encourage the students to use the new vocabulary they have learned about Chinese New Year and other traditional celebrations. Tell them to make their description as interesting as they can using strong adjectives and phrases. Remind them that this is an informal email so they can use informal language with contractions and a friendly, chatty tone.

Listening

Workbook page 53: Chapchar Kut

On page 53 of the Workbook, students hear two recordings about a different type of celebration, Chapchar Kut, which is a spring festival that takes place in India. The first recording is an informal conversation between two friends; the second is an extract from a holiday brochure. You may choose to listen to the recordings in class, stopping at any difficult vocabulary. Go through the answers in class, to check students' understanding.

Answers:
1. smart: neat and clean
   ancient: very old
   costume: clothing for a particular occasion
   bamboos: light, straight canes made from the stems of a plant
2. C festival
3. B Sherin's
4. A feathers
5. Sherin is a <u>dancer</u> at the festival.
6. The Cheraw is a <u>complicated</u> dance.
7. Some people think the dancers <u>represent</u> the wind in the trees.
8. C India
9. A February–March
10. A dance
11. B a good view of the ceremony

Extension

✏️ Writing a newspaper article

Ask the students to imagine they are Yin Ning and they have been asked to write an article for a newspaper in Shanghai about the New Year celebrations they have seen in Kowloon central square. Tell the students to include the following features:

- a headline that will grab the reader's attention
- bullet points highlighting the main events
- an account of the events, who was there and how they felt
- their own opinion about the celebrations
- a conclusion.

Use of English

Conditional sentences

Grammar

Conditional sentences

In this section students develop their understanding of the conditional by focusing on the use of 'if' and 'unless' in second conditional sentences. Start by reminding students that we use conditional sentences when we want to show that one event depends on another in some way and to make predictions or explore possibilities. Read through the examples in the first two sections of the language focus box on page 112 of the Student Book and write some more examples on the board. Draw students' attention to the commas after the conditional clauses in the examples and explain that if the conditional clause comes first in a sentence we use a comma before the main clause. Now explain that when we are describing an action that is unlikely, can't happen or impossible, we use 'if' followed by the past simple tense with 'would' or 'could' and the base form of a verb. Write the following example on the board, underlining as shown: 'If I ruled the world, I would give everyone more holidays.'

Elicit some more examples of sentences using the second conditional with 'if' or 'unless' to ensure understanding before the students complete the exercises independently.

Student Book answers

Using conditional sentences

Ask the students to complete the exercises and then check their answers with a partner.

Answers:

A If you go to bed late, you will be tired in the morning.

If they had a car, they would drive you there.

If I had more time, I would go to the party.

Unless you finish your homework, you can't watch television.

If you lived near me, you could visit me more often.

If it wasn't so cold, I would go for a walk.

If my computer wasn't so old, it would be more reliable.

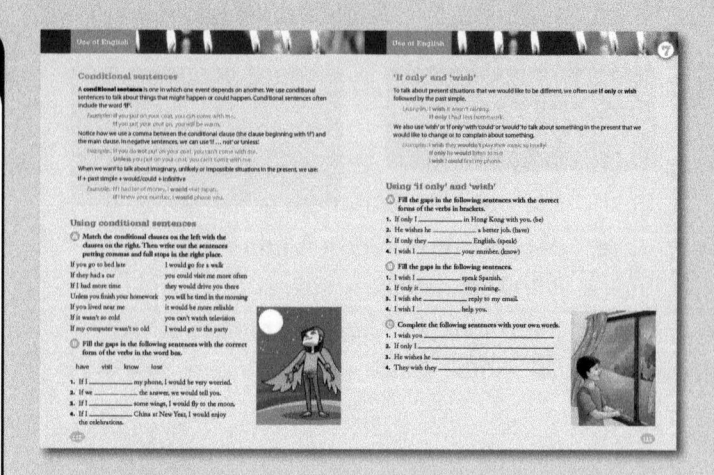

B 1. If I lost my phone, I would be very worried.
2. If we knew the answer, we would tell you.
3. If I had some wings, I would fly to the moon.
4. If I visited China at New Year, I would enjoy the celebrations.

Grammar

'If only' and 'wish'

In this section students develop their understanding of the use of 'if only' and 'wish' to talk about regrets or things we would like to change. Read through the first part of the language focus box on page 113 of the Student Book together, along with the examples. Explain that when we talk about things we would like to be different in the present we use 'if only' or 'wish' followed by a past simple tense. (Examples: I wish you lived nearer to me. If only it wasn't raining. If only I had a car.) Now read through the second part of the language focus box. Explain that we can also use 'if only' or 'wish' with 'would' or 'could' to make complaints and to talk about things we would like to change in the present. (Examples: If only it would stop raining. I wish I could play the piano. I wish you would stop shouting.) Elicit some more examples to ensure students understand before they complete the exercises independently.

106

Use of English

⑦

Student Book answers

Using 'if only' and 'wish'

Answers:

A 1. If only I <u>was</u> in Hong Kong with you.
   2. He wishes he <u>had</u> a better job.
   3. If only they <u>spoke</u> English.
   4. I wish I <u>knew</u> your number.

B 1. I wish I <u>could</u> speak Spanish.
   2. If only it <u>would</u> stop raining.
   3. I wish she <u>would</u> reply to my email.
   4. I wish I <u>could</u> help you.

C Example answers:
   1. I wish you would stop doing that.
   2. If only I had sent you an invitation.
   3. He wishes he had gone to the party.
   4. They wish they had seen the fireworks.

Explain that these sentences are often switched in the negative, with the conditional clause coming after the main.

Example: We shall not call in and see you if we don't have time.

3. Accept any accurate sentences that describe imaginary, unlikely or impossible situations in the present that use would/could + infinitive without 'to'.

   Example answers:
   a If I ruled the world, I <u>would give</u> everyone more holidays.
   b If I had a rocket, I <u>could fly</u> to the moon.

4. Accept any accurate sentences.
   Example answers:
   a I wish I could <u>play basketball</u>.
   b If only you would <u>listen to me</u>!

Use of English

Workbook page 54: Conditional sentences

Page 54 of the Workbook gives students practice in using conditional sentences. Students complete the work on their own at home or in class. Go through the answers in class to check their understanding. Make sure they also understand how to use 'I wish' and 'if only'.

Answers:

1. If we have time, <u>we will call in and see you</u>.
   If the ball crossed the line, <u>that was a goal</u>.
   If you are careful, <u>you can have one of mine</u>.

2. If Klara <u>isn't</u> good, she <u>can't</u> have an ice-cream/ <u>Unless</u> Klara is good, she <u>can't</u> have an ice-cream.

   If you <u>don't</u> finish your homework early, you <u>can't</u> see your friends later/<u>Unless</u> you finish your homework early, you <u>can't</u> see your friends later.

Extension

Practising the second conditional

In this exercise students will practise using the second conditional. Write the following sentence on the board: 'If I had enough money, I would buy a new bike.' Then write 'If I bought a new bike ...' and tell the students that they are going to write a paragraph using this pattern. Explain that each new sentence should begin with the idea from the end of the last sentence. Give them time to brainstorm in pairs to work out possible things that could happen. The paragraph might go something like this:

If I had enough money, I would buy a new bike. If I bought a new bike, I would ride my bike to school. If I rode my bike to school, I would become more fit. If I became more fit, I would be better at running. If I was better at running, I would be able to run to school!

Speaking

Traditional festivals

Prior knowledge

In this section students discuss ways in which different times of year are celebrated in countries around the world, from springtime to harvest. They then consider what these ancient traditions represent and whether they should be preserved. Begin by discussing what the students know/ have learned about Chinese New Year or Spring Festival. Then broaden the discussion to include other traditional celebrations around the world. Introduce some of the names – Holi in India, Nowruz in Iran, Hanami in Japan, Chuseok in Korea – and invite students to explore for themselves. They are going to discuss what we mean by 'the culture' of a region and how celebrations that happen every year help to keep certain traditions going from one generation to the next. In preparation for this, ask the students to look at the pictures on page 114 of the Student Book and say what they show. Discuss with them briefly the celebrations that are taking place.

Speaking

Speaking

In this speaking exercise students will move through examples of celebrations from a wide variety of cultures to thinking and discussing what they represent.

1. In small groups, students discuss each picture in turn and then match each one to the correct caption. Begin by asking them to read each caption carefully and discuss its meaning with the group. As they begin to look for matches between what is shown and the descriptions in the captions ask students to explain to each other what they see and how exactly this corresponds to the captions. Encourage them to go on to think about the origins of the traditions.

   Answers:
   a Nowruz
   b Mid-Autumn Festival
   c Hanami
   d Chuseok
   e Chapchar Kut – Cheraw/bamboo dance
   f Holi

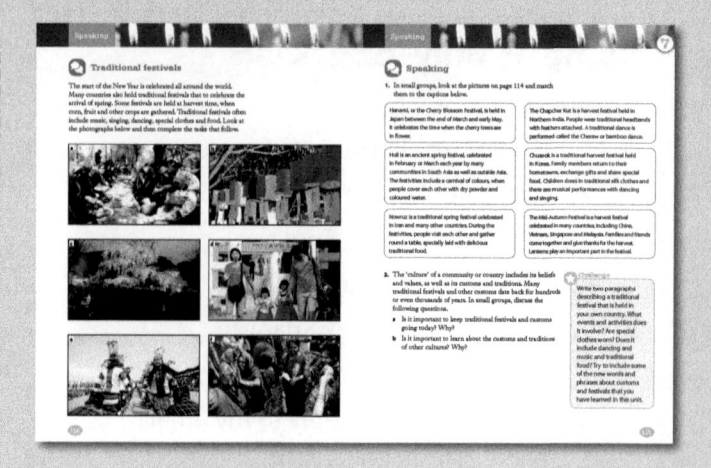

2. To prepare students for the discussion ask them:
   - What traditions they still keep.
   - Why are these festivals still celebrated?
   - How can knowing about the traditions help us to understand the people involved?

   The important thing is the discussion – encourage students to use vocabulary and material they have studied in this unit, to listen to each others opinions, ask questions and give reasons for their own opinions.

   a In discussing this question students might refer to:
      - traditions and customs they keep
      - what these mean to their families and friends
      - their importance nationally.

   b In this discussion students might refer to:
      - global society – for example, the shrinking world of the Internet
      - how it is interesting to learn about different peoples
      - the importance of history – where people have come from etc.
      - how learning about other cultures helps understanding and breaks down barriers.

108

Speaking

⭐ Challenge

In this activity students write two paragraphs describing a traditional festival that is held in their own country. Before they start writing, ask the students to find out more about the festival they have chosen to write about on the Internet or in a library. Tell them to include details such as whether special clothes are worn and what events are involved. Encourage them also to explain what they know about the festival from their own experience. Tell them to use new words and phrases about customs and festivals that they have learned in this unit.

Speaking

Workbook page 55: A conversation with Sherin

On page 55 of the Workbook, students listen again to the recordings that were introduced on page 53, and then imagine a conversation between two friends. In class, students can practise saying their questions and answers in pairs. Circulate, listening to their conversations and checking for correctness. Encourage the use of both open and closed questions.

Extension

✏️ Writing a diary entry or blog

In this activity students will write a diary entry or a blog about a visit to one of the cultural events pictured on page 114 of the Student Book. This activity can follow up the research project but is meant to provide an opportunity for them to reflect on the occasion and record their thoughts and feelings, picking up on some of the discussion points.

Ask students to imagine that they are attending one of the events depicted on page 114 of the Student Book and write a short diary entry or blog about their visit. Before they start their writing, ask them to think about:

- how did they come to be there? – invited by a friend, perhaps
- what did they see/hear?
- why was the event taking place?
- what did they learn?
- what were their thoughts/feelings/reflections? – understood friend better etc.

Example diary entry/blog:

I have just attended the most amazing event. Lal in my class invited me to a Spring Festival with her family. It was called Chapchar Kut. It was lively and noisy with lots of drums and instruments I had never heard before. The main event was a bamboo dance called the Cheraw. It was so skilful. It was a wonderful time that helped me understand more about Lal and her family.

Reading corner

Reading corner

Prior knowledge

In this section students read a poem about a festival held each year in Western Australia to celebrate nature and the history and culture of the Aboriginal people of Australia. Begin by asking the students what they know about the Aboriginal people of Australia. Explain that Aboriginal people have a rich cultural heritage, with traditions and ceremonies that date back for thousands of years. Some of these are based on the Aboriginal peoples' feelings of deep respect for nature and the land. They have also developed some unique musical instruments, such as the didgeridoo.

Reading

The Boab Festival

Before reading the poem with the students, go through the Glossary words and their definitions and check that the students understand the words clearly. Read the poem 'Tree Festival' through, stopping after each verse to discuss its meaning, along with the meaning of any other difficult vocabulary and phrases. When you have finished the first reading, read through the whole poem again and ask the students to describe the Boab tree and what the festival involves. When you are confident that students understand the poem's meaning, read the poem again, and ask them what they notice about the way in which the poem is written:

- there is no story, just a suggestion of what happened
- the description is brief – a few descriptive words and phrases
- the event is only hinted at through the choice of words: weirdest, freaks, odder, relic, Dreamtime, grim, hollow, prison cell
- the celebrations are also only hinted at and contrast with the event.

Students will find it useful to write this information down for future reference.

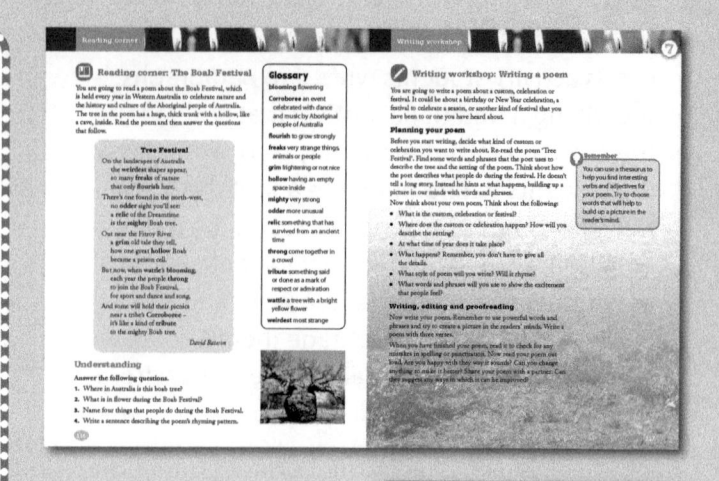

Student Book answers

Understanding

Answers:

1. near the Fitroy River/north-west Australia
2. the wattle (tree)
3. sports, dance, song, picnic
4. The second and fourth lines of each verse rhyme.

Writing workshop

Writing

✏️ Writing a poem

In this exercise the students write their own poems on the theme of a custom, celebration or festival. Begin by asking the students to read 'Tree Festival' again and refresh their memory about the points they noted about the way it is written. Explain that they should aim to include some of these features in their own poem (for example, no story, just a suggestion of what happened; descriptive words and phrases that hint at what is happening). Go through the details of the poem writing exercise on page 117 of the Student Book carefully with the students. Give them time to prepare individually and to write their first drafts. When they have finished, ask them to read their poems out loud. Are they happy with the way it sounds? Can they change anything to make it better? Ask them to share their poem with a neighbour before working on the final draft.

Writing

Workbook page 56: Writing an acrostic poem

Students complete the work alone at home or in class. Check their poems for correctness. You could collect students' poems into a book to be shared.

Extension

✏️ Writing a poem

In this activity students write a poem about a tree with a mysterious past. Before they start writing, tell them to picture a tree that they know, one near their house perhaps. Ask them to write down some words and phrases to describe it and then add some comparisons. They should try to build a word picture (examples: tall and graceful, like a dancer, swaying gently in the wind). Then ask them to think about something that might have happened to the tree in the past. Was it the scene of a crime? Did someone disappear? Does the tree have a secret to tell? Ask them to think of words and phrases that they can use to convey a sense of mystery (examples: but it has a guilty secret, only known to you and me).

Then ask them to write a poem with three verses. When they have finished their poem, they should read it to check for any mistakes in spelling or punctuation. Then they should read the poem out loud. Invite them to share their poem with a partner. Can they suggest any ways in which it can be improved?

Progress assessment

Progress check

Student Book answers

Progress check

1. One mark. b flour is thrown [1]
2. One mark. a decorations made from sugar [1]
3. One mark each. Example answers:
   a under <u>a bridge</u>
   b across <u>the table</u>
   c without <u>them</u>
   d between <u>the posts</u> [4]
4. One mark each. Example answers:
   a The road went under a bridge.
   b He passed the plate across the table.
   c We started without them.
   d He kicked the ball between the posts. [4]
5. One mark. b She did her best work as a teacher. [1]
6. One mark. c red [1]
7. Three marks. Accept any sentences that describe Chinese New Year traditions correctly. [3]
8. One mark each:
   a <u>I wish</u> I had more time.
   b <u>If only</u> you hadn't been late, you would have seen the performance.
   c <u>If only</u> he had read the instructions, he would know what to do. [3]
9. One mark. A prison cell. [1]
10. Two marks for each sentence. Students' own sentences. [6]

Total marks: 25

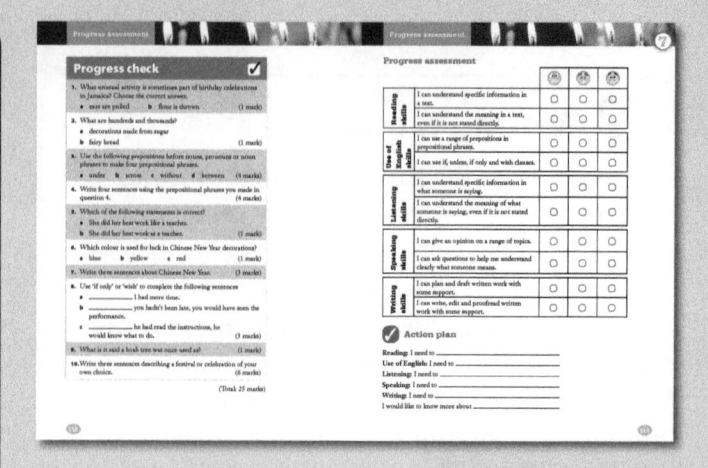

End-of-unit quiz

Workbook page 57: Culture and customs quiz

The end-of-unit quiz on page 57 of the Workbook is a summary of the content you have covered in the unit. You can set this as homework or to complete in class. Go through the answers in class, and check that there are no gaps in students' understanding.

Answers:

1. **C** around their bed
2. **A** curry and rice
3. The cake was cut <u>into</u> 12 pieces <u>by</u> Jamal. The cake had been made <u>by</u> his mother and hidden <u>under</u> the table.
4. **B** Her smile was like her mother's.
5. My friend Sherin comes from <u>India</u>. She told me about a <u>festival</u> or kut. It is held in the <u>spring</u> and celebrates new life. She will perform and will wear a colourful <u>costume</u>.
6. **C** birds
7. If only <u>I had more free time!</u>
   If you were me, <u>would you buy this coat</u>?
   If I knew her email address, <u>I would send her a message</u>.
8. Accept any appropriate acrostic.

Progress assessment

Reflection
Reflecting on your learning
Have a discussion with the class about how they will continue to use the different skills they have covered in this unit. Students should then work independently on the progress assessment task. For each of the skills, ask them to tick the box that they think most fits how well they are doing. Now move on to the action plan questions. The aim is to encourage students to identify which skills they think they need more practice in, while reinforcing the skills they can do well. Give students the opportunity to practise the skills they have identified and revisit the action plan after a few weeks, encouraging students to compare later attempts with the first.

Listening
🎧 End-of-unit activity
This activity allows students to evaluate what they have found easy and interesting in the unit. Explain that they are going to hear part of a telephone conversation between Sumaya, who is studying in Paris, and her friend Remi. Tell students that they should listen to Track TB7.1 twice and answer the questions on the photocopiable sheet (see CD).

Answers:
1. They might pull the person's ears.
2. Yes, 'like your sister' is correct.
3. They have fireworks for good luck.
4. Hanami is held in spring, when the cherry blossom is out.

Reflection
Teacher reflection
1. Which parts of the unit did the students enjoy the most? Why was this?
2. Was there anything that the students found difficult in this unit? How can I make sure this is easier next time?
3. Considering the learning objectives and content, what did the students successfully learn while studying this unit?
4. Considering the learning objectives and content, what did the students struggle with while studying this unit? Why was this? What could I do to help them more?
5. Which parts of the unit did I teach well? How did I achieve this?
6. Which parts of the unit did I struggle to teach well? What can I do to improve this?
7. Next time I teach this unit, is there anything I can do to improve the learning experience for my students?

8 Cookbook

Learning objectives

In this unit, students will:

- Recognise the attitude or opinion of the writer. **page 126** *7Re5*
- Recognise typical features at word, sentence and text level in a limited range of written genres. **pages 116–117, 126** *7Re7*
- Compose, edit and proofread written work at text level. **pages 117, 127** *7W2*
- Write, with some support, with moderate grammatical accuracy on a limited range of general and curricular topics. **page 127** *7W3*
- Develop coherent arguments, supported when necessary by reasons, examples and evidence. **page 127** *7W4*
- Use, with some support, style and register appropriate to a limited range of written genres. **page 127** *7W5*
- Use a growing range of future forms, including present continuous and present simple with future meaning. **page 123** *7Ug5*
- Use a growing range of reported speech forms for statements, questions and commands: *say*, *ask*, *tell*, including reported requests. **pages 118–119** *7Ug8*
- Use a range of relative clauses. **page 122** *7Ug11*
- Understand, with little or no support, most specific information in extended talk. **pages 120–121** *7L2*
- Understand, with little or no support, most of the detail of an argument in extended talk. **pages 120–121** *7L3*
- Understand, with little or no support, most of the implied meaning in extended talk. **pages 120–121** *7L4*
- Give an opinion, at discourse level. **page 115** *7S3*
- Interact with peers to negotiate classroom tasks. **page 115** *7S6*
- Use appropriate subject-specific vocabulary and syntax to talk about a limited range of curricular topics. **page 115** *7S7*

Setting the scene

Cookbook

Write the unit title on the board and explain that in this unit the students will be looking at cookbooks, recipes and food. First discuss the meaning of the words 'cookbook' and 'recipes' and show students a selection of cookbooks, or look at some recipes online. Ask the students to look at the photos on page 120 of the Student Book and discuss what they show. Read through the quotations and discuss their meaning (Maya Angelou: sharing food she has cooked with other people is a way for her to express herself and show people how much she cares for them; Cesar Chavez: when someone shares food with you in their home they are showing you friendship and expressing how they feel about you; Wolfgang Puck: styles of cooking depend a lot on the culture of a country and you can learn a lot about the people, place and culture from its food and style of cooking).

Thinking ahead

This activity introduces students to the theme of cookbooks generally by asking them to think about their own experience of cookbooks and their favourite foods. You could start by describing a cookbook you have used and a dish that you cooked using a recipe from the cookbook. How did the dish turn out? Was the recipe easy to follow? Why did you use the cookbook? Are there other dishes you can cook without a cookbook? Discuss the meaning of the words 'sweet' and 'savoury' and elicit some examples of sweet and savoury dishes. Now discuss each of the questions in turn with the whole class or ask the students to work in small groups.

Cookbook

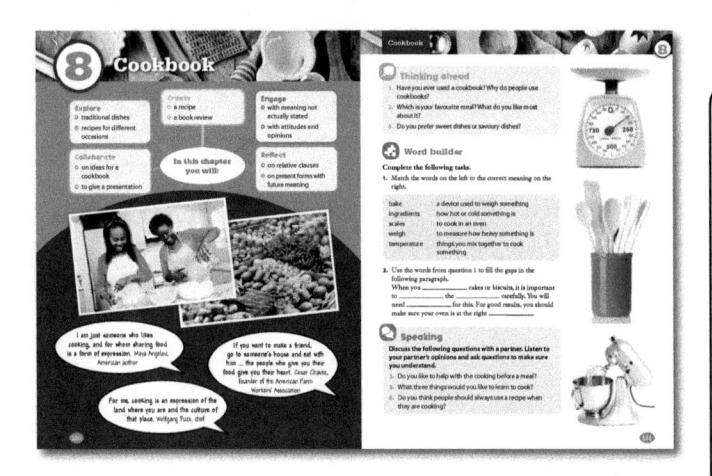

8

Vocabulary

🧩 Word builder

This exercise introduces students to some of the new vocabulary that they will find in the unit. In the first part of the activity students match the words with the correct definitions. They then use the words to fill the gaps in a paragraph, working on their own. When they have completed the activities, go through the answers with the class. Emphasise new vocabulary throughout the activities to reinforce learning.

Answers:

1. bake: to cook in an oven

   ingredients: things you mix together to cook something

   scales: a device used to weigh something

   weigh: to measure how heavy something is

   temperature: how hot or cold something is

2. When you <u>bake</u> cakes or biscuits, it is important to <u>weigh</u> the <u>ingredients</u> carefully. You will need <u>scales</u> for this. For good results, you should make sure your oven is at the right <u>temperature</u>.

Theme opener

Workbook page 58: Cookbook

Page 58 of the Workbook focuses on the theme of the unit. Students complete the work on their own at home or in class. Then, in class, discuss food alternatives for the menu. Use this as an opportunity to explain difficult vocabulary such as 'starter', 'main course' and 'dessert', and discuss particular meal choices such as meat, fish, vegetables, salad, etc.

Speaking

💬 Speaking

In this activity students work with a partner to discuss their own experience of cooking and the use of cookbooks. Encourage the students to give examples and reasons for their opinions and to ask each other questions to find out more. For example, when they are discussing question 1, they might ask their partner 'What do you like about it?' and reasons might be 'because it is satisfying to know you have helped to make food that tastes delicious' or 'because it is fun to learn how to make new dishes'. Remind them to use some of the subject-specific vocabulary they have learned already in this unit. You may wish to write some other vocabulary on the board to help in their discussions (examples: pudding, dessert, starter, main course, mealtime, treat, tasty, delicious, spicy, kitchen, utensils, equipment, pots and pans). Ask students to discuss each question in turn with a partner before sharing their ideas with the whole class.

Extension

Cook's dictionary

This activity will help students learn new vocabulary connected to the theme of cooking.

Tell the class they are going to be creating a cook's dictionary. Remind the students how a dictionary is laid out. (The words are listed in alphabetical order and beside each word there is a definition.) Ask the students to create their own dictionary based on words connected to cooking. Tell them they can draw a picture or stick a picture in beside each word (or they may wish to lay the dictionary out on a computer). Suggest some examples of words that could be included for the first few letters of the alphabet. (Examples: add – to put something into something; bake – to cook in an oven; cake – a sweet food made from a baked mixture, usually of flour, eggs, fat and sugar.)

115

Reading

Cookie recipe

Prior knowledge

In this section students will read and answer some questions about a recipe before using the recipe as a model for writing a recipe of their own. Ask the students if they have ever baked some cookies. If they have, did they use a cookbook or a recipe or did they already know how to make the cookies? Did the cookies taste nice? If they have never baked cookies, ask them whether they think a recipe would be necessary, and if so why? Ask the students what they know about the layout of a recipe. Explain that a recipe needs to be clearly laid out to help the reader know what ingredients are needed and what to do in order to achieve good results.

Reading

📖 Chocolate chip cookies

Before reading the recipe, read through the Glossary words and their definitions. Then read through the recipe together, stopping at any other difficult words and phrases. Remind students that recipes include instructional language and ask them to find some examples of command verbs or imperatives. Point out the title of the recipe ('Chocolate chip cookies') and explain that most recipes include a list of ingredients below the title. Draw students' attention to the heading 'Method' followed by the numbered steps. Explain that the use of words such as 'then' and 'next' help readers know what to do next. Discuss the piece of advice given in step 7 of the recipe. Explain that recipes often include extra bits of advice or information to help the reader achieve good results.

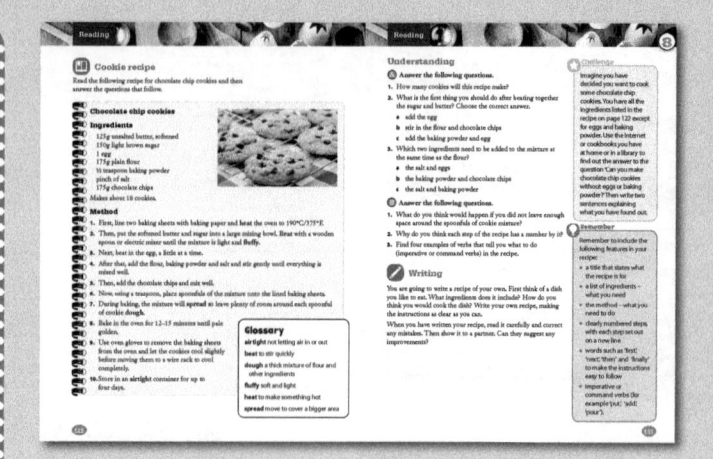

Student Book answers

Understanding

Ask the students to read the text again and then answer the questions on their own.

Answers:

A 1. 18

   2. a   add the egg

   3. c   the salt and baking powder

B 1. Accept any answer that refers to the cookies joining together as they bake and spread out.

   2. Accept any answer that refers to the numbers making the recipe easy to follow and helping the reader know what to do next.

   3. Accept any four of: line, heat, put, beat, sift, stir, add, mix, place, leave, bake, use, let, store.

116

Reading

Writing

Writing

In this activity students write a recipe of their own. They will first need to think about the dish they will write a recipe for. Explain that this does not need to be a recipe for a complicated dish: it could be a simple recipe for a sandwich filling. Before they decide what recipe to write, they may wish to look on the Internet or in cookbooks for inspiration or ask family members how to cook their favourite dish. Explain that they will need to make their recipe as clear as possible and include a title, a list of ingredients and a method with numbered steps as in the cookie recipe they have read. Draw their attention to the Remember feature in the margin on page 123 of the Student Book and ask them to try to include these features in their recipe. When they have finished writing, ask them to check their recipes carefully and correct any mistakes. Then ask them to share their recipe with a partner who should say whether anything can be improved in the recipe.

Challenge

In this activity students use the Internet or cookbooks to research whether it is possible to make chocolate chip cookies without eggs or baking powder. Ask them to see if they can find any recipes that do not include these ingredients (there are many recipes available). The students then write two sentences explaining what they have found out.

Example answer:

Yes, it is possible to make chocolate chip cookies without baking powder and eggs. Self-raising flour can be used instead of baking powder and there are many recipes for chocolate chip cookies that do not include eggs.

Reading

Workbook page 59: Grandma's cream dessert

On page 59 of the Workbook, students read the ingredients for a recipe, and then complete the instructions. Comprehension questions test their understanding of the text.

Answers:

1. <u>First</u>, add the egg and milk to a saucepan.
2. <u>Then</u>, stir the cornflour and sugar into the mixture.
3. <u>Remember</u> to add the chocolate powder or vanilla flavouring to add a flavour.
4. <u>Next</u>, stir the mixture in the saucepan on a low heat.
5. <u>After that</u>, slowly simmer until it begins to boil.
6. <u>Then</u>, pour into a tray or dish.
7. <u>Finally</u>, allow the mixture to set.
8. <u>Now</u>, decorate the dessert as you wish, with chocolate or fruit.
9. <u>Enjoy</u> this with your friends!
10. B pudding
11. 4 tablespoons
12. simmer

Extension

Role play

This activity encourages students to experiment with new vocabulary and practise using it in everyday situations. Ask the class to imagine that they and a friend are going to have a party. Tell them to role play a conversation in which they decide what kind of food they will have at the party, what dishes they will cook and what recipes they will need. Remind the class they will have to think of a variety of dishes. Remind them to use the vocabulary they have learned and to ask each other questions and give reasons for their opinions during the role play. You could write the following sentences as a starter for their role play on the board.

A: What recipes shall we make for the party?

B: I think we should include chocolate chip cookies. Do you agree?

Use of English

Reported speech

Grammar

Reported speech

In this section students develop their knowledge of reported speech forms. First they focus on reported speech for statements and look at how tenses sometimes change when we change direct speech to reported speech. Read through the language focus box on page 124 of the Student Book together. Explain that when we turn direct speech into reported speech, we do not always need to change the tense. For example, we do not need to change the tense if the situation is still true or we are talking about something that is generally true (examples: Mara said, "I love chocolate chip cookies."/ Mara said she loves chocolate chip cookies. The chef said, "Cookie dough often spreads out a lot in the oven."/The chef said cookie dough often spreads out a lot in the oven). However, sometimes a change of tense is necessary. For example, as described in the Student Book, the present simple sometimes changes to the past simple and the present continuous to the past continuous. The past simple usually does not need to change, but we sometimes change it to the past perfect. Draw students' attention to the examples that use 'that' to introduce the reported words. Explain that the use of 'that' is optional and when we use 'that' the meaning is the same as when we do not. Draw attention to the Remember feature in the margin, reminding students how to form the past perfect with 'had' and a past participle.

Student Book answers

Using reported speech

Ask the students to complete the answers in pairs and then check their answers with another pair.

Answers:

A 2. Mara said/told me (that) she needed some more flour.

   3. The chef said/told us (that) it was important to add the eggs gradually./The chef said (that) it is important to add the eggs gradually.

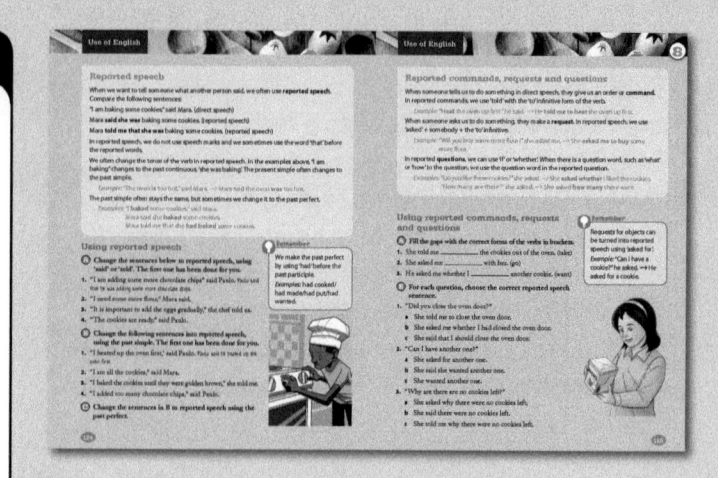

   4. Paulo said/told me (that) the cookies were ready.

B 2. Mara said/told me (that) she ate all the cookies.

   3. She said/told me (that) she baked all the cookies until they were golden brown.

   4. Paulo said/told me (that) he added too many chocolate chips.

C 2. Mara said/told me (that) she had eaten all the cookies.

   3. She said/told me (that) she had baked the cookies until they were golden brown.

   4. Paulo said/told me (that) he had added too many chocolate chips.

Grammar

Reported commands, requests and questions

In this section students develop their knowledge of reported speech forms further by focusing on reported commands, requests and questions. Ask students to read the language focus box on page 125 of the Student Book. Remind students that in reported speech we often change the tense of the verb. Explain that we also do this in reported questions (examples: "What are you doing?"/He asked me what I was doing. "Did you eat all of your breakfast?"/She asked me if I had eaten all my breakfast). Explain that if the situation is still true, we do not need to change the tense. (Example: "Do you like bananas?"/She asked me if I like bananas.)

118

Use of English

To ensure understanding before the students move on to the exercises, write some more examples of direct commands, requests and questions on the board and ask students to turn them into reported speech. For example:

Chef: Make sure the oven is at the right temperature. (The chef told us to make sure the oven is at the right temperature.)

Alex: Please can you turn on the oven, Joe? (Alex asked Joe to turn on the oven.)

Sunita: Did you use a recipe? (Sunita asked whether we used a recipe.)

she said to pour a carton of orange juice over the fruit and finally she told Anna to serve it in a large bowl.

2. **A** The Chef <u>told</u> the waiter <u>to</u> take the pizza to the customers at table number 10.

   B Thomas <u>asked if/whether</u> he could have fish and chips.

   C Maria <u>asked</u> the waiter <u>to</u> bring her the dessert menu.

Student Book answers

Using reported commands, requests and questions

Ask the students to complete the activity independently and then check their answers with a partner.

Answers:

A 1. She told me <u>to take</u> the cookies out of the oven.
2. She asked me <u>to go</u> with her.
3. He asked me whether <u>I wanted</u> another cookie.

B 1. b She asked me whether I had closed the oven door.
2. a She asked for another one.
3. a She asked why there were no cookies left.

Use of English

Workbook page 60: Reported speech

On page 60 of the Workbook, students practise using reported speech in the form of instructions, requests, commands, and questions. Students complete the work on their own in class or at home. Go through the answers in class to check their understanding.

Answers:

1. Example answer: Gabriella told Anna to first peel the oranges and bananas, and then cut all of the fruit into small pieces. She then said to add all the fruit to a fruit bowl. After that,

Extension

Practising reported speech

Ask the students to think of four questions to ask a friend or family member about their favourite meal or dish. Then tell them to interview the friend or family member, asking the questions and recording the four answers. Then tell them to rewrite the answers as reported speech.

You could provide a model on the board. For example:

Interviewer: What is your favourite meal or dish?
Friend: My favourite dish is sushi.
Interviewer: What do you like about this dish?
Friend: I like sushi because it is so fresh and tasty.
Interviewer: How often do you eat this dish?
Friend: I eat sushi more than once a week.
Interviewer: Do you use a recipe or cookbook to make this dish?
Friend: I would need a cookbook, but my mother knows how to make sushi without a recipe or cookbook.

In reported speech this could be rewritten as:

I asked my friend what her favourite dish is. She said that her favourite dish is sushi. I asked her what she likes about it. She replied that she likes sushi because it is so fresh and tasty. I asked how often she eats this dish. She replied that she eats sushi more than once a week. I asked whether you need a recipe or cookbook to make this dish. She told me that she would need a cookbook, but her mother knows how to make sushi without a recipe or cookbook.

Listening

Class cookbook

Prior knowledge

In this activity students listen to a conversation between two students. The students, Chloe and Alexa, are discussing what kind of recipes they would like to include in a class cookbook. As a pre-listening activity, ask the students to imagine they are going to make a class cookbook.

- What recipes would they like to include?
- How would they organise the cookbook?

Introduce the idea of implied meaning and read through the language focus box on page 126 of the Student Book together. Ask students to say what the phrases below actually mean or what they tell us about the opinion of the person who uses the words:

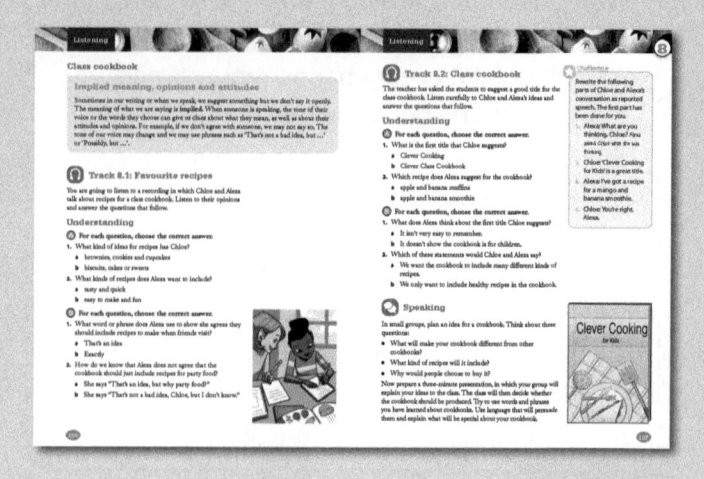

- "That's not a bad idea, Chloe, but I don't know …". (I don't agree with you/I've more to add.)
- "That is an idea." (I might agree with you/It's a possibility.)
- "Exactly." (I agree strongly.)

Listening

🎧 Track 8.1: Favourite recipes

Play the recording once and ask the students for two pieces of specific information about the recipes Chloe and Alexa decide to include in the cookbook. (Examples: recipes for all different occasions; healthy snacks.) Now play the recording again and ask students to listen for examples of implied meaning. (Examples: "That is an idea, Alexa, but …", "That's not a bad idea, Chloe. But …".) A transcript of Track 8.1 can be found on the CD.

Student Book answers

Understanding

Answers:

A 1. a brownies, cookies and cupcakes
   2. b easy to make and fun
B 1. b Exactly
   2. b She says "That's not a bad idea, Chloe, but I don't know."

Listening

🎧 Track 8.2: Class cookbook

Now listen to Track 8.2 in which Chloe and Alexa discuss a good title for the class cookbook. Tell the class to listen carefully and think about the detail and specific points of the conversation as well as the implied meaning behind what they are saying.

Student Book answers

Understanding

Ask the students to listen to Track 8.2 again and answer the questions.

Answers:

A 1. a Clever Cooking
   2. a apple and banana muffins
B 1. b It doesn't show the cookbook is for children.
   2. a We want the cookbook to include many different kinds of recipes.

120

Listening

Speaking

Speaking

In this activity students work in small groups to plan an idea for a new cookbook. Read through the questions on page 127 of the Student Book together and discuss them as a class. Then ask the students to discuss them further in their groups and prepare a three-minute presentation, in which their group will explain their ideas to the class. Remind the students to use language that will persuade the class that their cookbook should be produced. After each presentation, encourage students to ask questions and suggest ways in which the presentations could be made even better and the arguments even more convincing.

Challenge

In this activity students change part of Chloe and Alexa's conversation into reported speech.

Answers:

2. Chloe said that 'Clever Cooking for Kids' was a great title.
3. Alexa said she had a recipe for a mango and banana smoothie.
4. Chloe said that Alexa was right.

Listening

Workbook page 61: Implied meaning

On page 61 of the Workbook, students listen to a conversation which tests their understanding of implied meaning. You may choose to listen to the recording in class, stopping at any difficult vocabulary, before setting the work for students to complete alone at home or in class.

Answers:

1. A chocolate, cream and sugar
2. C It is the first time his colleague Ahmed will meet Eleni.
3. A That's not bad at all.
4. C Possibly, but have you thought about …
5. B because it is healthy
6. A I almost agree
7. 8 o'clock
8. He has heard so much about her.
9. He is Marios's work colleague, he is sporty and always eats healthily, he has never met Eleni before and is excited about meeting her.

Extension

Writing a conversation script

Ask the students to write a conversation between Chloe and Alexa during which they discuss what they would like to include on the front cover of the class cookbook. Chloe would like to include lots of pictures of different foods. Alexa would like one large picture of an apple and banana muffin. Encourage the students to include words and phrases that imply meaning, opinions and attitudes without explicitly stating them. You can write some examples on the board (examples: That's not a bad idea but …/Exactly/Possibly/Perhaps/Yes, but …/Maybe but have you thought about …).

Use of English

Relative clauses

Relative clauses
Grammar

In this section students will develop their knowledge of relative clauses. Tell the students that we use relative clauses to give more information about nouns. They make it clear which person or thing we are talking about. Explain that a relative clause is connected to the rest of a sentence with a word (a relative pronoun) such as 'who', 'that' or 'which'. Read through the first part of the language focus box on page 128 of the Student Book with the students, explaining that 'who' and 'that' are used when we are talking about people and 'that' or 'which' when we are talking about things. Then read through the last paragraph of the language focus box explaining that a relative clause beginning 'why' can be used to give a reason.

Using relative clauses
Student Book answers

Ask the students to answer the questions independently and then check their answers with a partner.

Answers:

A 1. that you need
   2. which includes ideas for healthy salads
   3. who was helping with the cooking

B 1. This is a dish <u>that/which</u> is very easy to make.
   2. I like to eat food <u>that/which</u> is healthy.
   3. What is the name of the chef <u>who/that</u> wrote the book?
   4. There are many reasons <u>why</u> people use cookbooks.

C Hi Alexa – My Grandma says she knows someone <u>who/that</u> has a good recipe for vegetable soup. It's a recipe <u>that/which</u> includes lots of healthy ingredients. Do you think it's the kind of recipe <u>that/which</u> would make people want to buy the cookbook? Chloe x

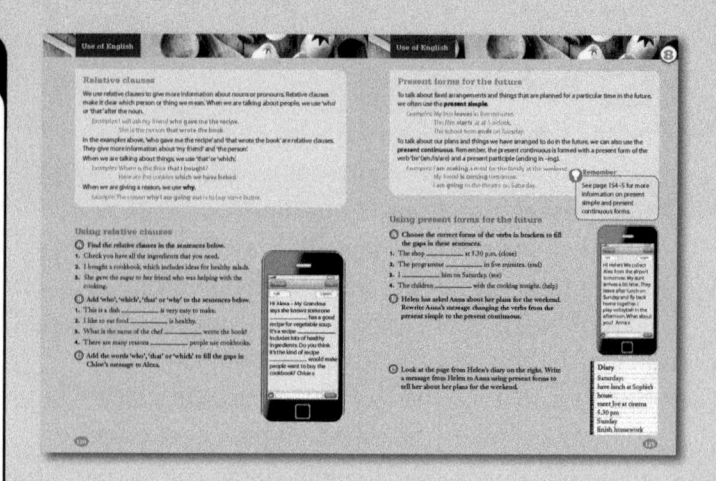

Present forms for the future

In this section students develop their knowledge of the use of present forms with future meaning. Read through the language focus box on page 129 of the Student Book with the students and remind them how to form the present simple and present continuous. Explain that the present simple is used to talk about fixed and timetabled future arrangements. The present continuous is also used to talk about future plans and arrangements, such as what we are doing tomorrow or next week. Explain that the present simple is usually used for timetables, events and programmes, while the present continuous is usually used for people. Read the examples in the Student Book and write some more examples on the board. (Examples: present simple: What time does the bus leave? The bus leaves in five minutes. What time does the concert finish? The concert finishes at 6 o'clock; present continuous: What time are you leaving? I am leaving in five minutes. Are you going to the concert tomorrow? I am going to a concert tomorrow.)

Use of English

Student Book answers

Using present forms for the future

Ask the students to complete the exercises independently and then check their answers with a partner.

Answers:

A 1. The shop <u>closes</u> at 5.30 p.m.
   2. The programme <u>ends</u> in five minutes.
   3. I <u>am seeing</u> him on Saturday.
   4. The children <u>are helping</u> with the cooking tonight.

B Hi Helen! We <u>are collecting</u> Alex from the airport tomorrow. My aunt <u>is arriving</u> a bit later. They <u>are leaving</u> after lunch on Sunday and <u>are flying</u> back home together. I <u>am playing</u> volleyball in the afternoon. What about you? Anna x

C Example answer:

   Hi Anna

   How are you? I've got a busy weekend. On Saturday, I am having lunch at Sophie's house and then I am meeting Joe at the cinema at 5.30. On Sunday, I am finishing my homework. When can we meet?

   Love Helen x

6. Tarik <u>who is your brother's</u> friend is fantastic at skateboarding.
7. Is this the street <u>which we walked along yesterday</u>?
8. I want to wear the dress <u>that I wore for my birthday last year</u>.
9. The train departs at 2 p.m.
10. The new football coach is starting next month.
11. My grandparents are arriving on the weekend.
12. The canoeing lesson starts at 4.30 p.m.

Extension

Practising present forms for the future

This task will give students some extra practice in using present forms for the future.

Ask the students to imagine that the school term ends on Friday. Tell them to write a diary page with their plans for next week and then write an email to a friend about their plans using the present simple or present continuous. Write the following diary suggestions on the board to help them, but explain that they can use their own ideas:

Monday	10 a.m. – dance class/football training
Tuesday	1 p.m. – swimming with friends
Wednesday	2 p.m. – lunch at friend's house
Thursday	Morning – shopping with Mum
Friday	Help Mum with cooking for party
Saturday	3 p.m. – birthday party!

Use of English

Workbook page 62: Relative clauses and present forms for the future

Page 62 of the Workbook gives students practice identifying relative clauses in sentences, and using present forms for the future. Students complete the work alone at home or in class. Go through the answers in class to check their understanding.

Answers:

1. I am going to the party with Amy <u>who lives near me</u>.
2. He is the person <u>that won the race</u>.
3. The boy <u>who won the prize</u> was eating a chocolate bar.
4. The girl <u>who lost the book</u> was buying another cookbook.
5. Those girls <u>who are twins</u> left ten minutes ago.

Speaking

Favourite dishes around the world

Prior knowledge

In this section students will use the photos on page 130 of the Student Book as stimuli for discussions about different national dishes around the world. They then watch a poet perform a poem about food before performing a poem of their choice. As an introduction you could perhaps ask the class what kinds of food they associate with different countries.

Some suggestions:

Italy – pizza

Spain – paella

Greece – moussaka

Japan – sushi

India – curry

Now ask students to look at each picture in turn and describe what kind of dish they think it is. Ask them whether they have ever eaten any of these dishes. If they have, did they enjoy the dish?

Vocabulary

Word builder

In this activity students learn some vocabulary that they can use in the following speaking activities. First students match the words in the left-hand column to the definitions on the right working on their own. When they have finished, ask them to check their answers with a partner.

Answers:

culture: the ideas and customs of a particular country or community

cuisine: a style of cooking, especially in a particular community or country

national: to do with a particular country

traditional: following or belonging to customs that have continued for a long time without changing

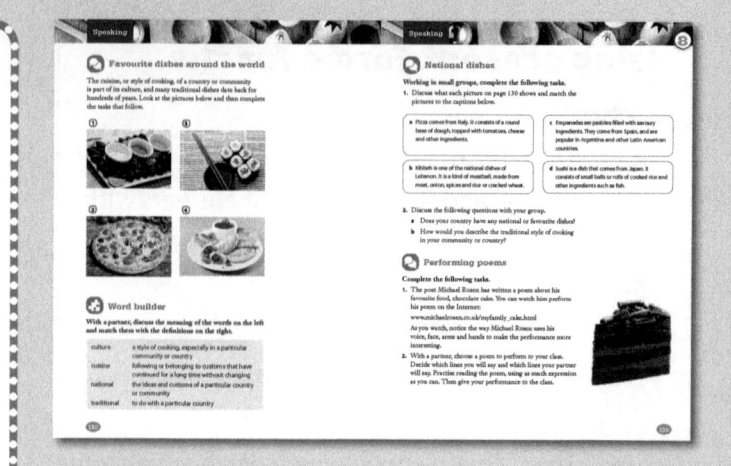

Speaking

National dishes

Ask students to work in small groups for this activity. Remind students to use words from the Word builder activity as they discuss their opinions and to ask each other questions to find out more about each other's ideas.

1. This speaking activity gives students an opportunity to use the new vocabulary they have learned and encourages them to express their opinions and ideas by making links between the photographs and captions. Remind students about the traditional celebrations and customs they learned about in Unit 7 and then move on to reading the captions on page 131 of the Student Book. In small groups, students discuss the pictures on page 130 and then match each one to the correct caption. Ask them to explain to each other what they see in the pictures and how exactly the pictures correspond to the captions.

   Answers:
   1. b kibbeh
   2. a pizza
   3. d sushi
   4. c empanadas

2. In the second part of the activity students discuss their own national dishes and cuisine. First they discuss whether their country has any national or traditional dishes and then they discuss the style of cuisine in their country more generally. Ask them to think about the kinds of occasion when traditional dishes are eaten in their country. Are they eaten on special days or for particular celebrations?

Speaking

Speaking

💬 Performing poems

1. In this activity students watch the poet Michael Rosen perform one of his poems about food. The activity encourages students to think about the way words are used to communicate ideas and thoughts and share opinions. It also models strategies they can use in their own presentations to keep the audience involved in a presentation. Ask students to think about how Michael Rosen performs the poem and write down what words he emphasises during his performance. Remind them also to watch how he uses his face and hands and body language to communicate his ideas. Encourage students to discuss how he adds interest to his poetry performance.

2. In this activity, students work with a partner and choose a poem to perform together. You may want to use this as an opportunity to differentiate and give different poems to different groups or you may choose to focus on one poem to allow for a deeper exploration.

   Students may wish to perform a poem written by Michael Rosen. He can be seen performing many of his poems on his website (www.michaelrosen.co.uk).

Speaking

Workbook page 63: Food for sale

On page 63 of the Workbook, students practise using reported speech, written and spoken. Students imagine that they are members of the Student Council at their school, which is organising a food sale at break time to raise funds for the school. Students are reporting back on the success of the first sale. Set the work for students to complete alone at home or in class. Then, in class, students can act out their work as a role play in pairs. Check for correct use of reported speech.

Extension

✏️ Writing a poem

In this activity students use Michael Rosen's poems as inspiration to write a poem of their own about food. Remind them of the poem they wrote at the end of Unit 7 about a celebration and write the following questions on the board to help them.

- What does it look like?
- What does it smell like?
- What does it taste like?
- What can you hear?
- What does it feel like?

Reading corner

Prior knowledge

In this activity students read a review of *Roald Dahl's Revolting Recipes* and then answer some questions before using the review as a model to write their own review. Start by reminding students of the meaning and function of a book review. If possible, bring in a range of book reviews or ask students to find some online. You might like to show a number of different reviews on the same book (these could be printed out, online or shown on the board). Explain that book reviews usually include certain features. For example, a cookbook review might contain:

- the title of the book and some general information, such as who wrote it
- some details about the contents of the book, such as the layout, photographs or particular recipes the reviewer has tried or wants to try
- an opinion about whether the book is good or not
- a short conclusion, summarising the reviewer's opinion and saying whether they would recommend the book.

Reading

Cookbook review: *Roald Dahl's Revolting Recipes*

Read the review with the class. Ask the class to find words and phrases that tell us the opinion of the reviewer (examples: 'recipes are easy to make and lots of fun', 'beautiful colour photographs', 'delicious food', 'recipe for every occasion', 'great to see', 'special', 'excellent', 'recommend').

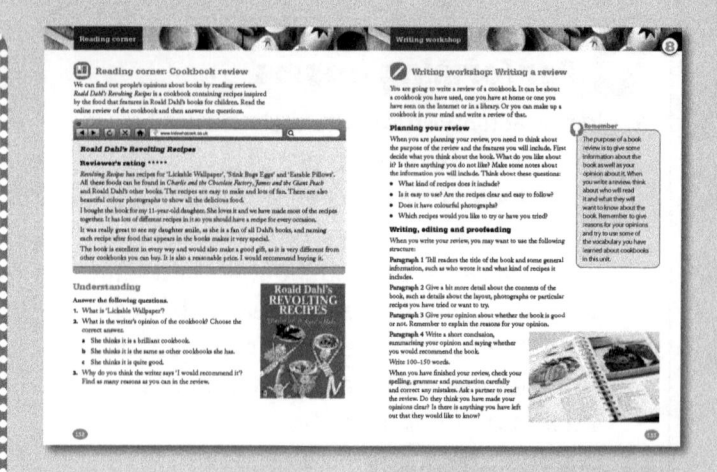

Student Book answers

Understanding

Ask students to read the review again and then answer the questions on their own before checking their answers with a partner.

Answers:

1. A recipe in the *Revolting Recipes* cookbook.
2. a She thinks it is a brilliant cookbook.
3. Example answers:

   Because she thinks the recipes are easy to follow and fun, there are beautiful colour photographs, it includes lots of different recipes for all occasions, the recipes are named after food that appears in Dahl's books, it is different from other cookbooks, it is a reasonable price.

126

Writing workshop

✏️ Writing a review
Writing

Tell the students that they are going to write their own review. Work through the step-by-step guide on page 133 of the Student Book and remind the class of the features they need to include in the review. You could ask students to work with a partner and share ideas at each point of the drafting process. When they have finished, they should check their reviews carefully for mistakes before sharing them with their partner.

Workbook page 64: Writing a review
Writing

On page 64 of the Workbook, students practise writing a review of a recipe. Set the work for students to complete alone at home or in class. In class, check their work to make sure the review format has been followed, and that students are using language to state their opinion.

⭐ Challenge

Ask the class to write another review on the same book as they reviewed in the writing task. This time tell them to write a review with the opposite opinion, for example changing the review from a positive review to a negative review. Ask the class to think about ways they can turn their reviews from positive to negative using antonyms. Write some examples of antonyms on the board: good (bad), tasty (tasteless), attractive (ugly), interesting (boring), fast (slow). Ask the class to underline positive words in their reviews and turn them into negative words. Students can read their positive and negative words in class.

✏️ Writing a book of reviews
Extension

Ask the class to produce a class book full of reviews of books or films the students have read or seen. This is a good opportunity to introduce the idea of collaborative group work. Roles can be differentiated to encourage students to work on different aspects of the book. Some examples of roles that could be given are editor, illustrator, introduction/contents/conclusion writer and marketing. Students can also be encouraged to consider genre and write a brief introduction for each book or film which is reviewed.

Progress assessment

Progress check

Student Book answers

Progress check

1. Three marks. Accept any three of: (unsalted) butter, (light brown) sugar, egg, (plain) flour, baking powder, salt. [3]
2. Two marks. a Beat in the egg, a little at a time. and
   c Bake in the oven for 12–15 minutes. [2]
3. One mark. Recipes for all occasions/many different kinds of recipes. [1]
4. One mark. a meaning that is suggested but not directly stated [1]
5. One mark each.
   a He told me (that) he had cooked the meal/He told me he cooked the meal.
   b She asked me to close the door. [2]
6. One mark each.
   a I like recipes which/that are easy to follow.
   b Have you heard of the chef who/that wrote the book? [2]
7. One mark each.
   a They are meeting you tomorrow at the airport.
   b We are playing football on Sunday. [2]
8. One mark each.
   a no
   b no [2]
9. One mark each. Example answers (accept any four): your opinion, the name of the book, the name of the author, details of the contents, examples of the contents, reasons for your opinions, the cost of the book, whether you would recommend the book [4]
10. Two marks for every sentence with an opinion and an explanation. [6]

Total marks: 25

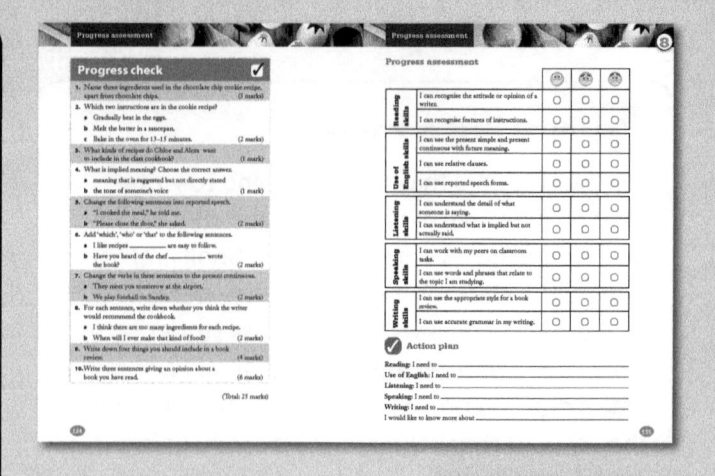

End-of-unit quiz

Workbook page 65: Cookbook quiz

The end-of-unit quiz on page 65 of the Workbook is a summary of the content you have covered in the unit. You can set this as homework or to complete in class. Go through the answers in class, and check that there are no gaps in students' understanding.

Answers:

1. ingredients: foods that are put together to make a particular dish

   recipe: a set of instructions for preparing a particular dish

   dessert: a sweet course you eat at the end of a meal

2. A Tenisha asked her dad if they could go out to eat tonight.
   B Gabriella told Anna to remember to buy some fruit juice.
3. A I met the girl who won the competition.
   B I went to the restaurant which has prize-winning desserts.
   C The school that won the education award was on the news the other day.
4. A I am playing the trumpet in a concert on Saturday.
   B The supermarket shuts at 6 p.m.
5. A "That's not bad, but it is rather bitter."
      dislike
   B "Fabulous – I'd like another slice, please."
      like
6. C That's not a bad idea, but can you …
7. B the reviewer's opinion of the book

Progress assessment

Reflection

Reflecting on your learning

Have a discussion with the class about how they will continue to use the different skills they have covered in this unit. Students should then work independently on the progress assessment task. For each of the skills, ask them to tick the box that they think most fits how well they are doing. Now move on to the action plan questions. The aim is to encourage students to identify which skills they think they need more practice in, while reinforcing the skills they can do well. Give students the opportunity to practise the skills they have identified and revisit the action plan after a few weeks, encouraging students to compare later attempts with the first.

Answers:

1. Who visited us on Tuesday.
2. I am going to see the manager on Friday.
3. She said that she really liked the recipes and she wanted to cook all of the dishes at the same time. She also said that she wanted to share the recipes with her friends.
4. 'I didn't quite understand', 'possibly' and 'that's not a bad idea but …'
5. Positive

When they have answered the questions, ask them to write down everything they have learned about interviews. You can recap on use of questions, opinions and specific points. A transcript of Track TB8.1 can be found on the CD.

Listening

End-of-unit activity

This activity will allow students to evaluate the unit and consolidate their learning.

Explain to the students that they will hear a telephone conversation between Dan and his publisher about reviews on his new cookbook.

Listen to Track TB8.1 together and then ask them to answer the questions below (see also the photocopiable sheet on the CD):

1. What relative clause is used to describe Susan B?
2. What example of present continuous is used by the publisher?
3. What examples of reported speech are used with Susan B?
4. What examples of implied meaning are there from the reviewer Eleni?
5. What does the word 'favourable' mean?

Let the students answer the questions while they are listening. Give them the answers when they have listened to the recording twice.

Reflection

Teacher reflection

1. Which parts of the unit did the students enjoy most? Why was this?
2. Was there anything that the students found difficult in this unit? How can I make sure this is easier next time?
3. Considering the learning objectives and content, what did the students successfully learn while studying this unit?
4. Considering the learning objectives and content, what did the students struggle with while studying this unit? Why was this? What could I do to help them more?
5. Which parts of the unit did I teach well? How did I achieve this?
6. Which parts of the unit did I struggle to teach well? What can I do to improve this?
7. Next time I teach this unit, is there anything I can do to improve the learning experience for my students?

9 Communication

Learning objectives

In this unit, students will:

- Understand the main points in texts on a limited range of unfamiliar general and curricular topics, including some extended texts. **pages 132–133** *7Re1*
- Understand the detail of an argument. **pages 132–133** *7Re3*
- Recognise the attitude or opinion of the writer. **pages 132–133** *7Re5*
- Begin to recognise inconsistencies in argument. **page 142** *7Re10*
- Compose, edit and proofread written work at text level, with some support, on a range of general and curricular topics. **page 143** *7W2*
- Develop coherent arguments, supported when necessary by reasons, examples and evidence. **page 143** *7W4*
- Use, with some support, style and register. **page 143** *7W5*
- Use infinitive forms after a limited range of verbs and adjectives; use gerund forms after a limited range of verbs and prepositions; use a limited range of prepositional verbs and begin to use common phrasal verbs. **pages 134–135** *7Ug9*
- Understand, with little or no support, most of the detail of an argument in extended talk. **pages 136–137** *7L3*
- Deduce, with little or no support, meaning from context in extended talk. **pages 136–137** *7L6*
- Recognise typical features at word, sentence and text level in a limited range of spoken genres. **pages 136–137** *7L7*
- Ask questions to clarify meaning. **pages 140–141** *7S2*
- Give an opinion, at discourse level. **pages 140–141** *7S3*
- Respond, with some flexibility, at both sentence and text level, to unexpected comments. **pages 140–141** *7S4*

Setting the scene

Communication

Write the title of the unit on the board and explain to the students that in this unit they will be considering various ways in which we communicate with one another – from the most basic, non-verbal to the latest state-of-the-art technology. Begin by writing some different forms of communication on the board and ask the students to add to the list. Ask them to think first of non-verbal communication (gesture, eye contact, body language, smiling, laughter).

Direct students' attention to the quotations. Ask them what they think they mean. What does Peter Drucker mean by 'hearing what isn't said'? Explain that we sometimes say something but mean something else, and remind students of the work they did on implied meaning in Unit 8. Ask them to give some examples.

Point out that two of the quotations emphasise the importance of listening. Why do students think that is? What do they think makes a good listener? Why is listening an important part of communicating?

Thinking ahead

Direct the students' attention to the Thinking ahead questions. Begin by asking students to write down as many different ways that people communicate as they can. Then ask them to compare lists with their neighbour before going on to think about the other questions. You may find this works best as discussion in small groups (5/6). Ask the students to think of examples when a lack of communication or a breakdown in communications led to problems. Remind them that in the twenty-first century we have more means of communicating than ever – refer to their lists and to the list on the board. Does that mean we are better communicators?

Communication

Theme opener

Workbook page 66: Communication

Example answers:

Allow any reasonable answer.

1. A best friend   B friend/acquaintance
   C someone in a position of authority
   D friend/family member

2. A Hi, great to see you!
   B Hello Auntie, I'm so pleased to see you again!
   C Good morning, sir.

3. A Lou – guess what? That competition you told me about. Well, you won't believe it – I won! I'll tell you all about it when we meet tomorrow.
   B Dear Ms … . I am delighted to tell you I won the writing competition you encouraged me to enter. Thank you for all your help and support.

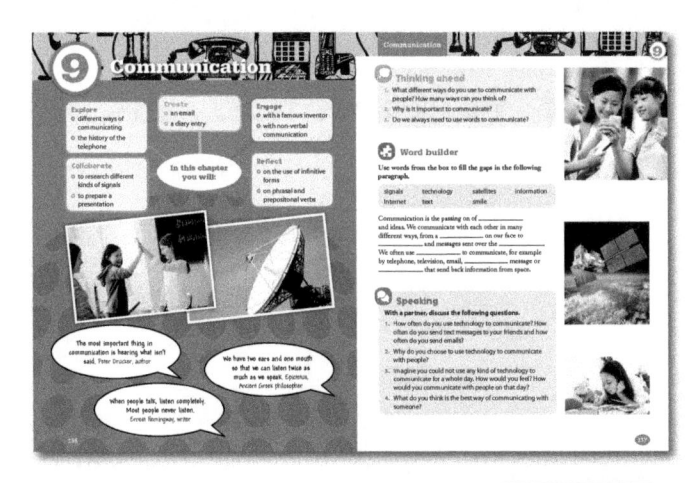

Vocabulary

Word builder

This exercise introduces students to some of the words they will find in the unit. Read through the word box with students, checking their understanding of the words, especially those they may be unfamiliar with. Ask students to fill in the gaps in the paragraph, working on their own. When they have finished, ask them to compare answers with a partner. Then ask them to read the paragraph out loud while you listen. Check their pronunciation is correct so they will be able to use the words when they speak as well as in their written work.

Answers:

Communication is the passing on of <u>information</u> and ideas. We communicate with each other in many different ways, from a <u>smile</u> on our face to <u>signals</u> and messages sent over the <u>Internet</u>. We often use <u>technology</u> to communicate, for example, by telephone, television, email, <u>text</u> message or <u>satellites</u> that send back information from space.

Finally, ask students to use these words in sentences of their own that indicate their meaning. (For example: Satellites gather information in outer space and beam it back to Earth.)

Extension

Communicating without language

Ask students to imagine that they are given the job of looking after a new student with whom they have no common language who has just joined their class. They have to communicate various messages to that student – but of course cannot use language. They need to remember, too, that the student will be trying to communicate with them as well. Ask them to work in small groups and discuss how they will do this and then put together a mime sequence of the occasion. First they will need to decide on the setting, for example, a typical school morning. Then they should plan the information they are going to use. Are they going to try to teach some words in their language? Perhaps they can think of one unexpected circumstance – the fire alarm going off, perhaps. When the groups have agreed what they are going to do and how they will present it they should act out the sequence, preferably to the class. Allow some time afterwards for discussion in groups about what they learned about communication.

Speaking

Speaking

This exercise prepares students for the Reading exercise that follows by directing attention to technology and communication. It also gives an early opportunity for students to practise using the vocabulary they have just learned. Begin by discussing the use of technology in communication. Then ask students to discuss the questions in pairs. After five minutes ask the pairs to share their answers with the class.

Reading

The first telephone call

Prior knowledge

Students will read a description of a famous breakthrough in the invention of the telephone: the precise moment when the first telephone message was successfully communicated. Ask the students what they already know about the development of the telephone and write some of the key words and phrases on the board. These might include 'telegraph', 'telephone exchange', 'landline', 'network', 'mobile' (or 'cell phone'). Ask the students to imagine the time before the invention of the telephone, to try to picture how significant a moment this invention was.

Reading

📖 The first telephone call

Read the text with the students before they start to work independently on the Understanding questions. Ask them to focus on the words in the Glossary box. Make sure that they have understood these words and any other unfamiliar words in the text (examples: laboratory, ability).

Student Book answers

Understanding

Answers:

A 1. a Mr Watson
   2. a 1876
   3. a transmit sound through a wire

B 1. a Mr Watson came into his room and said he had heard and understood what Bell had said.
   2. b loud but unclear

C Example answer:
   He felt pleased because it suggested his experiment had worked. He wrote in his diary that he was delighted.

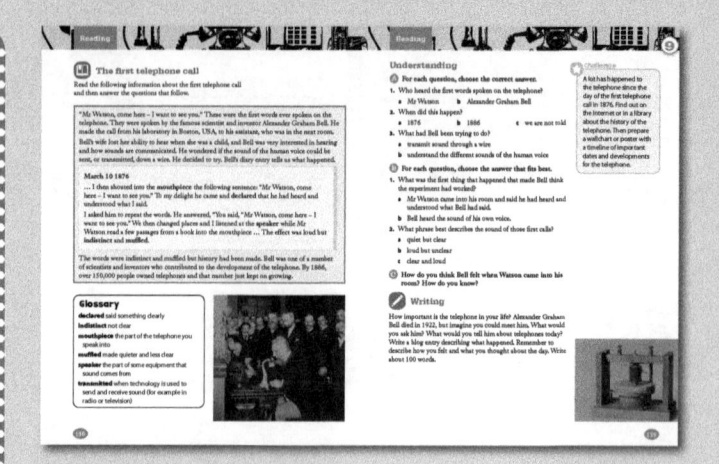

Writing

✏️ Writing

In this activity students will write a blog entry for 'the day they met Alexander Graham Bell'. They will be drawing on the information they have gathered from reading 'The first telephone call' and from their own research into the history of the telephone. Go over the earlier parts of the unit with them and guide their thinking – what questions might they ask him (how he felt about his discovery, or he thought the telephone would be used); what they would tell him about modern phones (everyone has one, uses it all the time …). Ask students to write their blog entries independently and to compare entries with their neighbour when they finish.

Example answer:

10 March 2016

I met Dr Bell today. It was amazing. I asked him about that day when he said those famous words. He told me that he was so delighted when Mr Watson came and told him what he had shouted into the mouthpiece. He asked me if I knew what a telephone was. I told him that everyone had one and showed him mine. He was very surprised. "It's very small," he said and asked where the speaker was. I showed him how to get on to the Internet, and searched for his name. He couldn't believe it when we found so much information about him.

Reading

⭐ Challenge

In this activity students find out what the key events in the history of the telephone have been from that first telephone message to today. Explain that in a library they should look in an encyclopedia or other reference books to find the necessary information. If students use the Internet for their research then BBC websites (www.bbc.co.uk) could be a good place to start. Suggest that they aim to produce an interesting timeline (with illustrations) with about five key dates and developments.

Example answer:

1876	Alexander Graham Bell makes first telephone call
1890	candlestick phone
1930	first rotary (dial) phone
1963	first push-button phone
1984	first mobile phone

Ask the students to share their findings with the class.

✏️ Writing about another invention

Extension

In this activity students will research and write a paragraph about the invention of another form of communication such as the radio, television, computers or the Internet. Ask them to decide what they want to write about and use the Internet or books in a library to find out about its history and development. Ask the students to make notes and then write a paragraph on their findings.

Reading

Workbook page 67: Alexander Graham Bell

Answers:

1. B speech therapy
2. B all telephones went silent
3. No. He thought it would distract him from his work.
4. Allow any reasonable answer.

Use of English

Infinitives and –ing forms

Grammar

Verbs and adjectives followed by infinitives

In this section students work on the use of the infinitive after some verbs and adjectives. Begin by reminding them that an infinitive is the base form of a verb, and infinitives usually begin with 'to' (examples: 'to be', 'to run').

Read through the first part of the language focus box on page 140 of the Student Book with the students, explaining that certain verbs are followed by the 'to' infinitive. These verbs include many verbs that refer to thinking, feeling, and saying. Read through the examples in the Student Book and give some examples of how these verbs can be used followed by a 'to' infinitive (examples: 'I chose to send an email'. 'I forgot to put a stamp on the letter'). Now read through the second part of the language focus box, explaining that the 'to' infinitive also follows many adjectives. Explain that these adjectives often express feelings, reactions or opinions. Read through the examples in the Student Book and give some examples of infinitives that can be used after the adjectives (examples: 'It is good to meet you', 'I am happy to hear that').

Student Book answers

Using 'to' infinitives after verbs and adjectives

Answers:

A 1. He said he was <u>pleased</u> to win the race.
   2. She was speaking very quickly, so I found it hard <u>to understand</u> what she was saying.
   3. Did you remember <u>to take</u> your book home?

B 1. She looked at the menu and <u>decided to order</u> a pizza.
   2. Please <u>remember to be</u> more careful next time.
   3. After the lesson he <u>forgot to take</u> his book home.

C Accept any two sentences that use infinitives correctly after the verbs or adjectives in the box.

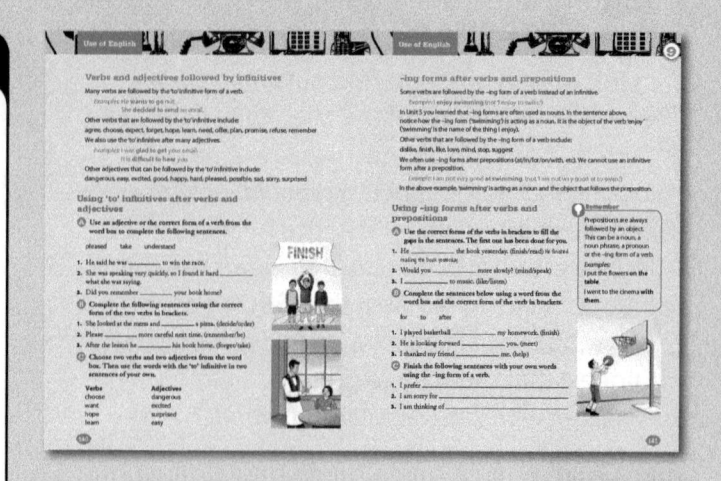

Grammar

–ing forms after verbs and prepositions

Students next go on to consider verbs that are followed by gerunds instead of the infinitive. Read through the first part of the language focus box on page 141 of the Student Book and remind students that they learned about –ing forms used as nouns in Unit 5. Explain that when an –ing form of a verb is used as a noun it is called a gerund. Read the example in the Student Book ('I enjoy swimming') and explain that the –ing form 'swimming' is the object of the verb 'enjoy'. It is acting as a noun. Give the students some more examples of gerunds following the verbs mentioned in the Student Book (examples: 'I dislike writing letters', 'I finished reading the email', 'I like talking to my friends').

Now read through the section in the language focus box explaining that we cannot use 'to' infinitives after prepositions. Draw students' attention to the Remember feature in the margin and remind them that prepositions are always followed by objects. The object can be a noun, a noun phrase, a pronoun or an –ing form of a verb (a gerund). Ask the students to find the preposition in the example (at) and the gerund (swimming).

Give some examples of gerunds following prepositions that stand alone (examples: 'After finishing my homework I played football', 'By working hard I achieved good results') and gerunds following adjectives and prepositions (examples: 'I am not very good at football', 'I am excited about seeing the film tonight').

134

Use of English

Student Book answers

Using –ing forms after verbs and prepositions

Ask the students to complete the exercises independently and then check their answers with a partner.

Answers:

A 2. Would you <u>mind speaking</u> more slowly?

    3. I <u>like listening</u> to music.

B 1. I played basketball <u>after finishing</u> my homework.

    2. He is looking forward <u>to meeting</u> you.

    3. I thanked my friend <u>for helping</u> me.

C Accept any sentences that use gerunds correctly after the verbs.

Use of English

Workbook page 68: Infinitives and –ing forms

Answers:

1. My plan was that I would learn <u>to ride</u> a bicycle that year.
2. Paolo found the questions <u>easy</u> to answer.
3. He <u>forgot</u> to leave the key for his brother.
4. They were <u>excited</u> to have the day off.
5. Yesterday Naia <u>decided to go</u> on the science trip.
6. It was better after he <u>agreed to follow</u> the rules.
7. If you won't change your mind, then I <u>(shall) refuse to answer</u>.
8–10. Allow any correct answer.
11. Cheng was very good <u>at finding</u> the right answers.
12. Sam was remembered <u>for scoring</u> the winning goal.
13. <u>After talking</u> for an hour, he sat down.

Extension

Practising infinitives and –ing forms

In this activity students practise using infinitives and –ing forms after verbs. Ask them to write a sentence using the correct form of each of the following pairs of verbs. Explain that they will need to decide which form they need to use.

regret/leave	learn/play	promise/visit
mind/walk	expect/finish	imagine/win
miss/see	offer/show	avoid/speak
agree/lend		

Example answers:

I regretted leaving so early.

He was learning to play the guitar.

She promised to visit me today.

He doesn't mind walking to school.

I am expecting to finish my course soon.

They imagined winning first prize.

I missed seeing you on Saturday.

She offered to show me round the city.

She avoided speaking to her friend.

I agreed to lend him my book.

Listening

Signalling

Prior knowledge

Explain to students that they are going to hear some recordings about different types of signals that are used to communicate information. Ask them what signals are and how we might use them. Ask them to think of times when they use signalling (riding a bicycle, travelling by bus, answering questions in class).

Word builder — Vocabulary

Direct students' attention to the Word builder exercise. Ask them to fill the gaps in the sentences, working on their own. When they have finished, ask them to check their answers with a partner.

Answers:

A **signal** is a way of communicating information or **instructions** from one person or place to another. Signals can be **movements**, actions or sounds. Many kinds of signals are used to **guide**, warn or simply inform **travellers**.

Signalling — Listening

Explain to the students that they are going to listen to four tracks, each one giving information about a different kind of signal: track 1 – smoke signals; track 2 – flags at sea; track 3 – flag semaphore; track 4 – traffic signals. Before they listen go over the Glossary words with them, making sure that they understand the meaning of each one. Play each track through twice and before each one ask the students to answer the questions as they listen. To avoid any confusion, only move on from one recording to the next after the questions have been completed.

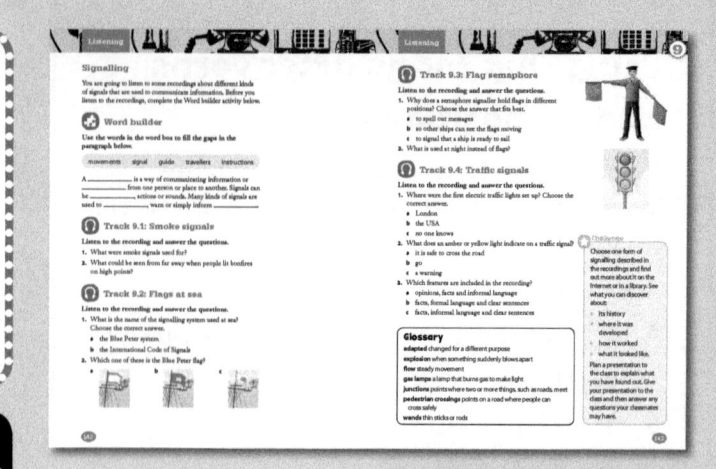

Student Book answers

Understanding

Answers:

Track 9.1: Smoke signals

1. sending news, messages and warnings
2. smoke

Track 9.2: Flags at sea

1. b   the International Code of Signals
2. b   plain blue flag with a white square in the middle (picture)

Track 9.3: Flag semaphore

1. a   to spell out messages
2. battery-powered light wands

Track 9.4: Traffic signals

1. b   the USA
2. c   a warning
3. b   facts, formal language and clear sentences

136

Listening

⭐ Challenge

In this Challenge activity students will plan and give a presentation on one form of signalling described in the recordings. Ask them to research different aspects as listed in the Student Book (history, where developed, how it worked, what it looked like) and then put their findings together as a presentation. They need to plan how they are going to make the presentation (Will they have any visual aids? How will they handle questions from the class?). Ask them to give their presentations, allowing two minutes plus question time.

Extension

Developments in signalling

Ask the students to take the research project into forms of signalling a stage further by researching, planning and giving an additional presentation on more recent developments in signalling. Ask them to choose satellite signalling, radio or the Internet and in small groups to carry out their research and planning as they did previously in the Challenge research project. This could be a task for an able group to undertake alongside the research project and the presentation could be given as a final part of the series of group presentations.

Listening

Workbook page 69: Sign language

Answers:

1. gestures: using arms or hands to convey meaning

   combinations: putting together two or more things

   facial expressions: movement of eyes, lips, and so on to show meaning

   regional: belonging to a particular area (of a country)

   dialects: local differences in speech

   petition: a formal written request, signed by many people

2. **B** deaf people
3. **C** Sign language is found in many different forms around the world.
4. **A** available for many TV programmes
5. **C** Let Sign Shine
6. **A** She uses sign language.
7. **B** by having sign language taught in schools

Use of English

Phrasal and prepositional verbs

Grammar

Phrasal verbs

In this section students develop their knowledge of phrasal verbs – verbs that consist of a main verb and a particle (words such as 'down', 'away', 'off', 'up' and 'in'). Together, the main verb and particle have a single meaning that may be different from the meaning of the main verb (for example, 'fall through' meaning 'not happen' or 'put off' meaning 'postpone'). Read through the first paragraph of the language focus box on page 144 of the Student Book. You may wish to give some more examples of phrasal verbs used without objects. (Examples: The band broke up. I stayed in last night.) Can students identify the main verb and particle in each example?

The second paragraph of the language focus box explains that phrasal verbs sometimes have objects. See if students can identify the object in the example given (my coat), the main verb (put) and the particle (on). Use the second example ('I put my coat on') to help students understand that the two parts of a phrasal verb can be separated by the object. You may wish to give some more examples. (Examples: She filled the form in. He took the rubbish out.) Ask the students to identify the main verb and the particle in each example. Draw students' attention to the penultimate paragraph of the language focus box, explaining that when the object of a phrasal verb is a pronoun, it must come before the particle. (Examples: She filled it in. He threw it away.)

Now read through the final paragraph of the language focus box, explaining that some phrasal verbs are followed by prepositions. Can the students identify the phrasal verb in the example ('looked up') and the preposition ('at')? Students may have some difficulty with this, so to ensure understanding give some more examples and ask the students to identify the phrasal verbs and prepositions in each case. (Examples: We are looking forward to the meal. I sent off for an application form.)

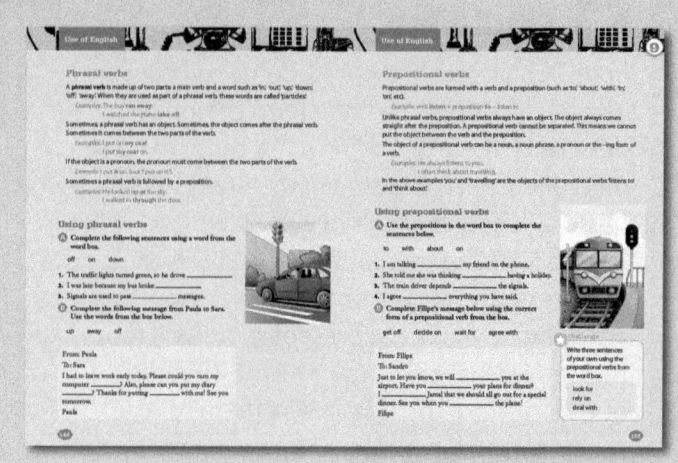

Student Book answers

Using phrasal verbs

Ask the students to answer the questions independently and then compare their answers with those of a neighbour.

Answers:

A 1. The traffic lights turned green, so he drove <u>off</u>.

2. I was late because my bus broke <u>down</u>.

3. Signals are used to pass <u>on</u> messages.

B I had to leave work early today. Please could you turn my computer <u>off</u>? Also, please can you put my diary <u>away</u>? Thanks for putting <u>up</u> with me! See you tomorrow.

Paula

Grammar

Prepositional verbs

In this section students focus on prepositional verbs – phrasal verbs that consist of a main verb followed by a preposition. Prepositional verbs differ from other phrasal verbs in that they must always have an object, and the verb and preposition cannot be separated: the object must always follow the preposition.

Before reading through the language focus box on page 145 of the Student Book, remind students that prepositions are words such as 'in', 'over', 'on' or 'through' that we use with nouns and other words in prepositional phrases. Remind students that prepositions always have objects.

Now read through the language focus box together along with the examples. To ensure understanding,

Use of English

write the following sentences on the board: 'I looked after the visitors', 'I've been looking for you', 'I looked over my notes before giving my talk'. Explain that these sentences contain prepositional verbs. In each case, the object follows the preposition and the verb cannot be separated (for example, we could not say 'I looked the visitors after').

5. Allow all correct answers.
7. He was not <u>listening to</u> her.
8. They both managed to <u>jump on</u> the bus.
9. Guess who has just <u>walked through</u> the door?
10. Will you <u>look after</u> my house while I am away?

⭐ Challenge

In this activity, students write three sentences using the prepositional verbs 'look for', 'rely on' and 'deal with'. Make sure that students understand the meaning of the prepositional verbs before they complete the activity. Accept any correct answer.

Student Book answers

Using prepositional verbs

Ask students to complete the questions and then compare answers with a neighbour.

Answers:

A 1. I am talking <u>to</u> my friend on the phone.
   2. She told me she was thinking <u>about</u> having a holiday.
   3. The train driver depends <u>on</u> the signals.
   4. I agree <u>with</u> everything you have said.

B Just to let you know, we will <u>wait for</u> you at the airport. Have you <u>decided on</u> your plans for dinner? I <u>agree with</u> Jamal that we should all go out for a special dinner. See you when you <u>get off</u> the plane!
   Filipe

Extension

Practising phrasal and prepositional verbs

This task gives practice in distinguishing and using phrasal verbs and prepositional verbs. Refer students to the information in the language focus boxes and then write the list of phrasal and prepositional verbs on the board. For the first part of the activity, write the following sentences on the board and ask the students to identify the sentences that include prepositional verbs.

1. I am counting on your support.
2. If you are going to the football match, please count me in.
3. Everyone was counting down the seconds to the New Year.
4. The teacher said the marks would count towards the final result.
5. I hope this won't count against me.

Answers:

Sentences 1, 4 and 5 contain prepositional verbs.

For the second part of the activity, write the following phrasal and prepositional verbs on the board and ask the students to use them in sentences of their own.

Phrasal: bring up, close down, dig up
Prepositional: care for, deal with, hear from

Use of English

Workbook page 70: Phrasal and prepositional verbs

Answers:

1. Max <u>gave up</u> and said he didn't know the answer.
2. The shop had none left so had to <u>send away</u> for a replacement.
3. Aaron was told to <u>switch off</u> the lights before he left.
4. Antonio <u>called out</u>, but no one heard him.
5. Finish <u>off</u> your answers for homework and hand them <u>in</u> tomorrow morning. Please leave <u>out</u> the final question, as we shall go <u>through</u> that in our next lesson. Make sure you look <u>up</u> all the words that are new to you and write <u>down</u> their meaning in your notebook.

Speaking

Communicating without words

Prior knowledge

In this section students use the picture on page 146 of the Student Book as a stimulus for discussions about the use of body language and other means of non-verbal communication. Begin by referring back to the introductory discussion of the quotation from Peter Drucker, "The most important thing in communication is hearing what isn't said" and any work done on the Extension activity (see page 131). Discuss the meaning of the phrase 'non-verbal communication' and ask students to think of other ways in which we can convey our thoughts and feelings other than by words. Give practical examples – exaggerating your non-verbal response to their suggestions, perhaps. Ask them in pairs to spend two minutes talking about these and when they would use them. Remind them about poems they watched being performed by Michael Rosen and how he used his face, hands and arms to add meaning to his performances. Remind students to think about the importance of listening during a conversation and ask them to think about the ways they can convey attitudes and opinions without using words during a discussion. For example, how do they show non-verbally they are interested in what someone is saying? How do they convey the idea they agree with someone? Discuss other attitudes and opinions that can be expressed without using words (for example, surprise shown perhaps by raising eyebrows; lack of interest or boredom shown by yawning or turning away, etc.).

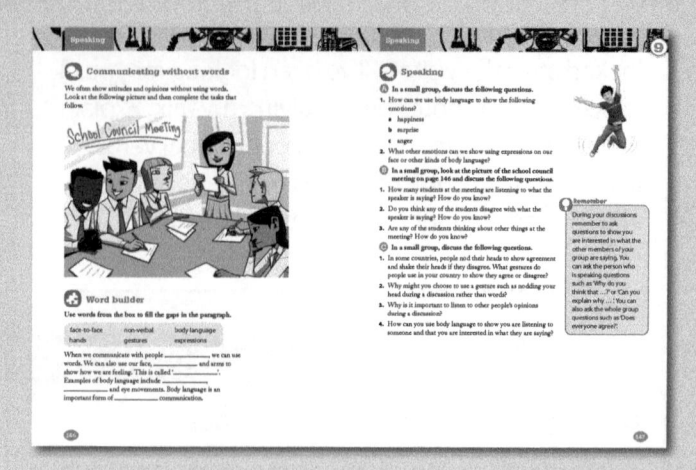

Vocabulary

Word builder

This activity introduces students to some vocabulary and ideas associated with non-verbal communication. Read through the word box with students, checking their understanding of the words. Ask students to fill in the gaps in the paragraph, working on their own. When they have finished, ask them to compare answers with a partner.

Answers:

When we communicate with people face-to-face, we can use words. We can also use our face, hands and arms to show how we are feeling. This is called 'body language'. Examples of body language include gestures, expressions and eye movements. Body language is an important form of non-verbal communication.

Speaking

Speaking

In this speaking exercise students will look at different examples of non-verbal communication and consider how we use them to convey feelings, attitudes and opinions. Ask the students in small groups to look at the picture on page 146 of the Student Book and say what they think is taking place. Tell the students to look at each of the students at the school council meeting in turn. What are they doing? Are they listening to the speaker? What attitudes and opinions is their body language conveying? The students should then go on to discuss the questions. Remind them to make use of the vocabulary they have just learned, to listen to each other's ideas and give reasons for their opinions. Draw the students' attention to the Remember feature, explaining that, in discussions, questions can be as important as answers. As the point of these questions is to promote discussion, there are no 'correct' answers.

Example responses:

A 1. a smiling/jumping/dancing/waving arms
       b open mouth/wide eyes/raised eyebrows/standing/stopping still
       c scowling/tight lips/deep breath/ shaking head (in some cultures)
    2. fear: pulling back, moving away/open mouth; boredom: yawning/looking away; agreement: nodding head (in many cultures)/smiling; trust: smile/nodding head/relaxed, etc.

B 1. Two of the students are listening to the speaker. They are looking at her. Two of the other students are talking to each other and one is looking away from the speaker.
   2. One of the students has an expression on their face that suggests they disagree with what the speaker is saying.
   3. Three of the students seem to be thinking about other things. Two are talking to each other and one is looking away from the speaker.

C 1. Students' own answers, depending on how gestures to show agreement are shown in their culture.

2. You might choose to use a gesture rather than words during a discussion because the person has not finished speaking.
3. It is important to listen to other people's opinions during a discussion so you can understand their ideas and these might make you change your own ideas or develop your own ideas further. It also helps in a discussion if you listen to someone carefully because you can then ask questions about what they have said to help you understand more.
4. You can look at them directly, smile and if you are sitting at a table you can sit up with your body turned towards them.

Workbook page 71: Giving a talk

On page 71 of the Workbook, students prepare a talk in note form, and then practise giving their talk at home or in class. Make sure that students use the correct format, with an introduction and a conclusion. Check also that they use the right register – it doesn't need to be too formal, but should be persuasive with a strong beginning and ending.

Extension

What makes a good listener?

Ask students in small groups (5/6) to discuss the question 'What makes a good listener?' The aim will be for the groups to agree a short list (five bullet points) and to work together to give a presentation on the subject.

Points to consider:
- why listen?
- what to listen for
- how to listen
- how body language can help
- asking questions.

Reading corner

Prior knowledge

In this section students read an advertisement placed on a school noticeboard and two emails about the information in the advertisement. Begin by asking students how often they might use email as a means of communication. Ask them for examples of the kind of thing they would email about. What are the benefits (ease and speed of communication)? What drawbacks are there (lack of security, not as personal)?

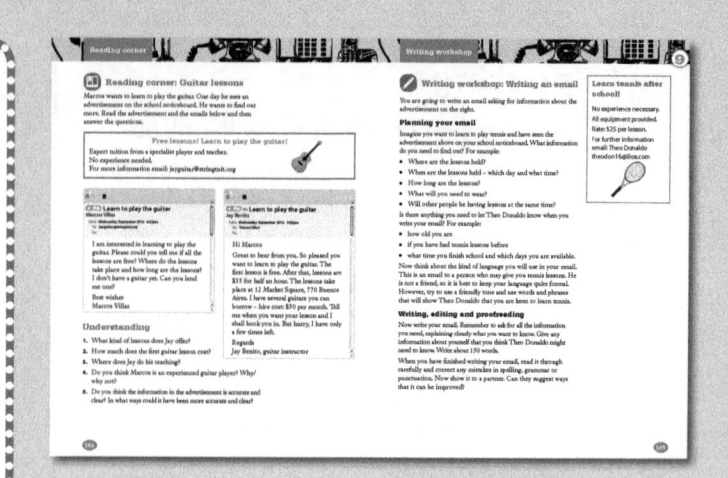

Reading

📖 Guitar lessons

Read the advertisement through with the students. Ask them what information is actually given. Is there any further implied information? If they were Marcos, what questions would they be asking? Read through the emails together and then ask the students to work independently at the questions.

Student Book answers

Understanding

Answers:

1. guitar lessons
2. nothing/free
3. 12 Market Square, 770 Buenos Aires
4. No, because he starts his email by saying that he wants to learn to play the guitar, and he does not have a guitar.
5. No. (Too little information/'free lessons' misleading/no details/no mention of instructor's qualifications.)

Writing workshop

Writing | Writing an email

Tell students that they are going to write an email in response to an advertisement. Explain that the advertisement gives only the minimum information so they will need to decide what else they should find out and what questions they should ask. Read through the advertisement with the students and the 'Planning your email' section on page 149 of the Student Book. Spend time talking with students about the appropriate style of language for the email. Ask them how they think they might show polite enthusiasm. Ask the students to plan and then write their email. Give them time to check spelling and punctuation before asking a neighbour to look it over.

Example response:

Dear Mr Donaldo,

I am keen to learn to play tennis and would like to know where you give lessons. Please can you also tell me when the lessons take place and how long they last? Will other students be having lessons at the same time? Will I need a tennis racket?

I am twelve years old and attend Lanos Secondary School. I am interested that you say that no experience is needed, as I have not played before but am keen to learn. We finish school early on Tuesdays and Fridays and I am free between 2 and 5 p.m. on those days. I do hope you can fit me in.

Kind regards

Sara

Writing | Workbook page 72: Writing an email

On page 72 of the workbook, students practise writing a semi-formal email, in response to an advertisement to learn sign-language. Check that students have used the correct format and register (formal, but friendly). Ensure also that they ask some questions about the course.

Extension | Writing an advertisement

Direct students back to the emails on page 148 of the Student Book. Ask them to imagine that Jay is in fact an experienced and well-qualified teacher, but he is not very good at advertising his skills. Ask them to prepare a more informative and persuasive handwritten advertisement for Jay to put up on the school noticeboard. Ask them to think about what information they need to include that was not in Jay's original advertisement (examples: cost of lessons, Jay's qualifications, where lessons are held and when). Then ask them to think of ways they can persuade people to reply to the advertisement and find out more (for example, they might suggest a special offer such as a free first lesson).

Progress assessment

Progress check

Student Book answers

Progress check

1. One mark. Alexander Graham Bell [1]
2. One mark. b not clear [1]
3. One mark each.
   a   They hope/are hoping to visit their friends this weekend.
   b   I shall remember to bring my book tomorrow.
   c   Please try to follow what I am saying. [3]
4. One mark each.
   a   She finished doing her homework.
   b   He decided to go for a walk. [2]
5. One mark. To signal that it is ready to go to sea. [1]
6. One mark. b by holding flags in different positions [1]
7. One mark. b at the beginning of the twentieth century [1]
8. One mark each.
   I got on the bus and sat down. I looked out of the window. When we reached the marketplace I stood up and got off the bus. [5]
9. One mark for each correct fact. [4]
10. Six marks. Accept any accurate email. [6]

   Total marks: 25

End-of-unit quiz

Workbook page 73: Communication quiz

The end-of-unit quiz on page 73 of the Workbook is a summary of the content you have covered in the unit. You can set this as homework or to complete in class. Go through the answers in class, and check that there are no gaps in students' understanding.

Answers:

1. B   It would distract him.
2. C   1922
3. He offered to carry my bag to the car, but I refused to let him in case he hurt himself.
4. Thank you for emailing me.

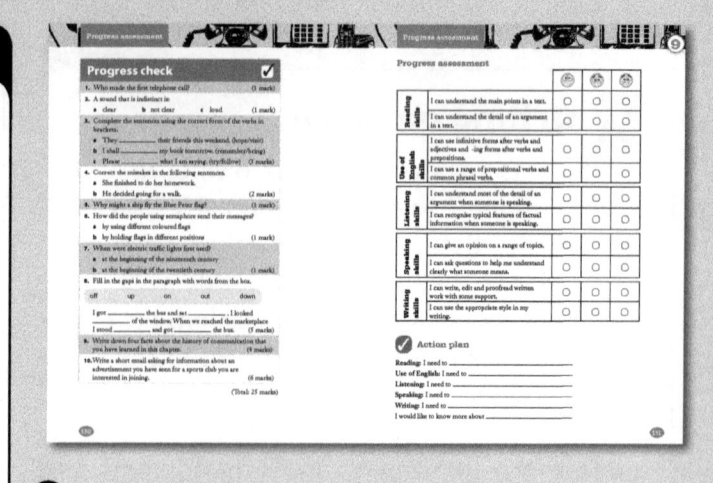

5. A   British Sign Language
6. Jade's eleven year old sister Laura cannot hear or speak. When she visits the doctor or goes shopping she communicates with sign language. Jade wants to help her and has started a petition called Let Sign Shine to collect signatures to have signing taught in schools.
7. Allow any correct sentences.
8. Allow any suitable ending.

Reflection

Reflecting on your learning

Have a discussion with the class about how they will continue to use the different skills they have covered in this unit. Students should then work independently on the progress assessment task. For each of the skills, ask them to tick the box that they think most fits how well they are doing. Now move on to the action plan questions. The aim is to encourage students to identify which skills they think they need more practice in, while reinforcing the skills they can do well. Give students the opportunity to practise the skills they have identified and revisit the action plan after a few weeks, encouraging students to compare later attempts with the first.

Progress assessment

Reading

📖 End-of-unit activity

This activity will allow students to evaluate the unit and what they have found easy and interesting in the unit. Ask the students to read the following email from Pepe to his friend Lou. Pepe has just completed this unit. Then ask them to answer the questions below (see also the photocopiable sheet on the CD).

From: Pepe

To: Lou

Subject: Re: Catching up

Hi Lou

Great to hear from you. We have just been finding out about different kinds of communication. Did you know that your birthday is on the same day as the first phone call in 1876? I really enjoyed learning about semaphore. I will try to find out more about it.

I am looking forward to seeing you next week. My sister is waving for me to join the family, so must go.

Cheers

Pepe

1. What is the date of Pepe's birthday?
2. What signalling does Pepe want to find out more about?
3. Which two –ing forms does Pepe use as nouns in his email?
4. What non-verbal communication does Pepe mention at the end of his email?

Answers:

1. 10 March
2. semaphore
3. 'learning' and 'seeing'
4. waving

Ask the students to discuss with a neighbour what they have found most interesting in the unit. Then ask them to share this with the class.

Reflection

Teacher reflection

1. Which parts of the unit did the students enjoy most? Why was this?
2. Was there anything that the students found difficult in this unit? How can I make sure this is easier next time?
3. Considering the learning objectives and content, what did the students successfully learn while studying this unit?
4. Considering the learning objectives and content, what did the students struggle with while studying this unit? Why was this? What could I do to help them more?
5. Which parts of the unit did I teach well? How did I achieve this?
6. Which parts of the unit did I struggle to teach well? What can I do to improve this?
7. Next time I teach this unit, is there anything I can do to improve the learning experience for my students?

Grammar reference

Forming comparative adjectives

For information on the use of comparative adjectives, see Unit 1 page 17.

Adjective	Rule	Examples
one syllable (most)	add –er	warmer, taller, quicker
one syllable ending with a silent –e	drop the –e and add –er	larger, nicer, later
one syllable ending with consonant + vowel + consonant	double the final consonant and add –er*	bigger, sadder, wetter
one or two syllables ending with –y	change –y to –i and add –er	drier, luckier, happier
two syllables, not ending with y (many)	'more' + adjective**	more careful, more patient
adjectives with three syllables or more	'more' + adjective	more possible, more expensive, more interesting

* Exception: we don't double the final consonant when an adjective ends in –y or –w; examples: slower, greyer.

** With some two-syllable adjectives, we can use 'more' or add '–er'; examples: cleverer/more clever; simpler/more simple; polite/more polite.

Irregular comparative adjectives

These common adjectives have irregular comparative forms.

Adjective	Comparative
good	better
bad	worse
many	more
much	more
little (quantity)	less
some	more
far	farther/further
well (healthy)	better

Grammar reference

Forming adverbs

For information on the use of adverbs, see Unit 4 pages 60–61 and 64–65.

Most adverbs are formed by adding –ly to an adjective.

Adjective	Rule	Examples
most adjectives	add –ly	slowly, carefully, quickly
adjectives ending with –le	remove the –e and add –y	possibly, simply, terribly
adjectives ending with –y	remove –y and add –ily	easily, luckily, happily
adjectives ending with –ic	add –ally*	realistically, enthusiastically, tragically
adjectives ending with –ly	use 'in a … way/manner'	in a silly way, in a friendly manner

* Exception: public → publicly

Irregular adverbs

Some adverbs have the same form as the adjective: hard, fast, straight, late, early, daily, wrong. 'Well' is the adverb that corresponds to the adjective 'good'.

Forming comparative adverbs

For information on the use of comparative adverbs, see Unit 4 page 61.

Adverb	Rule	Examples
adverbs ending with –ly	use 'more' in front of the adverb	more carefully, more patiently
short adverbs that do not end with –ly	add –er if the adverb ends in –e, add –r	faster, harder, later

Irregular comparative adverbs

Adverb	Comparative
well	better
badly	worse
ill	worse
little	less
much	more
far	further/farther

Grammar reference

Forming verbs + –ing

Verb	Rule	Examples
most verbs	add –ing	look → looking
verbs ending with consonant + –e	remove the –e and add –ing	move → moving
verbs ending with –ee	add –ing	agree → agreeing
verbs ending with consonant + vowel + consonant	double the final consonant and add –ing*	stop → stopping
verbs ending with –ie	change –ie to –y and add –ing	lie → lying

* Exceptions: We do not double a final –w or –x; examples: flow → flowing, fix → fixing. We do not double the consonant when the last syllable is not stressed; example: order → ordering.

Forming verbs + ed

Verb	Rule	Examples
most verbs	add –ed	look → looked
verbs ending with –e or –ee	add –d	move → moved agree → agreed
verbs ending in consonant + y	change –y to –i and add –ed	study → studied
verbs ending in consonant + vowel + consonant	double the final consonant and add –ed*	stop → stopped prefer → preferred

* Exception: We do not double the consonant when the last syllable is not stressed. Example: order → ordered.

Verb forms

Present simple

See Unit 3 page 44 and Unit 8 page 129.

Positive	I/you/we/they walk	He/she/it walks
Negative	I/you/we/they don't walk	He/she/it doesn't walk
Question	Do I/you/we walk?	Does he/she/it walk?

Grammar reference

Present continuous

See Unit 3 page 48 and Unit 8 page 129.

Positive	I am walking	He/she/it is walking	You/we/they are walking
Negative	I'm not walking	He/she/it isn't walking	You/we/they aren't walking
Question	Am I walking?	Is he/she/it walking?	Are you/we/they walking?

Past simple

See Unit 3 page 44.

Positive	I/you/he/she/it/they walked
Negative	I/you/he/she/ didn't walk
Question	Am I walking?

Past continuous

See Unit 3 page 49.

Positive	I/he/she/it was walking	You/we/they were walking
Negative	I/he/she/it wasn't walking	You/we/they weren't walking
Question	Was I/he/she/it walking?	Were you/we/they walking?

Present perfect simple

See Unit 2 pages 32–33.

Positive	I/you/we/they have walked	He/she/it has walked
Negative	I/you/we/they haven't walked	He/she/it hasn't walked
Question	Have I/you/we walked?	Has he/she/it walked?

Past perfect simple

See Unit 8 page 124.

Positive	I/you/he/she/it/we/they had walked
Negative	I/you/he/she/it/we/they had walked
Question	Had I/you/he/she/it/we/they walked?

149

Use of English glossary

abstract noun a noun that refers to an idea, quality or concept that cannot be seen, heard, touched, etc. Examples: happiness; truth; beauty. *See also* concrete noun.

active verbs are active when the subject of the sentence (the agent) does the action. Example: He *cleaned* the windows this morning. *See also* passive.

adjective a word that gives more information about a noun or adds to its meaning. Adjectives are often used in front of a noun. Example: They live in a *big* house. Adjectives can also be used after verbs such as 'be', 'feel' and 'look'. Examples: He is *hungry*; She feels *happy*; You look *tired*.

adverb a word that is used to give more information about a verb, adjective or another adverb. Examples: She speaks English *well*; He is *very* tall; He spoke *really* loudly.

auxiliary a verb such as 'be', 'have' or 'do' that is used with a main verb to form tenses, passive forms and questions. Examples: She *is* eating her lunch; She *has* eaten her lunch; Her lunch *was* eaten. *Did* she eat her lunch? *See also* modal verb.

clause a group of words that contains a verb and usually some other words, too. Clauses form part of a sentence or may be complete sentences on their own. Example: I went to school. *See also* conditional clause, relative clause.

command an order to do something. We often use imperative verbs in commands. Example: Stop talking. *See also* imperative.

comparative the form of an adjective or adverb that is used when comparing things. Examples: You are *taller* than me; Mara works *harder* than Jamal.

compound adjective an adjective made up of two or more words. Examples: She is a *prize-winning* writer; He bought a *second-hand* car.

compound noun a noun made up of two or more words. Examples: website, swimming pool.

concrete noun a noun that refers to something that can be seen, heard, touched, etc. Examples: school, house, apple. *See also* abstract noun.

conditional clause a clause that describes something that must happen in order for something else to happen. Conditional clauses usually begin with 'if' or 'unless'. Examples: *If I see her*, I will tell her what you said; *Unless it stops raining*, we will not go for a walk.

conjunction a word that is used to link other words or parts of a sentence, such as 'and', 'but', 'since' and 'as'.

continuous form a verb form used to describe an action that continues over a period of time. We make continuous forms using a form of the verb 'be' with the present participle of the main verb. To change the tense, we change the form of 'be'. Examples: I *am eating* my lunch; He *was reading* his book.

contraction a shortened form of a word or group of words. An apostrophe is used to show where letters have been missed out. Examples: I'm (I am); you're (you are).

countable noun a noun that refers to something that can be counted. Countable nouns have singular and plural forms. Examples: planet/planets; book/books. *See also* uncountable noun.

Use of English glossary

determiner a word that introduces a noun and forms part of a noun phrase. Examples: a/an, the, this, some, many, this, that, these, much, your.

direct speech the words spoken by someone and quoted in writing. To indicate direct speech, we use inverted commas, or speech marks. Example: She said, *"I will see you tomorrow."* See also reported speech.

future a verb form used to refer to something that has not yet happened. To talk about something that has been arranged in the future, we often use the present simple or present continuous. Examples: My piano lesson is at 4 o'clock. I am having a piano lesson tomorrow.

gerund a present participle of a verb when it is used as a noun. Example: I like *reading*.

imperative a verb form that expresses a command or instruction. Examples: *Be* quiet; *Close* the door; *Stir* the mixture carefully.

infinitive the basic form of a verb. Examples: read, be. The infinitive with 'to' is 'to' + base form: 'to read', 'to be'.

–ing form the present participle form of a verb ending in –ing. We use the –ing form in continuous forms. Example: I *am reading* a book. We also use –ing forms as nouns (gerunds). Examples: I like *reading*; *Reading* is relaxing. We also some use –ing forms as adjectives. Example: This is an *exciting* book.

irregular an irregular word does not follow the normal rules. Irregular nouns do not have plurals that end in –s. Examples: man → men; child → children. An irregular verb does not have a past tense and past participle that end in –ed. Examples: go → went/gone; be → was/were/been. See also regular.

main verb the verb that expresses the main meaning in a clause (unlike an auxiliary verb). Main verbs can be used with or without an auxiliary verb. Examples: I *read* a good book last week. I am *reading* a good book.

modal verb an auxiliary verb that we can use with another verb to express ideas such as ability, advice, possibility, permission, etc. The main modal verbs are: can, could, may might, must, ought (to), shall, should, will and would. Examples: He *can* play the piano very well; You *should* wear a coat; He *might* visit you next week. You *can* borrow my phone.

noun a word that refers to a person, animal, thing or idea. See also abstract noun, compound noun, concrete noun, countable noun, noun phrase, uncountable noun.

noun phrase a phrase that contains a noun. Noun phrases can contain determiners such as 'a/an' or 'the' and other words that give more information about the noun. Example: Have you seen *the blue shirt that I was wearing yesterday?*

object a noun or pronoun that is the person or thing that is affected by a verb. Example: He kicked *the ball* into the goal. See also subject.

participle See –ing form, past participle.

passive verbs are passive when the subject of the verb has the action done to it. Example: The windows *were cleaned* last week. See also active.

past continuous See continuous form.

past participle a form of a verb that we use to make some past forms and passives. Regular verbs have past participles that end in –ed. Examples: He has *delivered* all the leaflets; The windows were *cleaned* yesterday. Irregular verbs have different forms. Example: I have *sent* my friend a postcard. Past participles are also used to form adjectives. Example: They have mended the *broken* window.

past perfect (simple) a verb form that we make with 'had' and the past participle. We use the past perfect to talk about an event that happened before another event in the past. Example: The film *had* already *started*

Use of English glossary

when we got to the cinema. We also use the past perfect in reported statements. Example: She said she *had* just *arrived*.

past simple a verb form that we make by adding –ed to regular verbs. Irregular verbs have different forms. We use the past simple to talk about actions or events that happened in the past. Example: I *called* him yesterday.

past tense *See* continuous form, past perfect, past simple, tense.

phrasal verb a verb made up of a verb and a particle such as 'to', 'in' 'up', 'off', 'down', etc. A phrasal verb often has a different meaning from the verb alone. When a phrasal verb has an object, it can usually come before or after the particle. Examples: My car *broke down*; He *put on* his coat.

phrase a group of words that forms a unit within a clause. Examples: Have you seen *my blue coat*; I put the book *on the table*.

plural the form of a word that we use to refer to more than one person or thing. Examples: books; they.

preposition a word such as 'at', 'into', 'on' or 'for' that we use before a noun or pronoun to show place, direction, time, method, etc. Examples: The book is *on* the desk; He walked *across* the street; I will see you *at* 6 o'clock;
I went to Japan *by* plane.

prepositional verb a verb that is made up of a verb and a preposition. Prepositional verbs always have objects and we cannot separate the verb and the preposition. Examples: She *listened to* what her friend was saying. He cannot *do without* your help.

present continuous *See* continuous form.

present participle *See* –ing form.

present perfect (simple) the verb form that we make with a form of 'have' and the past participle of the main verb. The present perfect has many uses. For example, it is used to talk about something that started in the past and continues in the present. Example: She *has lived* in Paris for over ten years.

present simple the form of a verb that we use to talk about things that are true in the present and actions that happen regularly in the present. We make the present simple with the base form of the verb. With 'he', 'she' and 'it' we add –s to the base form of regular verbs and many irregular verbs. Examples: He *lives* in Hong Kong; I often *walk* to school. We also use the present simple to talk about something that is fixed in the future. Example: My lesson *starts* at 6 o'clock.

present tense *See* present simple, present perfect, continuous form, tense.

pronoun a word that is used in place of a noun. Subject pronouns usually come before a verb. Examples: I, you, he, she, it, we, they. Object pronouns come after the verb. Examples: me, you, him, her, it, us, them. Relative pronouns connect relative clauses to main clauses in a sentence. Examples: who, which, that. Possessive pronouns show who something belongs to. Examples: mine, yours, his, hers, ours, theirs.

quantifier a word that expresses the quantity, number or amount of something. Examples: all, both, many, several, lots of, little.

regular a word such as a noun or verb that follows normal rules. For example, regular nouns have plurals with –s, and regular verbs have past participles ending in –ed.

relative clause a clause that gives information about someone or something in the main clause. A relative clause is connected to a main clause by a relative pronoun such as 'that', 'which', 'who' or 'where'. Example: I read the book *that my friend lent me*.

Use of English glossary

reported speech the words someone uses to report what someone has said. Example: She said that she enjoyed the match. *See also* direct speech.

sentence a group of words that expresses a complete thought and makes complete sense. Sentences contain a main verb, begin with a capital letter and end with a full stop, exclamation mark or question mark. Examples: Paulo is playing football; That is great! Why did you do that?

perfect *See* present perfect and past perfect.

singular the form of a word that we use to refer to one person or thing. Examples: book; she.

statement a sentence that is not a question or a command. Example: The match has just started.

subject the person or thing that performs the action of a verb in a sentence. Example: *He* kicked the ball into the goal. *See also* object.

syllable a word or part of a word that contains one vowel sound and usually one or more consonants before or after the vowel sound. Example: meet (one syllable); meeting (two syllables 'meet' and 'ing').

tense the form that a verb takes to show when something happened or when someone did something. In English, there are two main tenses: present and past. There are four forms of the present tense: the present simple, present continuous, present perfect and present perfect continuous. There are four forms of the past tense: past simple, past continuous, past perfect and past perfect continuous.

uncountable noun a noun that refers to something that we cannot count. Uncountable nouns do not have a plural form. Examples: water, information. *See also* countable noun.

verb a word that describes what someone or something does, or what happens. Examples: look, read, seem, understand.